Willpower's Not Enough

Willpower's Not Enough

Understanding and Recovering from Addictions of Every Kind

ARNOLD M. WASHTON, PH.D.   DONNA BOUNDY, M.S.W.

1817

HARPER & ROW, PUBLISHERS, New York
Grand Rapids, Philadelphia, St. Louis, San Francisco
London, Singapore, Sydney, Tokyo

FIRST EDITION

Designer: Joan Greenfield

Library of Congress Cataloging-in-Publication Data

Washton, Arnold M.
  Willpower's not enough.

  Bibliography: p.
  1. Compulsive behavior. 2. Compulsive behavior—Treatment.
I. Boundy, Donna. II. Title.
RC533.W37 1989   616.85'227   88-45069
ISBN 0-06-015996-0

---

89 90 91 92 93 CC/RRD 10 9 8 7 6 5 4 3 2 1

To my father, Irving Washton (1909–1975), whose quiet generosity and kindness are remembered by all who knew him.

—A. M. W.

To my mother, Esther Phillips Boundy, and in memory of my father, Dean Boundy, for teaching by example the value of living with integrity.

—D. B.

Contents

List of Tables

Acknowledgments

MANY PEOPLE HELPED TRANSFORM this book from an idea into a reality, and we are grateful to each of them:

Our editor, John Michel, for skillfully shepherding the manuscript through its many incarnations, and for his patience and support;

Debra Elfenbein, production editor, for her conscientious effort in producing the best manuscript possible;

Larry Ashmead, executive editor, for having the confidence in us to support this project from beginning to end;

Connie Clausen, our agent, for seeing the merits of this book when it was just an idea and four pages of notes;

Kate Davis for her editorial skill, friendship, and humor—all of which proved invaluable to the completion of this project;

Erica Lindsay for her late-night readings of endless drafts, helpful feedback, and, most important, for sharing the vision;

Harris Breiman of The Mustard Seed Center for Healing in Woodstock, N.Y., for making key contributions to the manuscript and bringing to it his clarity and wisdom;

Rebecca Daniels, Carol Perkin, and Jane Letus for their various contributions to the research and Joan Munkacsi for her work on an early draft;

And a very special thanks to the many recovering people who agreed to be interviewed for this book so that others might identify and gain hope.

Loving gratitude to my wife, Nannette Stone, and my daughters, Tala and Danae, for their encouragement and support.

—A. M. W.

I wish to thank my family for their unwavering support and enthusiasm, in particular Marcia and Mary Beth;

Leona Trinin, for her wit, love, and reality testing, all of which has helped me write books and keep my sense of humor;

My partners in Reelizations, Tom Colello and Bart Friedman, for their patience while I worked on this book;

Finally, I thank Francesca, Elena, Howard, Nedra, Susie, and the many other friends, too numerous to name, who have—all in their own way—helped to provide the sense of community so necessary to thrive, create, and carry on.

—D. B.

Notes to the Reader

NOT ALL ADDICTIONS ARE EXACTLY the same. Important differences among them do exist. Chemical addictions, for example, uniquely alter the physical functioning of the human brain—unlike most other addictions. Despite these differences, however, we see great value in identifying the common threads that bind together seemingly different types of addictions. Addictions can look very different on the surface but can be generated by many of the same root causes underneath. We have chosen, therefore, to avoid the current academic debate about whether certain types of habitual behaviors are truly addictions or are better classified as compulsions. We view the similarities among different forms of addictions as being more important than the differences, at least in terms of what causes addictions and how to deal with them effectively. This book is about the similarities.

GIVEN THE GENDER LIMITATIONS of the English language, it is a challenge to write without a gender bias. Every time we refer to an indefinite person (such as "the addict") we are forced to chose between using the masculine pronoun "he," the feminine pronoun "she," or the awkward and cumbersome combination "he or she."

Our solution has been to alternate pronouns. With this approach, we hope to allow the maximum number of readers to benefit from the material presented—since addiction itself knows no bias.

Willpower's Not Enough

Introduction:
This Is Not a Quick-Fix Book

THIS IS NOT A QUICK-FIX BOOK. If you're looking for an easy, fast answer to addiction, you will not find it here.

Do you feel let down, or even cheated? Did you buy this book thinking that maybe *we* could provide you with an instant cure for your or someone else's addiction? If so, that could be part of the problem: a limited understanding of addiction and mistaken beliefs about how it can be overcome. Many people think that what the addict needs is greater self-control: "If she could just try harder, surely she could stop drinking (or overeating, or getting hooked on unavailable men, or using cocaine). What she needs is willpower."

Nothing could be further from the truth. What prevents an addict from recovering, in fact, is relying on willpower alone. Using willpower, you can get off an addiction—for a week, a month, or even longer. But sooner or later, when life gets stressful, you're very likely to relapse. Or, you might "conquer" one addiction with willpower—only to find yourself with a new one, as when Sally stops drinking, but starts abusing prescription drugs; or when Howard stops eating compulsively, but starts using cocaine. In other words, you can use willpower to get rid of the *symptom* of your addiction, but you'll still be vulnerable to relapse or to new compulsive behaviors until you make other—internal—changes in yourself.

Willpower isn't enough because it springs from the very thinking that causes addiction—the belief that there is a "quick-fix" to everything and that if we just exert enough control we can avoid

1

all pain and discomfort. Since we've all grown up in a society that relies heavily on quick-fix solutions, it's not surprising that when we try to break an addiction we approach it the same way. We think, "There's got to be an easy way."

Using willpower alone to break an addiction is what's called "first-order change."* It never works very well because the "solution" comes out of the same mindset as the problem. When an addict has already lost control over her use of a mood-changer, how can yet another attempt at *controlling* it be a lasting solution?

In "second-order change"* the problem—and the solution—are reframed within a different set of concepts and beliefs. Second-order change for addiction means *not* trying harder to control the addiction, but throwing up your hands and admitting defeat—admitting that you are not in control.

The addict finds this hard to swallow. "But that sounds like the opposite of what I should do. You're telling me to give up." We are, because that's what works. Trying harder and harder to be good enough, to be accepted, to perform better, to look like you're managing, to be "normal" is part of what makes a person vulnerable to addiction to begin with. So it's only when you *stop trying*, accept yourself right where you are (even if that's addicted), and admit that you're not in control, that you can begin to regain control. It's a paradox, but there are many in recovery.

The whole thrust of recovery, in fact, is not self-control, but self-acceptance. Only when you fully accept yourself as you are can you stop trying to control how things appear, clearly observe the destructiveness of the quick-fix approach, and honestly admit that it's not working for you. That's where recovery begins.

On a societal level, the War on Drugs is a prime example of attempted first-order change and is, in effect, an addictive society's approach to the drug problem. The strategy has been to try to control the supply of drugs (as if that were the problem) and to control whether people want them or not (as if that were possible).

---

*The terms "first-order change" and "second-order change" were introduced in *Change*, Paul Watzlawick, et al. (New York: W. W. Norton, 1989).

What's missing is self-observation and honesty. We haven't been able to admit that our attempts to control the epidemic aren't working and that the problem (like any addiction) is only getting worse. Instead we launch ever-more "initiatives," trying harder to control the problem. In the process, we side-step the more central issue: the fact that so many Americans crave quick-fixes of all kinds.

With this approach, we are like the spouse of an alcoholic who thinks that if she can just find the "right" tactic—throwing out the liquor supply or convincing the alcoholic that he's hurting his health—the problem will be solved. The fact is, the supply is not the problem, and neither is a lack of information. If the alcoholic craves alcohol, he'll find a way to get it. That's the nature of addiction; it's compulsive!

To overcome addiction—individually or as a nation—requires second-order change, a new way of thinking about it. Addictions to drugs, sex, shopping, work, food, people are not entirely unrelated phenomena. We read separate books about them and attend separate self-help groups trying to recover. But what is becoming increasingly clear is that the original source of addiction does not lie within the individual substance or activity so much as *within ourselves.*

We urgently need a model for understanding and recovering, not just from each separate *expression* of addiction but from the source of the problem—the "dis-ease" within ourselves that makes us so vulnerable to the appeal of mood-changers of all kinds.

This is what we have tried to provide in *Willpower's Not Enough.* In it we present a bigger picture of addiction than you might have been aware of before—like a road map with an arrow that says, "You are here." Of course, no map in and of itself can take you anywhere. It can only show you the direction you need to go in and some possible roads to take. You still have to do the traveling.

The good news is that recovery really is possible—once you give up on addictive solutions. And embarking on a recovery path will change your life in profound and positive ways that you can't even imagine yet. Perhaps the most important thing to know in advance is that recovery is not going to be about deprivation. Quitting your drug—whatever it is—doesn't mean you have to resign yourself to a life of joyless restraint or terminal boredom.

Quite the opposite. As you will see, recovery is about coming to know the inner ease that comes with self-acceptance. It means learning to face problems with confidence, knowing that you have the skills to deal with them responsibly, resourcefully, and creatively. And it's about finding more real gratification in life—a sense of meaning, belonging, and joy. In time, in fact, recovery will bring you more pleasure than your drug ever could.

You might get a little homesick along the way, and that's understandable. After all, you've probably lived with addictive illusions—like the idea that willpower's all you need—for a very long time. Letting go of these illusions in recovery is like letting go of a part of yourself. But when you miss the familiar old patterns, try to remember that they weren't getting you what you wanted anyway—just the fantasy of it. So allow yourself to get excited, and go forward with hope. It really is quite an adventure to be embarking on.

PART I

America on a Binge

1

The Many Faces of Addiction

IT'S NO NEWS THAT THERE'S an epidemic of compulsive drug use in America. But while politicians and police search in vain for ways to stem the tide, more and more people are beginning to realize that our national appetite for mood-altering chemicals is just one aspect of a more far-reaching national problem: an epidemic of many different types of compulsive behavior—*not just drug abuse.*

The number of Americans addicted to something has been increasing yearly since the sixties. Some 14 to 16 million of us now attend one of a half-million different self-help groups that have sprung up around the country to help people with one kind of addiction or another, and these numbers are expected to double in the next three years. Many of the "other addictions"—to food, work, gambling, shopping, sex, and even exercise—sound harmless enough, and at times even humorous. But for a growing number of Americans, the activity has become an end in itself, tyrannizing and controlling rather than enhancing their lives.

The examples are endless: the compulsive shopper who is unable to leave a store without buying something—anything! The compulsive gambler who plays the horses (or stocks and commodities) even though the mortgage is overdue. The sexual addict who seeks one empty encounter after another, despite a trail of broken hearts, venereal disease, and now even the deadly threat of AIDS.

What these and countless other stories have in common is their compulsiveness. Despite the negative consequences, the person is driven to repeat the behavior—as if responding to an inner command rather than to choice. The very mark of addictive behavior is that in trying to bring it under control, *willpower's not enough.*

BRIAN IS A CREDIT-CARD JUNKIE. Thirty years old and single, working temp jobs as a word processor, Brian's real addiction is to travel. Mostly, he uses his cards to buy airline tickets, taking trips by himself to destinations he doesn't even care about. The point, he says, is to keep on the go, no matter where. Sometimes he just takes out a map, closes his eyes, points to a place, then buys a ticket to go there.

He joined two "frequent flier" programs offered by the airlines and accumulated 93,000 miles on one and 40,000 on another. He once flew to Kansas City and back in one day just to get a triple-mileage special being offered. If there's space in first class, he gets upgraded. According to Brian, flying is the ultimate "high in the sky."

When he's flying, Brian says he's removed from all his worries—temporarily. No one can reach him (including his creditors), and he can literally escape his life. Unfortunately, each time he lands, Brian has more pressure than ever from which to escape. His credit card debts now total $28,000, though his annual income is only $26,000. Unable to make even the minimum payment on some of his cards, Brian has received several court summonses for non-payment and his salary has been attached.

Because all but two airline cards had been canceled (he pays on those selectively), he once went so far as to charge a round-trip flight somewhere just to "eat out" on the plane (Brian is also a compulsive eater). He says he knew while he was doing it that he was "out of control," but felt driven to do it anyway.

Recently, Brian's sister lent him $3,000 to cover his most urgent bills, but admonished him to go to Debtors Anonymous, a self-help group for people with compulsive spending and debting problems. Surprising even himself, Brian went to a meeting and actually found it helpful: "It was the first time I felt I could talk about my MasterCard and somebody knew, somebody could understand," he says. "I felt so accepted."

KIM, A TWENTY-EIGHT-YEAR-OLD free-lance writer, has never had a romantic relationship with anyone that lasted more than three or four months. As a teenager, she was in a serious car accident that left her with some unsightly scars on her legs and a slight but permanent limp. Even worse, it left her with emotional scars: Kim doesn't believe she is attractive to men. And in the process of trying to assure herself that she is, she's developed a sexual addiction.

Kim compulsively seeks to be sexually desired, pursued, and "consumed" by as many different men as possible, and she's developed a ritual to obtain it. Three or four evenings a week she dresses up stylishly, has a drink at home, goes to a bar downtown, has a couple more drinks, becomes flirtatious, and picks up a man—a different one each time. Then she takes him back to her apartment, where she has sex with him. Rarely does she see him again. Increasingly, both alcohol and cocaine have become part of the ritual too—so much so that Kim may have already crossed the invisible line into these physical addictions as well.

Recently Kim found out that one of the men, an intravenous drug user, has AIDS (she's never asked that condoms or any other "safe sex" practices be used). Terrified of what she could find out, Kim has been unable to get herself to go for an AIDS test. She is also unable to change her behavior. Kim is still picking up men, still drinking and using coke to numb her feelings—and still not practicing safe sex. For Kim, sex is a "drug," and she's hooked on the experience.

WHEN PAUL, A THIRTY-FOUR-YEAR-OLD engineer, inherited a moderate sum of money last year, he decided to try his hand in the stock market. The only other time he'd invested—five years earlier—he'd doubled his money, so it seemed like a good bet now.

Once again, Paul was very lucky. He put almost all his money into one very high-risk area—options—and hit it big. He made a phenomenal profit and was hooked. He quit his job and now stays home all day watching Financial News Network (for which he bought a satellite dish), running back and forth between the television and the phone. Most days, he can't even get himself to go to lunch because he's afraid he'll miss an important trade. He trades constantly, all day, every day. Unless he's made three or four trades a day, he's not happy.

Paul's moods, in fact, are tied in with the ticker tape. If his investments are up, he's elated; if they're down, he's despondent. In either case, by the end of the day, he's exhausted from the emotional roller coaster.

His relationship with his wife, Jeanne, now pregnant with their first child, has been affected too. She doesn't know anything about stocks, and since that's all Paul thinks about and wants to talk about these days, they don't seem to have much in common anymore. It's become a "separating thing," he says.

All the more separating, no doubt, because of the financial effects his stock-market gambling has had on the pair. At this point, Paul's luck has run out. He's lost all his original gain and most of the inheritance he began with—yet he doesn't stop. He keeps putting more money in, believing that he can make it back. Now he feels he *has* to play the market regardless of whether he wins or loses. "It takes me out of my present reality," he says. And that's what he's banking on now.

MARCIA, A FORTY-YEAR-OLD college administrator, lives in a wealthy California suburb. Married for five years to an alcoholic professor she met in college, she recently separated and says she's glad she did—even though it means raising their two-year-old alone. But Marcia has her own way of dealing with the stress in her life: she eats.

After her son is tucked into bed at night, Marcia brings massive amounts of food—cakes, ice cream, submarine sandwiches, candy, and doughnuts—into her bedroom and downs them in one sitting (or rather, she points out, reclining). Then she feels "drugged" and falls into a deep sleep. If she wakes during the night, she binges some more and goes back to sleep again. Sometimes, the day after a binge, she takes Ex-lax—up to thirty in a single day.

As Marcia's weight approaches the 300 mark, friends and colleagues often remark that she must have a "glandular problem," because they never see her overeat. They don't realize that she eats in secret—like most compulsive overeaters—where no one can interfere with the "orgy." At work, Marcia sometimes steals food from the department kitchen—not because she can't afford to buy her own, but just because it's there and she can't resist it. She lives in fear that she'll be found out and humiliated.

All this is taking its toll on Marcia physically. She has pains in her feet and shoulder blades from carrying so much weight. Her joints ache if she exercises, and she's increasingly short-winded. She's also had colitis now for six months.

Marcia's tried every diet around, lost "thousands" of pounds, and gained thousands back. She says she keeps "trying to eat normally," but just can't. "Food is too comforting," she admits. Recently, Marcia joined Overeaters Anonymous and says it's the first time she's felt any real hope.

WE ARE ALL VULNERABLE

What is most striking about these true—and increasingly typical— stories is that few bear out the stereotype we once held of the addict. The addict used to be some other guy, that poor unfortunate, a derelict, the product of an impoverished upbringing or someone obviously mentally disturbed. The addict was not someone like me, not someone who functioned, for the most part, "normally" in society. No, the addict was not me—not my brother, my parent, my wife, my neighbor, or my child.

But we can no longer maintain this denial about who is vulnerable to addiction. This epidemic of compulsive behaviors is not just happening in urban ghettos, or to poor people, the uneducated, or to one particular race. It's happening in every small town and big city in America; behind the doors of sprawling mansions, suburban tract houses, and high-rise apartments alike; among the highly educated as well as those barely out of grade school; among people of all colors and all classes. We don't have to look any farther than our own hometown, our own block, and often even our own family to find stories of addiction and the pain it carves into people's lives.

In fact, the addictive personality exists on a continuum. As we have all grown up in an addictive society amidst conditions that, as we shall see, generate addictive vulnerability, most of us exist somewhere on the continuum. We are vulnerable to different degrees based on who we are *inside*—not where we live, how much money we make, or the color of our skin. *What* we get addicted to may be influenced by some of those factors, but not *whether* we get addicted.

Differences between the "faces" of our addictions—how the disease expresses itself—do exist. Some addictions are obviously more overtly destructive than others. Few would dispute, for instance, that addiction to freebasing cocaine has more serious ramifications than workaholism or that the sexual addict who molests children is more destructive and dangerous than the compulsive shopper. Differences—in the severity and effects—of different addictions are enormous.

But when we allow ourselves to take seriously even the "nonserious" addictions like workaholism, stock-market gambling, shopping, or exercise, we find people who are not only failing to reach their potential, they are suffering greatly. But because their drug is socially acceptable, there is little pressure to get help.

Let's look now at some of the many expressions of addictive behavior prevalent in our society today.

THE MANY FACES OF ADDICTION

Few would argue that we are fast becoming a nation of compulsive drug users, a "chemical people," if you will. As Americans, we consume over 60 percent of the world's production of illicit drugs—more than any other nation. At last count, some 6 million of us regularly use cocaine, the street drug with the highest addiction potential of all. And the number of users of cocaine's most potent and addictive form—crack—is still climbing.

Then there are the legal drugs. We've had a blindspot about the negative consequences of these—especially our two favorites, alcohol and nicotine. Yet together they kill some 450,000 of us each year (compared with 6,000 or so deaths from illegal drugs). And let's not forget the 5 to 10 million Americans who abuse prescription medications such as tranquilizers, painkillers, and sleeping pills.

But since addiction is *any* self-defeating behavior that a person cannot stop despite its adverse consequences, the term can accurately be applied to almost any behavior that meets this criterion. Some 40 to 80 million Americans, for instance, are thought to suffer from compulsive overeating, bringing upon themselves a host of health problems—from obesity, diabetes, and hypertension to heart disease, stroke, and digestive disorders. (Five to 15 percent of all people with compulsive eating disorders actually die from these side effects.) Because many undertake an endless series of diets in a largely futile attempt to "control" the addiction, a $20 billion weight-loss industry thrives.

For sex addicts, sex is the drug that's used in a never-ending search for relief, distraction, comfort, excitement, and a sense of power, or other effect having little to do with sex itself.

At one end of the scale are those driven from one sexual encounter to the next, despite a constant lack of fulfillment (and now even the deadly threat of AIDS), those who compulsively seduce (the Don Juan complex), seek prostitutes (or prostitute themselves), or masturbate compulsively. Those with more severe sexual addictions engage in behaviors such as exhibitionism or voyeurism. And at the extreme are those who seek domination and power over others through such violent acts as rape and sexual abuse.

No one knows for sure how many sex addicts there are, but the fact that reports of sexual abuse have literally skyrocketed (from 6,000 in 1976 to 200,000 in 1988) tells us that there are a lot even at that end of the scale. Some 60 million Americans—one

13

quarter of us—are sexually abused by age eighteen. Tragically, young victims of sex addicts often go on to develop sexual or other addictions themselves, perpetuating the cycle in our society.

There are no statistics on how many Americans are in addictive relationships, where the relationship is used (like a drug) to avoid certain feelings and to play out power and control issues, among other things—but judging by the brisk sales of *Women Who Love Too Much,* Robin Norwood's book on the topic, and the rapid proliferation of self-help groups with this focus, there are lots.

Typically, the relationship addict stays hooked on partners who cannot provide many of the usual comforts of a relationship (security, intimacy, consistency) because they are themselves addicted to something, have intimacy phobias, are married, or are otherwise unavailable. Relationship addicts (also known as "codependents" because of their tendency to get addicted to addicts) can waste years, sometimes decades, looking for water in a dry well. Many suffer emotional, physical, or sexual abuse in the process.

"Loving too much," however, doesn't really accurately describe the problem in relationship addictions. The fact is, those of us who suffer from this disorder are ourselves unable to love intimately, let alone "too much." Staying with a partner who victimizes us or is unavailable in one way or another keeps us from having to face our own intimacy problems and reinforces the core belief "I am not enough."

There are more compulsive gamblers these days than most of us realize—about 12 million to be exact—and another 50 million, such as spouses and children, are affected by someone's compulsive betting. Not even counted among these figures are stock-market junkies, another "growth" addiction. Most often, people in over their heads in stocks, options, and commodities have even more denial than other gamblers, because they can rationalize that they're not gambling, they're "investing."

Those with gambling addictions stand to lose a lot more than money: 38 percent develop cardiovascular problems from the stress, and the suicide rate for this group is twenty times higher than the national average.

As our credit debts spiral upward, spending-related addictions are increasingly recognized as a serious problem. Collectively, we owe some $650 billion in consumer debt—twice our indebtedness in 1981! In part, this addiction reflects our mounting preoccupation with the process of shopping itself. Less than half of what we buy is to replace worn-out items. Mostly, we're just "shopping around" for something to fill us up, to make us feel better.

To pay for these mounting debts, an estimated 12 million Americans have become workaholics. This affliction can be a lot more serious than it sounds because it robs a person of his most valuable resource—time. As more and more of us commute long distances, work longer hours, and take work home with us in the evenings, we are losing our health, family life, and *joie de vivre.* The work ethic has gone overboard, and we're rapidly becoming a nation of workaholics.

What's the carrot in workaholism? Why do we do it? There are two chief reasons: (1) to gain a sense of competence and power *somewhere,* since we feel increasingly inadequate, bewildered, and insecure in our intimate relationships, and (2) to pay for the truckloads of consumer goods we think we need (even though we're never home to play with them). This addiction is probably the most difficult to identify because it's actively encouraged and rewarded in our culture. To resist workaholism is like turning down a drink at some parties: you have to be willing to be the oddball.

Compulsive exercise sounds harmless enough, but when someone is "driven" to get this fix above all else in his life—it takes a toll too. Addicted runners often injure themselves, and their personal relations and work productivity can suffer from their single-minded focus. What sets healthy exercise apart from the compulsive variety is that—like workaholism—the process of *striving* (for more mileage, faster time, more lifts on the Nautilus, or whatever) is the fix, so that as soon as one goal is reached, it's on to the next. Like other addicts, exercise "junkies" can't get enough—because they don't feel *they're* enough.

With the pronounced emphasis on appearance in our society, it's not surprising that millions suffer from preoccupations with

15

body image. Sad caricatures of this exaggerated concern are the 4 percent of American women who become anorectic (self-starving) at some point in their lives. (The rates are lower for men, but rising—especially among gays.) This is no harmless primping; anorectics have one of the highest mortality rates—5 to 10 percent—of any psychiatric illness. And bulimia, a disorder in which binge eating is followed by self-induced vomiting or other "purging" measures—affects even more, perhaps as many as 8 percent.

There are also the swelling ranks of scalpel slaves, those addicted to altering their looks with serial plastic surgery. Such people use tucks, lifts, and other procedures the way an addict uses a drug: they get a temporary high, but can never get enough. Then they keep coming back for more, trying to make themselves feel better.

Some behaviors not usually identified as addictions may, in fact, qualify. Some 10 to 11 million Americans might be called religious addicts. Unlike others with spiritual or religious interests, religion junkies use their church or cult activities not so much for spiritual growth and devotion but as a way to compulsively structure and control their lives—often because they feel out of control if they don't. And like any addiction, religion can be used as a way to exert control over others, as many who grew up in families with religion addicts can verify.

Another behavior not commonly thought of as addiction but which may, in some cases, be one is compulsive violence. For a "rageaholic," lashing out at someone—a child, a spouse, a stranger—provides a temporary mood-change by discharging inner tension. The perpetrator has little control over the impulse, feels intense guilt and shame afterward, but inevitably repeats it again, despite the consequences. Willpower, it appears, is not enough to stop it.

LIVING IN AN ADDICTIVE SOCIETY AFFECTS US ALL

Not one of us is unaffected by the current addictions epidemic in America. If we aren't ourselves driven by self-defeating cravings for some drug, food, or activity, then someone we know probably is, for every addict directly affects at least ten others, people with whom he or she regularly interacts.

An astounding 41 percent of Americans surveyed in a recent Gallup poll said they have already suffered physical, psychological, or social harm during their lifetime as a result of someone else's drinking. This is twice the level reported in 1974 and says nothing about those affected by addicts of other drugs. Neither does it take into account the growing ranks of infants damaged *in utero* by drugs or in childhood by parents too preoccupied with their drug—whatever it is—to provide proper care.

But even if we don't ourselves know someone seriously addicted, we are still victims of the epidemic just because we live in a society among so many out-of-control people. Less and less can we depend on people in the work force, for instance, to be concentrating on their job and not on their addiction. (Three quarters of cocaine users calling a hot line admitted using the drug on the job, a quarter of them daily.) Some addicts will be teaching our children, assembling our cars, running our government, and performing other tasks that we count on for quality.

Living in a society of addicts also means living among people increasingly unable to enter into or maintain close relationships. Growing up in an addictive family, as more and more of us do, we often don't learn how to be intimate, and those who become addicts themselves become even less capable of loving, honoring, or protecting anything beyond their next fix—of whatever sort.

As the rate of addiction climbs, so does the safety risk to everyone—addicted or not—who steps out the door in the morning. Addiction-related crime is on the upswing; so much so that the Justice Department grimly predicts that three of four homes will be burglarized in the next twenty years and 83 percent of current twelve-year-olds will be the victim or intended victim of a violent crime.

Our daily safety is jeopardized too by addicted train, plane, bus, and car drivers. In just one fatal train crash last year, all five railroad employees involved were found to have illicit drugs in

17

their blood. And in 1986, nearly 24,000 of us died in alcohol-related car crashes.

There are also more hidden, yet far-reaching ramifications of our addictions epidemic: some $200 billion is drained from our economy each year, the result of lost work productivity, addiction-related medical care, and crime. And the amount of money spent on our drugs directly is mind-boggling ($150 billion a year on cocaine alone). This epidemic may even jeopardize our national defense, for the rates of drug and alcohol use among those who enter our armed forces are thought to be substantial.

Like the individual addict, we, as an addictive society, are increasingly out of control. And because our collective cravings have such extensive consequences, this problem must be addressed before we as a nation can begin to thrive again. For just as an alcoholic often cannot resolve his debt, work, and relationship problems until first he is sober, so we as a nation will make little headway with our other domestic problems until we reverse those trends within our culture that foster addiction.

But just as the individual addict can recover, so too is there hope for our addictive society. As we shall see, the problem is not just the drugs themselves (or the credit cards, or the food, or the sex), but our insatiable appetite for mood-changers. That's why the so-called War on Drugs isn't working; it doesn't address the widespread "dis-ease," the quick-fix mentality that makes so many of us vulnerable to addiction. We *can* get better—both individually and collectively—but only after we admit that we are ill.

2

Is It an Addiction?

WHEN DOES A HABIT BECOME an addiction? How does one tell the real thing from a harmless activity not worth worrying about? Some people think of an addict as a "desperate fiend," chasing a fix twenty-four hours a day, every day. The guideline they apply is: if you're doing it every day, you must be addicted. What follows from this erroneous belief is the equally erroneous converse: if you're *not* doing it every day, then you can't possibly be addicted.

The fact is, whether or not something is used daily is *not* an accurate measure of whether a person is addicted. The *majority* of addicts, in fact, are not daily users of their drug, but use it in sporadic binges, alternating periods of daily use with periods of abstinence or controlled use.

It's important to understand this, because, based on this erroneous measure, people who are addicted often reassure themselves and others that they don't have a problem. "I don't even drink every day, so how can I have a problem?" Or "I only use coke on weekends. If I was addicted, I'd be doing it all the time."

With some drugs and activities it is even theoretically possible (though unlikely) for a person to use every day and not be addicted. In *A Nation of Gamblers,* for example, Stuart Winston and Harriet Harris point out that it is possible to place a bet every day and not be a compulsive gambler—if the amount bet is within one's financial means and *causes no negative consequences.*

With many substances, though (nicotine, caffeine, sugar, cocaine, and alcohol among them), daily use does often *lead* to addiction. With a highly addictive drug like cocaine, for example, it would be very unusual for someone to use it every day for, say, six months and not become addicted—given this drug's profound biochemical effects on the brain. Whether a person uses a drug every day, then, is not an accurate yardstick in determining addiction.

Neither is how much one uses (snorts, spends, drinks, bets). A person can be alcoholic, for instance, and have only a couple of drinks a day—if she is exerting tight control over the urge to drink more. Likewise, people have become cocaine addicts on as little as one gram a week, while others who use more of the drug may not show signs of addiction (at least yet).

As we shall see, then, it's not the amount nor the frequency that matters so much as *how the drug affects you,* both at the moment and in its overall effect on your life. Basically, use of a drug or activity is an addiction *if it's causing problems in your life but you keep doing it anyway.*

The other key distinguishing factor is *what you're using the drug or activity for.* If you're drinking to quell an inner "tension," for instance, chances are it's not "social drinking." If you're having sex to distract yourself from intolerable feelings more than to express yourself sexually, it's probably addiction. If your main reason for being in a particular relationship is to avoid being alone, you're using it addictively. Basically, if you are using something as a mood-changer because your own mood is intolerable, it's going to lead you in the direction of addiction.

THE FOUR CARDINAL SIGNS OF ADDICTION

Addiction to anything is diagnosable. Its symptoms can be recognized and described. There is a point at which the disease does not yet exist and a point at which it does. The problem is diagnosing someone else's addiction is that this disease is best left *self-diagnosed.* That's because unless the addicted person is ready to see it, he will probably dismiss and resent your "labeling" anyway. Unfortunately, though, the addict is usually the last to know about his problem because of a defense known as *denial.* Still, hammering someone with your diagnosis of his addiction is usually a futile exercise.

The best thing you can do—rather than label him—is give the person concrete feedback about his behavior and how it affects you. For example, a man concerned about his wife's recent cocaine use might say something like, "When you used cocaine the other night and then missed work the next day, it affected me. I'm worried that cocaine's starting to take priority over other things in your life and that it'll affect our relationship too." With this, he hasn't diagnosed, hasn't labeled, but has simply and honestly stated what he's observed and how he feels about it.

If the addictive behavior continues, there may be a need for a more planned or professionally guided confrontation, or "intervention." Many treatment centers today offer this and other forms of help for the person *affected* by someone else's addiction.

Let's look in more detail now at the four cardinal signs (symptoms) of addiction.

1. Obsession

Addictive behavior is usually quite compelling and consuming. If you're addicted to something (or someone) you often can't stop thinking about it and planning for your next "fix." When you're close to being able to engage in the activity, you may get a feeling of anxiety and excitement that doesn't let up until you actually get to do it. And if your use is blocked, you'll probably become frustrated and perhaps panicky. In general, your obsession consumes a good deal of your time, energy, and attention.

If you're addicted, you'll also increasingly arrange your life in ways that facilitate getting your drug. Depending on the addiction, you might make sure nothing interferes with getting to the track to gamble, line up a supply of cocaine for the evening, or bring alcohol to a dinner party to make sure it's served. You'll protect the supply of your drug at any cost.

Richard, a compulsive gambler who got help through Gamblers Anonymous, looks back on how compelling his urge to gamble was and how it completely overrode any other values:

> One day when my wife was doing the dishes she cut her hand on a broken glass. She was bleeding all over the place from a big gouge and was going to have to go to the hospital. I had a *fit* because I was planning on going to the races. "How dare she do this to me!" I thought. I got a neighbor to take her to the emergency room on the pretext that I couldn't get the car started. Soon as they were out of the driveway, I was off to the races.

The compelling urge that an addict experiences has been described as a "command from within." It's as if you are driven to do it despite any more "rational" considerations. Debbie, a compulsive spender, recalls that there was no decision involved: "I felt totally compelled to buy and spend—regardless of the reality of my resources. There wasn't even any struggle in my mind about it. I would just block out the reality, go to the bank machine, and punch my card through. I was *going* to do it. Period."

And Jerry, a sex addict whose compulsion drove him to ride the subway so that he could rub up against women's bodies in the crowded cars, describes how his negative moods became compelling urges: "It just felt like a necessity, that's the best way I can describe it. There wasn't even a thinking process to it that I was aware of. I'd be in the depths of depression, and the next thing I knew I was finding some way to get out of those depths—which for me was through this ritual."

2. Negative Consequences

Suppose you squeeze a glass of fresh orange juice every day. It tastes so good that pretty soon it becomes a habit. Now if you don't have your o.j., you really miss it. You start making sure you've got enough oranges at night for the next day. Could this be considered an addiction, albeit a positive one? Not at all. It's just a habit, a repetitive pattern of behavior from which you derive some benefit—without any negative consequences.

What makes an addiction an addiction is that it turns against you. You start off getting some apparent benefit, just as you do with a habit. But sooner or later your behavior starts having negative consequences in your life—yet you keep doing it anyway. Addictive behaviors produce pleasure, relief, and other payoffs in the short run but pain, grief, and more problems in the long run.

Stanton Peele, author of several books on addiction, notes that "the criteria that establish if an individual is addicted . . . must focus on the involvement's *harmfulness* [emphasis added] to the individual . . ." Such harmfulness, he continues, might include "its limiting of other sources of gratification, the perception by the individual that the involvement is essential to his or her functioning, and the upset to the person's overall social, psychological, and physical system from deprivation of the involvement."

The negative consequences associated with addictions affect many different areas of a person's life, including:

Relationships. An addicted person often takes time away from family and friends to pursue the drug or recover from it, resulting in broken plans, sexual disinterest, arguments, and increasing resentment. Communication breaks down as the addict withdraws and becomes emotionally distant, trying to eliminate any interference with her use. Less and less can she be counted on to keep her word, so distrust grows—creating an atmosphere in which no relationship can thrive. Estrangement, separation, and divorce are common long range consequences

Work. The person suffering from addiction may start taking time away from work (to pursue the drug or recover from it), resulting in frequent tardiness, absences, lost productivity, lowered quality of work, tension with coworkers, missed promotions, and sometimes loss of work itself.

Finances. Funneling money into addictive pursuits such as drugs, betting, sex, and shopping inevitably leaves less money for other things. It drains savings and leads to unpaid bills and borrowing. Income suffers too when someone loses work because of the addiction.

Psychological health. Addicts often suffer a wide range of psychological consequences, including negative moods and irritability, defensiveness, loss of self-esteem and confidence, and intense feelings of guilt and shame (though these may be covered up). As if this were not enough, one's self-esteem often further plummets because of the problems building at work, at home, and in finances. And because the addict can't seem to bring these problems under control, feelings of being a failure, of powerlessness, depression and despair often ensue. Then it becomes a circular process: these feelings lead to a greater desire to use the drug again and again—to escape the pain and suffering.

Judgment and behavior. In the grips of addiction, people do things they wouldn't ordinarily do, because getting and using the drug become more important than almost anything else. As a result, addicts are often considered "selfish and self-centered," caring about no one but themselves. While this may be true on the surface, it's an inaccurate explanation for their behavior, which is motivated more by desperation than purposeful disregard. "The drowning man," writes Leon Wurmser, noted addictions theoretician, "has commonly little regard for questions of integrity."

Physical health. The compulsive pursuit of a mood-changer —whatever it is—often results in the neglect of one's physical health. This, combined with a build-up of stress, can easily lead to a myriad of physical symptoms, including appetite disturbances, ulcers, high blood pressure, loss of sleep, and fatigue, to name a few. Then there's the physical effects of the drug or activity itself, whether it is anorexia, bulimia, overeating, or compulsive exercise. Drug and alcohol addicts are subject to certain illnesses due to the specific chemical effects of their drug.

3. A Lack of Control

Despite these negative consequences, if you're addicted, you're usually unable to control or stop the behavior—once you "pick up" (have that first drink, place that first bet)—despite all good intentions and vows to yourself and others. The very mark of addictive behavior is that in trying to bring it under control, *willpower's not enough!* The substance or activity is controlling *you* rather than you controlling it.

For example, once the compulsive spender stops at the mall, she will very likely be unable to control her spending; once the gambler places that first bet, he is not in control of the amount bet; and once the alcoholic picks up that first drink, she is finishing the bottle. Personal accounts of this abound. Joyce, a compulsive eater, remembers:

> Every time I started a diet, I was convinced my willpower would triumph. I figured I was intelligent, so therefore I should be able to control my eating if I wanted to. But it never worked. Whether it lasted a day or six months, I always started bingeing again. It would start with one bite off my food plan, and then I couldn't stop. And it ended with the despair that I'd done it again.

Steve, a sex addict whose addiction consisted primarily of compulsively pursuing sex with prostitutes, has some interesting insights into the whole issue of willpower and addiction:

> Occasionally after doing it [having sex with a prostitute] I would say, "This is it. I'm disgusted, I've had enough, this is the last time." Until the next time. Willpower doesn't mean a thing with this stuff. In fact, it's the enemy . . . the absolute enemy. It doesn't work. If willpower worked, no one would be a sex addict, an alcoholic, or anything else.

But the idea of self-control gets confusing, because some people who are addicted *are* able to exert some degree of control for varying periods of time, which only feeds the illusion that there is no problem. This may be denial masquerading as discipline or control. For instance, a cocaine addict often can go for several weeks without getting high, especially if trying to prove to someone such as a spouse or therapist that the addiction isn't a problem. Likewise, compulsive gamblers have been known to have episodes of control, as have compulsive eaters on a new diet.

Unless the person's addictive disease is being healed within, however, a return to the drug—or another one—is usually inevitable. So in the end there is no control. Or the addict can continue to exert strained control over his addiction—theoretically for the rest of his life. But again, if he isn't healing the disease within, he's likely to be still suffering from the emotional pain that made him crave a mood-change in the first place. There's a saying among recovering alcoholics that if you want to know how bad the disease of alcoholism really feels, don't drink and don't get help. For that's when the mental and emotional aspects of the addictive personality are experienced—without the "anesthesia" of a drug.

Cathy, for example, is the child of an alcoholic and was "determined" never to become an alcoholic herself. As a teenager, when she found herself drinking in the morning a couple of times, she got scared and decided she'd better cut back. Her reasoning, she recalls, was "to get it under control now, so I could drink for the rest of my life." And control she did, cutting back to about two beers a day.

Yet a decade later, at age twenty-eight, Cathy's life seemed to be falling apart: she suffered from excruciating feelings of inadequacy in her job as a social worker, had few friends, and was generally not functioning up to her potential. But she couldn't figure out what was wrong with her.

Then, one day, she heard a speaker from Alcoholics Anonymous talking at a conference she went to for work. He said that he had been able to control his drinking for years, but that the *mental* part of the disease—the low self-esteem, the feelings of isolation, the self-consciousness—still made his life unmanageable. Cathy's denial was pierced:

> The veil lifted. I said to myself, "I'm an alcoholic." I just knew it in that moment. I remember thinking, "So that's what's wrong with

me." I finally understood what was wrong with my life. This guy was describing ways I felt that I had no idea had anything to do with alcoholism. Since I had been controlling my drinking, it hadn't occurred to me that I still had the disease of alcoholism. I realized then that while I was in control of the physical part, the mental part was still raging in me.

The addict, then, is either out of control or trying to control his use. In either case, it's not a nonissue. Not using, for the addict, is effortful. He has to think about not using and apply himself, because he is still compelled by it. No matter how much willpower he exerts over his actual use, he is powerless over the disease within. The key question, then, is not so much "Are you able to control it?" but "Can you take it or leave it?" If you can truly leave it—not use and not care, not crave it, not think about it—then you're probably not addicted.

4. Denial

As addicts begin to pile up problems at work and at home—virtually everywhere—as a result of their addiction and their neglect of ongoing problems, they inevitably begin to deny two things: (1) that the drug or activity is a problem they can't control and (2) that the negative consequences in their lives have any connection whatsoever to the drug use or activity.

Denial takes many forms, and Terence Gorski, author of *Staying Sober,* has identified some of the most common:

1. *Absolute denying.* "No, I don't have a problem."
2. *Minimizing.* "It's not that bad."
3. *Avoiding* the subject altogether (ignoring it, refusing to address it, or distracting others from the subject).
4. *Blaming others.* "Sure I do it—who wouldn't if they had my wife/boss/kids, etc."
5. *Rationalizing and intellectualizing.* "I'm not as bad as Joe." Or "Cocaine is not addictive anyway."

Examples abound of just how powerful denial can be. When Arthur's drinking caused him to be committed to a psychiatric hospital, for example, he was *still* unable to see that alcohol had anything to do with it. As far as he was concerned, alcohol was his "best friend":

> Just because I was in the "nut house"—while I certainly would allow that things had taken an "unfortunate turn"—I was not about to tell you that alcohol was the core problem here. In fact, I still remember my interview with the social worker, and her looking across the table at me saying, "Alcohol is your problem." And I said, "Wait a minute, dearie, alcohol is not my problem. Alcohol is the glue that keeps me together in the face of all these problems." And I believed that.

Like Arthur, addicts typically blame other people and circumstances for the problems in their lives: a boss who's making life miserable, an unfaithful husband, a nagging wife, a lack of money, and on and on. The idea is that if other people and circumstances would just cooperate, life would straighten out.

Since denial is a delusional thought process, to be in denial about one's addiction or its consequences is to literally be out of touch with reality. The moment that the cocaine addict, for example, makes a decision to buy another gram of coke—despite the fact that he has no money left to buy his children's school clothes or pay the mortgage—he literally enters a delusional state. There is a blocking of his rational mental faculties.

To the extent that denial represents an actual break with reality, it is nothing short of a "micro-psychosis," as Harvard psychiatrist Margaret Bean-Bayog suggested recently. Only in a psychotic person, she says, do we observe a split with reality that comes anywhere close in magnitude to that observed in an addict. She calls it micro-psychosis because the person is not usually psychotic otherwise. The addict has this psychotic-level break with reality in this one circumscribed area only: maintaining the addictive activity.

The key point here is that addicts are not just trying to manipulate and "get over" on everyone. At the moment that they are

28

denying, they really believe they are telling the truth. They block from consciousness the facts that would point otherwise. In a sense, the addict is saying, "If reality is painful, I don't want to see it. Therefore I will close my eyes, and it will go away."

For the person who must interact with an addict—spouse, child, parent, coworker, friend—the addict's denial can be maddening. Unless you are aware that denial is a *symptom* of addiction and that it exerts a very powerful unconscious pull on the addict, you can become very confused. The addict's arguments and rationalizations may be so convincing that you even start to question your own perceptions. Obviously, you should trust your own inner voice in this situation rather than the claims of a person rendered literally out of touch with reality.

The main function of denial is to keep anything from interfering with one's use. The addict has to avoid seeing the problems the addiction is creating because if she sees them, she'll have to do something about them, and that thought is intolerable once she's addicted, as Beverly, a compulsive overeater who once tipped the scales at 325 pounds, attests:

> When I was really fat, I literally didn't know how fat I was. I was in denial about it, I guess. I would look in the mirror and just be able to see the center third of my body . . . yet I didn't realize how distorted that was. It was only after I'd lost 75 pounds or so and saw a photo of myself that I realized how bad I'd gotten.
>
> If I acknowledged it then I would have had to do something about it, because the reality of it was really intolerable. I mean, it was hard just to get around the room. And I "knew" it then, but I couldn't stand to know it, so I blocked it out.

The addict denies, then, because it is effective to do so, as Gorski points out, *in the short run* (which is all the addict is concerned with). While the addiction itself is creating unmanageability in the addict's life, denial helps him keep out of touch with that fact and maintain the illusion that "everything's O.K.," that he's in control. Denial allows the addict to maintain some good feelings about himself by blocking out awareness of the growing chaos in his life.

29

In other words, when the addict's illusions, her idealized image of herself, come under assault from the invading reality, the wall of denial *must* go up. For in the black-and-white world of the addict, as we shall see, those who do not maintain the illusion of being "O.K." will drop to the depths of self-loathing and be left with feelings of utter worthlessness, shame, and humiliation.

Thus, denial is a self-protective effort, given what addicts believe about themselves and the world around them. It's an attempt to retain some integrity of self, no matter what. The addict is operating under a faulty belief system and doesn't know (1) that it's not necessary, or even possible, to be perfect, (2) that the quick-fix doesn't work, and (3) that he *can* get help from others.

The main destructive effect of denial is that it prevents the addict from correcting his behavior—because he is out of touch with it. As one noted expert puts it, "Gone are the feedback loops." Though the addict's problems are growing worse, and the signs of addiction more glaring, this information is not getting through to him. He is diverted and distracted and cannot see himself and say, "Oh, this substance/behavior is affecting my job/marriage/health so I'd better stop doing it." The addict can't do this because he isn't getting the information. And that's why all addicts are destined to hit a brick wall; they never saw it coming.

The question many readers may have at this point is "How is it possible for an average person—a person not in obvious psychological pain, who functions fairly well at work and in other areas of life, to become addicted and not 'see it coming'?" In the next chapter, we'll look at just what does happen when an "ordinary person" gets trapped in a cycle of addictive behavior.

3

How Ordinary People Get Trapped

YOU DON'T HAVE TO HAVE EVERY element of an addictive personality or be emotionally disturbed to become trapped by addictive behavior. All it takes is your brain's memory, or imprint, of an experience with some activity or substance that was inordinately comforting, relief-giving, or pleasurable. Later, when you experience a high level of stress (as we all do at one time or another), you may be unconsciously compelled to seek that substance or activity again. Without your even realizing it, a vicious cycle can be set in motion. With alcohol, drugs, and perhaps even arousing activities like gambling, actual biochemical effects on the brain reinforce the dependency, as we shall see.

In many ways, the process of addiction can be likened to a developing relationship. As we proceed through each stage, our involvement intensifies and the pull it exerts on us becomes stronger. Since this relationship is something like a bad marriage, we've outlined the stages accordingly.

Stage 1: Infatuation. Our early experiences with a drug or activity leave an imprint on us—if it provides a welcome effect.

Stage 2: The Honeymoon. Under stress, we seek out that remembered experience for comfort or relief. We get only its positive effects and expect them to last.

31

Stage 3: Betrayal. The drug or activity that has served us so well turns on us. We no longer get the "high" from it.

Stage 4: On the Rocks. Ignoring mounting evidence of the drug or activity's negative effects, we try to recapture the honeymoon by increasing our involvement with it.

Stage 5: Trapped. Now, the more we struggle to break the addiction by willpower alone, the tighter its grip becomes.

STAGE 1: INFATUATION

The addict's early encounters with the drug to which she later becomes addicted leave her starry-eyed and in love. Usually, it has an effect on her that is outstanding in some way—thrilling, euphoric, or soothing. It brings a mood-change, one that, in many cases, is felt viscerally.

With alcohol and drug addictions, of course, this mood-change is caused by an actual alteration of brain chemistry. Any substance that makes you feel "high" is altering your brain chemistry—that's what *causes* the sensation of being "high." Those substances most likely to cause addiction upset the brain's neurotransmitter balance and in time cause an actual biochemical dependency on the substance, as we shall see.

For the person who becomes addicted to an arousing activity like gambling, the "thrill" sought is said to be similar to a drug high. Very often it involves a release of adrenaline. So to the degree that brain biochemistry is affected, even activity addictions may have a physiological component. But because there has been insufficient research in this area, we can only offer a best guess theory at this time.

What experts in gambling do know is that a big win early on makes gambling addiction much more likely to develop. The win (and perhaps the adrenaline rush that accompanies it) becomes the hook. Even if the gambler loses his next several wagers, the memory of that early win keeps him coming back to try again and again.

He keeps thinking, "This will be the time."

Infatuation with a mood-changer can happen at any age. Six-year-old Sally, for instance, feels loved when her mother rewards her with cookies. That first beer makes fourteen-year-old Allan feel socially at ease—"normal" for the first time. Teenage Jill feels better about herself as she shops for new clothes. Joe, at twenty-two, goes to the racetrack for the first time and finds it an unexpected thrill. And Ellen, in her thirties, tries cocaine and loves the feelings of self-confidence and power she gets from it. From these examples, it is easier to see how a particular drug or activity will have continuing appeal to the person who has had such a positive early experience with it.

The Brain's "Reward Center" and Imprinting

It could be said that our brains go by the maxim "If it feels good, do it." That's because they're "wired" to reinforce pleasure and avoid pain, undoubtedly to help us meet basic survival needs such as hunger, thirst, warmth, and sleep.

What sets the biological stage for addiction, then, may be some type of learning that takes place on a cellular level in our brain's reward center. The brain, in effect, "reads" our response to a substance or activity. If we are infatuated with it, find it inordinately comforting or relief-giving (usually because it meets some needs not being met otherwise), it releases neurotransmitters that convey the message "This has survival value—recommend repeating." The next time we engage in the activity or ingest the substance, we are again rewarded with releases of these "feeling-good" neurotransmitters and experience a sense of well-being, as if we have satisfied a basic drive.

This mechanism clearly has adaptive value. If we were starving, specific brain messages would help us to survive by sending us off in single-minded pursuit of food. We would become so intent on getting food that we'd put it first above all else. We would take time away from work if necessary and withdraw from social activities until we found the food we needed.

33

If what we are starving for is not food, however, but a sense of power, control, and confidence, cocaine (or any experience which provides the illusion of these goals) will cause the brain to register *it* as something to be sought after as a top priority. In effect, our brain gets misprogrammed into reinforcing an addictive behavior as if we need it to survive.

Steve, a sex addict who compulsively sought prostitutes, recalls how his first sexual experience formed an imprint in his mind that propelled him into addiction:

> The first time I had sex with a woman I was about sixteen. My parents were away and all the guys I hung out with were over and we were drinking beer and Jack Daniels. One of my friends announced that he knew this girl who was a nymphomaniac. He said he could go pick her up and bring her back to the house. He did, and he wasn't kidding. All twelve of us took turns with her all afternoon.
>
> So my first sexual experience was in this really insensitive, totally degrading situation. It had nothing to do with the girl at all. I actually ejaculated before I even penetrated her.
>
> But this experience taught me that seeking out prostitutes was my thing. I found out that in being with prostitutes I could get a girl to be with me . . . it was a sure thing; and I could get held, I could get caressed, I could get the orgasm which became my substitute for feeling whole and complete.

Who Falls for What?

Why do we gravitate to one substance or activity, finding *it* a welcome effect and not another? For the same reason that we're attracted to one person over another. This is a complex interaction based on how the effects of the addictive object match up with the needs of the addict, influenced by life-style/personality predisposition, physical predisposition, attitudinal predisposition or expectations, and availability.

For example, how satisfied do we feel with our lives? The more "hungry" we are for certain effects and gratifications, the more attracted we will be to a substance or activity that provides them, just as a five-course meal will have more appeal to someone who hasn't eaten all day than it will to someone who has just gotten up from the table.

But in some cases there is also a physical predisposition, a preexisting biological vulnerability, either inherited genetically or perhaps acquired through the effects of diet and chronic stress. This vulnerability can be compared to an allergy, and it has been positively identified not only in some alcoholics (an estimated one- to two-thirds of those who develop alcoholism, for instance, are thought to have inherited a genetic vulnerability) but in compulsive gamblers, compulsive runners, and other addicts. If a person has this preexisting vulnerability and is exposed to the substance or activity, she skips straight to the end of the addictive process— where the physical component of the disease kicks in. It's a little like getting a GO DIRECTLY TO JAIL, DO NOT PASS GO card in the game of Monopoly.

Whether a drug is widely accepted within our social milieu affects whether we try it or not—and thus whether we get addicted to it or not. For instance, if alcohol was widely used in our home growing up, we will be more likely to use it, and thus be more likely to get addicted to it.

We also learn from our environment the degree to which a desired *result* of a drug or activity is approved of and rewarded. Among the upper-middle-class and highly educated, thinness, a youthful appearance, material success, and accomplishment are highly valued. Hence, it is no surprise that anorexia, compulsive exercise, and workaholism are more common in this group too.

We can't fall in love with a person we never meet. Similarly, whatever activity or substance is easily available to us affects what addiction or addictions we may pick up. A person who has a large disposable income has greater access to such quick-fixes as shopping, cocaine, and stock-market gambling.

But once—for whatever complex of reasons—we have "fallen in love" with a certain mood-changer, the groundwork is laid for a crippling dependency to develop. The memory of this early love— with its comfort, security, and excitement—remains imprinted in

35

our brain's reward center. If we lack the self-awareness to observe the delusion involved, we may "wed" ourselves to it as a technique for coping with life—and take off on a honeymoon.

STAGE 2: THE HONEYMOON

Once a person has learned—from family, society, or her own experience—that such activities as food, sex, gambling, or shopping can provide that magical transportation away from uncomfortable feelings or moods, it's a short hop to the next circular path down the vortex of addiction. Inevitably, stressful times will occur in any person's life. Having "learned" at Stage 1 that a certain experience of relief or pleasure is available through the addictive substance or activity, the person may be compelled to try and blot out the uncomfortable or painful feelings with something positive.

Remember Joe, who during Stage 1 went to the racetrack and liked it because it took his mind off things? A few months or a year later when he's troubled because he failed to get an expected promotion at work, what does he feel like doing? Gambling at the racetrack! When Jill, who found buying a new dress gave her a lift, finds herself in the midst of a painful marital separation, she goes shopping. Sally goes to the cookie jar, Allan reaches for a beer, and Ellen buys some cocaine.

Paul, the engineer who had a big win in the stock market his first time out, didn't play again for a while. But his brain stored away the memory of the power and control he felt from playing. A few years later, he ran into a particularly stressful time: Paul's father, with whom he had had a close relationship, died suddenly and Paul's wife became pregnant—both within a couple of months. He started to play the market again. This time, he threw himself into it with a vengeance:

> There definitely was a high with it, a very enthusiastic feeling. But in a way it was also a distraction. It took me out of my present reality. I didn't think about any of the problems in my life while I was watching that ticker. It was a release from other things, kept my

mind busy, and took it off everything else. It gave me something to focus on.

The trigger for turning to the mood-changer as a way of coping can be any life crisis, an experience of failure (or success), feelings of isolation, the death of someone close, career stress, relationship problems, or any other situation that engenders uncomfortable feelings or moods. The relationship with the drug or activity can develop slowly over a period of years or, in acute stress, escalate quickly.

Thirty-year-old Bruce is a sex addict who compulsively masturbates and frequents peep shows. After early experiences with masturbation brought him comfort, Bruce returned to this fix whenever feelings of insecurity overtook him, such as during high school when he was picked on by his peers:

> I wanted so much to be accepted and I just couldn't understand why I was being picked on. It was very upsetting to me. And that just reinforced the escape of the masturbation. There was something about looking at those naked women—the connection that I felt— that made me feel so connected and loved. It's hard to explain.

Quite normally, we all have a desire when we are in a bad mood to change it to a good one. Faced with circumstances that create uncomfortable mood states such as fear, anxiety, or anger, it is natural to want to do something to change or obliterate the feelings. Feelings we call negative are signals that alert us to a situation (either internal or external) that needs attention.

Without a "magical solution," we have basically two options if we are to find relief: we can take some action to change the circumstances that are having this negative impact on us (by problem-solving, negotiating, communicating), or—if that is not possible or desirable—we can change ourselves, our relationship to the circumstances.

Unfortunately, many of us are inadequately trained in either of these coping modes. We know little about making effective changes in our environment because we have not learned to communicate directly what we want and feel (oftentimes not even knowing ourselves) and have not learned problem-solving techniques such as reflection, self-observation, negotiation, and cooperation. We are much more accustomed to denying our true feelings, avoiding reflection and self-observation, and blocking out any awareness that threatens to break through by stringing together a series of mood-altering experiences.

Likewise, we have been raised with belief systems that make it all the more difficult to change our relationship to the circumstances. The first step in such a process is to pause, reflect, self-observe, and take stock of ourselves. This reflective posture is one we have had little training in, growing up as we have in an action- and achievement-oriented culture. We learn from our models that if you don't like what someone is doing, you stop him by being stronger and more controlling than he is.

The result of being unskilled in either external or internal problem-coping skills is our increasing susceptibility to copping out, changing our moods by temporarily removing ourselves from the problem. As Stanton Peele puts it, "More and more people seek to modify internal emotional states rather than working to modify the external conditions of their lives."

During the honeymoon, the addict-to-be experiences all the payoffs with none of the negative consequences: he feels in control, feels the activity is harmless, feels he deserves it. He can instantly feel better, enjoy the sense of oblivion, the loss of awareness, the relief or the high. What he doesn't realize is that no marriage based on delusion and fantasy can work in the long run.

STAGE 3: BETRAYAL

The real irony of addictions is that what you see during the honeymoon is not really what you get. Eventually you are betrayed.

At first, addictions seem to serve us well: we feel more attractive, at ease, less isolated, more productive, powerful, removed from our problems, or whatever else we're looking for. But this feeling is based upon an illusion, for the drug can't really provide these results. And while we're trying to maintain that illusion, our problems are actually mounting and our hunger for gratification intensifying. Because the addict has withdrawn whatever long-term coping efforts he did have in favor of the quick-fix, the original problems are now worse.

The addict's greatest fear—being inadequate—is compounded by the very real failure that is occurring now in most areas of her life as the result of her compulsive drug use or activity. If she had reason to feel inadequate to begin with (often she doesn't, but has an exaggerated sense of her own failure), she has *real* reason to feel so now: her productivity at work is down due to preoccupation with the addiction; perhaps her job, promotion, or income is threatened; her relationships are also affected because she has made the addiction her priority love affair; rejection or abandonment may be imminent; and so on.

In addition to the deterioration of major areas of her life, the addict at this point is probably doing things she wouldn't ordinarily do in order to maintain her addiction. The compulsive debtor is now writing bad checks, manipulating bank accounts to cover insufficient funds, reneging on loans. The compulsive eater may be stealing food or taking food out of garbage cans (both acts are more common that most people realize). The drug addict is stealing money, participating in other criminal acts, or trading sex for drugs. All of these compromises of values contribute to plummeting self-esteem and give the addict all the more negative moods from which to escape. Grant, a compulsive debtor, describes it this way:

> My self-esteem was affected in so many ways. I didn't want to walk downtown, I owed so many people and was bouncing checks all over the place. I found it very hard to face people. Once a bank manager called me in for kiting checks. Two banks got together and realized what I was doing. He looked at me from across the desk and said, "Grant, what you're doing is a criminal offense." I was so humiliated. But it didn't stop me. In fact, I kept spending money I didn't have, maybe more than ever after that. I was in so much pain.

39

As the ability to assess realistically either the original problems or the negative effects of the addiction is lost, denial (remember, the fourth cardinal sign of an addiction) sets in. Blame for both the original stresses and for any new problems related to the addiction get placed on others and on external circumstances. With denial operating at full force, the addict is no longer able to accurately perceive the negative consequences of his drug use. The communication lines have been severed.

At this or an earlier stage, the addict can receive messages from the family system that encourage him—however unwittingly—to proceed down the path of addiction. Usually these messages come from someone who relates as a codependent. (The term "codependent," while originally used to describe the person addicted to an addict, is now used more broadly to refer to anyone from a dysfunctional family who's developed a vulnerability to other addictions. We are using the original, narrower sense here.) For the codependent, such a payoff might be a feeling of being needed, of being a good caretaker, or of being in control and powerful.

Debbie, a compulsive spender and debtor, recalls how her money addictions developed hand in glove with her mother's codependency:

> When I was just getting on my own, in my early twenties, I remember my mother would periodically pay off my bills. Sometimes all I had to do was mention that I had a big bill or expense to meet, and I could count on a check showing up in the mail a couple days later. Once I bounced ten checks in one week and I called her because I couldn't cover the bank charges. She sent it right off to me, no questions asked.
>
> We had a little ritual we went through, though, whenever she bailed me out. I would call her and say, "Well, this has to be a loan, I have to pay you back." She would reluctantly agree even though she'd offer to just give it to me. But when I did get any money the next time, it would be gone quickly and I would never pay it back. Neither of us would ever mention it again, but we would go through this same dance again the next time, as if it had never happened before!

This kind of "enabling" allows the addict to escape facing the consequences of her behavior. As long as Debbie was being bailed out by her mother, she didn't have to face her compulsive spending. When there is an enabler in the picture, the addiction is often prolonged.

STAGE 4: ON THE ROCKS

Even after the flaws in the relationship become evident, the addict continues to chase her losses, to "throw good money after bad." That's because she still clings to the memory of the honeymoon and hopes—against all evidence to the contrary—that she can recapture it. The situation is similar to the battered spouse who denies being beaten up and stays in the relationship, hoping to recapture what she had on the honeymoon.

The addict must use more and more in order to keep the mounting negative moods and feelings from piercing her consciousness and to try to maintain the diminishing high. She is developing tolerance. And no matter what the mood-changer is, increasing tolerance signals addiction. Compulsive gamblers, for instance, tend to place larger and larger bets as their addiction progresses in an effort to "win back" what they've lost and achieve the sense of excitement that once attracted them to gambling. Paul, the engineer turned stock-market gambler, continues his story:

> After I started losing, I just kept upping the amount of investment I made. I traded every day. The amounts became unrealistic. But it wasn't even about the profits anymore, it was the *process*. I felt I could make it back. The idea is that you have the power. I came to trust in my own personal power to do it.

Now just about anything becomes a trigger for addictive use: the crash and withdrawal from the last binge, demands from the boss, complaints by the spouse, mounting bills, fear of failure, legal pressure, and on and on. Even seemingly positive events (marriage, childbirth, promotion, financial gain, professional recognition) spawn overwhelming feelings—particularly fear of

41

loss—that are every bit as much a trigger for "picking up" as obviously negative events.

At this stage, at least three processes begin to reinforce a person's continued relationship with his addictive activity:

The desire to avoid withdrawal. It seems that most addictions do cause some kind of physical or psychological withdrawal symptoms, if only irritability and feelings of "emptiness."

Conditioning. Once a feeling of excitement or relief gets associated with certain cues, those cues (people, places, and things) set off cravings for the substance or activity whenever they are encountered.

Altered brain function. After a while, the brain can become depleted of the neurotransmitters it has been misprogrammed to release whenever a person uses his drug. A depletion of these feeling-good chemicals, necessary for maintaining feelings of well-being, cause the addict to suffer from chronic negative mood states, including substantial depression.

STAGE 5: TRAPPED

Eventually the addict reaches a point of desperation in his relationship with the addictive substance or activity. At this point he is obsessed with the activity to the exclusion of almost everything else. He is increasingly impulsive and compulsive about it, doing things he never thought possible earlier. Steve, a sex addict who compulsively sought prostitutes, offers us insight from his experience:

> There was a point at which I was driving around, looking for prostitutes and masturbating in my car. When people saw me doing it, I was embarrassed, but it didn't stop me. I stopped caring about anything; I didn't care if I got arrested, I didn't care if I lost my business,

I didn't care about myself or anyone else. All I wanted was to have my orgasm.

This stage of the addictive relationship is a descent into despair. The addict sees no way out, loses the ability to cope in any other way, and remains preoccupied with the mood-changer. He has lost control. His moods depend almost entirely now on whether or not he is able to use the mood-changer. All areas of life deteriorate. The choice is between the addictive behavior—which brings no relief or pleasure anymore but is repeated ritualistically—and terror and despair.

The addict can remain stuck in this stage indefinitely; he is trapped in a self-perpetuating downward spiral that can go on for years unless something happens to stop it.

At this point, the addiction is a full-time obsession. Rachel, a compulsive overeater, describes this:

> At the times I am planning a binge, I am thinking of it nonstop, even while working, talking or driving. I am "driven." Because of the preoccupation I am working at half efficiency at work. I have lost time from work from bingeing myself sick and from sugar-induced depressions more times than I can even estimate.

Any use of the mood-changer plunges the addict right back into the cycle. That's why attempts at controlled use are never successful. Even a little bit sets off cravings for more. The addict takes this as proof that she has no willpower and is a failure.

It's not the fear of withdrawal, however, that keeps the addict from seeking help and stopping her addiction. It's pure terror at facing the unknown. The addiction is predictable. Facing the real world, on the other hand, requires time, patience, and sometimes serious discomfort. Since the addict usually doesn't believe she *can* cope successfully, the prospect of trying produces terror and keeps the cycle going.

At this point, the addict feels as if her survival depends on her drug, so there's no real incentive to give it up. For Dana, a sex and relationship addict who becomes obsessed with different men, it's the fear of slowing down, stopping the incessant action/distraction in her life, that scares her the most: "I almost think I'm going to die when I give it up. There's a physical high that one gets from having these obsessions and rushing around all the time for it. It's a high. Without it, I don't know what I'd do with myself."

The despair and depression that follows each use of the drug at this point gives the addiction further momentum. Jerry, a sex addict who molested women on subway trains for fifteen years before finding help in Sex and Love Addicts Anonymous, shares how despair perpetuated his cycle of addiction:

> At the end, I'd wake up in the mornings and practically the first thought I would have would be of killing myself. I'd be shaving, looking in the mirror, and thinking about really doing it that day. And the second thought would be about getting to the subway so I would touch someone. "Who am I going to molest? What am I going to see? What am I going to do?" And I would get into the routine and the ritual of it and that would take me right away from the intolerable feelings of despair.
>
> I had such a quick-fix as soon as I got into it and once I got into it the rest of the day was just, well, I was immersed in it. In the subway, I'd get down to the station and if it was crowded, whoopee. Then I'd start my pacing and find somebody I felt comfortable to do my acting out with. I wouldn't be thinking about suicide anymore.

GETTING DIVORCED

Getting out of this destructive "marriage" is what part three of this book is all about. But here's a hint: no one files for divorce without first admitting that the marriage is a problem. And no one gets out of an addiction without admitting it either. Paradoxically, only by accepting that we've "lost it," that we are utterly powerless over our addictive behavior, can we even begin to make the types of decisions that will lead to solid recovery.

4

The Source of Addiction Is Within Us

WE KNOW THAT MANY PEOPLE don't have just one addiction, they have a cluster of them. Indeed, some addictions seem to go together. Sexual addiction is often associated with alcohol or drug abuse. Similarly, anorectics and bulimics are often compulsive exercisers. Some compulsive spenders are workaholics, and gamblers often overeat. One addiction seems to fuel the other.

As more and more people are discovering, stopping one addiction does not automatically "cure" others; in fact, it often results in the *emergence* of a new one. Like a bump in a rug, when it's flattened out in one place it simply pops up somewhere else. Seth, an alcoholic and sex addict who attends Alcoholics Anonymous, reports, "I thought my sexual obsession would stop with the drinking, but it didn't. I also started overeating and put on forty pounds. I finally saw that it's my own *attitude,* not just a particular chemical or behavior, that's addictive."

Seth discovered for himself a key to understanding compulsive behavior: the problem is not always in the mood-changer itself. For too long we have blamed the drugs themselves for drug addiction. We have chosen to believe that just getting rid of the drugs— making them unavailable—would solve the problem. But the fact that we are now getting addicted to activities that don't involve chemicals, such as shopping, work, and TV, proves it can't just be the chemical action of a drug that causes addiction.

Neither can we assume anymore that addiction is caused solely by a desire to avoid withdrawal, as once thought by experts.

That's where the idea for short detoxification programs came from, in which the patient was weaned off drugs and in a few days sent home "cured." It was thought that all an addict had to do was stop using the drug, complete the physical withdrawal process, and the addiction was behind him.

We now know that there's a lot more to recovering from addiction than just stopping the habitual behavior. It has more to do with changing life-style and attitudes than anything else. By lifestyle, we don't mean whether you like to vacation at the beach or in the mountains, eat out a lot or prefer cooking at home. We mean how you see the world (your belief system), how you approach problems, and how well you're able to meet your physical, emotional, social, and spiritual needs. In other words, when we get rid of one addiction we will simply get another—or get *that* one back—unless we begin to *change how we live.*

So all addictions—however different they appear on the face of it—have more in common with each other than they do differences. They are different versions of the same phenomenon. In other words, *it's all one disease.*

What *is* the common denominator in every instance of addiction then? It's not one particular chemical, or whether the substance causes withdrawal, or how it affects the brain. All of these vary considerably from one addiction to the other. But what's present in every case of addiction is the addict! It is our "dis-ease" within—our lack of ease—that renders us so vulnerable to addictions, not the substances or activities themselves. *The true source of addiction lies within us.*

That's why even when addicts turn to positive activities, such as meditation, exercise, or eating health foods, they can wind up doing *that* compulsively too. People who have the predisposition to addictive disease can become addicted to almost anything. Until we are able to create a less addictive life-style for ourselves (a lifelong process, by the way), we will continue to be vulnerable.

WHAT IS THE "DIS-EASE"?

Part of having an addictive "dis-ease" means that we hold certain contradictory beliefs that set the stage for inner conflict and struggle—such as believing simultaneously that we are not enough and that we *should* be perfect. Or believing that we *should* be able to control everything and yet feeling utterly powerless to affect our lives. Having an addictive dis-ease also means being unable to tolerate frustration and demanding immediate gratification, lacking the skills necessary to cope with ordinary life crises and processes, and not having enough support from others or ourselves.

There are five major factors (in addition to genetic predisposition in some chemical dependencies) that put people at high risk for turning to a mood-altering drug or activity, finding it a welcome effect (becoming infatuated), and being compelled to repeat it over and over again. They are shown in the figure Addictive "Dis-ease."

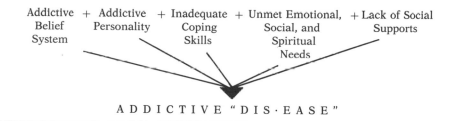

Addictive + Addictive + Inadequate + Unmet Emotional, + Lack of Social
Belief   Personality   Coping   Social, and   Supports
System   Skills   Spiritual
                                                     Needs

A D D I C T I V E " D I S · E A S E "

Addictive Belief System

A faulty belief system lies at the root of addiction. This belief system, as we shall learn in chapter five, embraces the idea that it is possible to be perfect, that the world should be limitless, that our *image* is more important than who we really are, that we are not enough, and that externals (people, drugs, and other things outside of ourselves) hold the "magic" solutions to life's problems.

These beliefs set us up to be seduced by the promise of immediate gratification (the quick-fix) even while they deprive us of more substantial, lasting gratification in the long run. Addictive thinking is increasingly common in today's society and in our families.

Addictive Personality

Certain personality traits emanate from addictive beliefs and worsen our addictive dis-ease. These include perfectionism, emotional numbness, approval-seeking, hypersensitivity to criticism and rejection, easily tapped reservoirs of shame, mismanaged anger, an inability to tolerate frustration, feelings of powerlessness, an inordinate need for control, a passive approach to problems, self-neglect (despite what appears to be self-*indulgence* in the addiction), isolation, and a tendency to live in self-delusion (among other traits). We will see in chapter five exactly how each of these increases our likelihood of finding relief or comfort in addictions.

Inadequate Coping Skills

Because we live in an increasingly addictive society and in addictive families that transmit faulty beliefs, we are not learning adequate coping and problem-solving skills. We have few role models, for instance, for learning to tolerate ambiguity and frustration, evaluate options, communicate directly and honestly, cooperate, and take constructive action.

Instead, we are learning from both society and family models to turn to quick-fix, short-term solutions.

Unmet Emotional, Social, and Spiritual Needs

Chronically unmet needs for unconditional acceptance (for who we really are, not for our image), intimacy, community, security, meaning and purpose, autonomy, and play leave us with chronically negative moods and feelings. Exacerbated by our lack of coping skills, inability to tolerate frustration, and our belief in the quick-fix, these feelings, such as anxiety, anger, loneliness, depression, become the triggers that send us seeking relief, comfort, or distraction in addictions. In part two of this book we look at what it is about our families and our society that leaves so many people with so little gratification in their lives.

Lack of Social Supports

Without a sense of belonging to a support network—whether it is family, extended family, community, or other group—coping and problem-solving can be overwhelming (especially if one's skills are poor to begin with) and the comfort of the addiction is that much more appealing.

It is no surprise that the self-help movement of the 12-step programs—Alcoholics Anonymous, Gamblers Anonymous, and others—is successfully helping people recover from addictions. A crucial benefit of belonging to these groups is the fellowship they offer. Members are helped to peel away the mask and relax the relentless self-scrutiny that has existed in the service of maintaining an image. Likewise, it is the lack of this sense of community and unconditional support that is contributing to our vulnerability to addictions and the current epidemic. Isolation feeds addiction.

An Explosive Mixture

Chances are, if a person is in a state of dis-ease given the above five high-risk conditions, she will develop an addiction to *something*. What form it takes will depend, as we have seen in chapter three, on what substances and activities she is exposed to, the messages received about addiction from family and cultural role models, and what kind of effect is desired.

Addiction is analogous to the process of combustion: the "dis-ease"—the addiction-proneness in the person—is the fuel, and the drug or activity is the spark. When you put the two together, you have an explosive mixture. If the spark is a drug like cocaine, one that causes rapid physiological addiction, combustion occurs more rapidly and more intensely. Other "sparks," like sex or eating, build up slowly, often over years.

But you need *both* the spark and the fuel to create combustion. Obviously, you can't become drug-addicted unless you take the drug in the first place. And you're not likely to keep taking it—given the possibility of negative effects—unless there's some major payoff you get from it, one that you hunger for, fueled by your own "dis-ease."

WHAT MOOD-CHANGERS DO FOR US

To understand why addictions are so epidemic, we must examine what mood-changers *do* for us, what are the payoffs? After all, they must be meeting some of our needs—however self-defeating—or we wouldn't keep turning to them, risking our careers, health, family life, and peace of mind.

Superficially it seems that people engage in addictive behaviors because they find them fun, pleasurable—at least in the beginning. But when a person's drug has potentially negative consequences and he continues using it anyway, we must conclude that he is deriving deeper, unacknowledged payoffs from it—secondary gains for which he is willing to risk a lot.

Let's look at what—collectively—we may be getting out of our mood-changers, at some of the ways they "serve" us. This will help us understand the persistence of the addictions epidemic and why current approaches to it (like the War on Drugs) are unlikely to work.

Relief from Isolation

In a society where people have a lot of trouble with intimate relationships and lack a sense of community support, drugs and other mood-changers provide welcome relief. Although in the long run addiction causes greater isolation, in the short run it provides contact and often camaraderie with other addicts—or numbs feelings of loneliness. Thus, the addictive involvement creates its own sense of belonging and community, albeit a self-destructive one.

Distraction from Feelings

Addictions provide activity and rituals that keep us busy so we don't have to feel our feelings or the emptiness inside. They insulate us from despair, from the lack of deeper meaning and purpose in our lives, and from the feelings and conflicts that we fear may overwhelm us.

Pseudopleasure

In a society where work values have heavily invaded recreation (making it goal-oriented, rather than creative or fun), moodchangers give us a chance to "lose ourselves," to be temporarily released from self-consciousness and time-consciousness. They keep us from confronting just how little genuine pleasure and joy we actually have in our lives.

Illusion of Control

In a technological society in which people feel they have less and less control over the conditions of their lives, and yet revere power and "performance," many of our mood-changers prop up feelings of being in control, competent, and powerful—or numb us from feelings of impotence and helplessness. Addiction is a sign that we are "looking for power in all the wrong places."

Constant Crisis

Addiction-prone people don't want to feel their real feelings but at the same time don't want to experience the emotional "deadness" inside that results from repressing these feelings. Addictions provide constant excitement and crisis, substituting for a real sense of being fully alive.

Predictability

The ritual of drug use and its dependable outcome eliminate choices and make life simpler and more predictable, which is particularly appealing for people who feel unable to cope with current stresses and responsibilities. Instead of achieving a simpler, saner life, we turn to addictive behaviors of all kinds.

Image Enhancement

In a society based largely on projecting an image that is acceptable to others rather than on being honest and authentic, mood-changers help us feel more acceptable to others, mask fears that we are not enough as we are, or numb us from painful feelings of self-judgment and measurement. They substitute, then, for self-acceptance.

Suspended Animation

In the trance of the high, the addict is frozen in time. The past cannot haunt him nor the future worry him. There is just the here and now of the drug experience. With so many people lacking the skills to face normal life problems, mood-changers put life on hold, thereby substituting for problem-solving skills.

AN ATTEMPT TO ADAPT TO A DYSFUNCTIONAL SOCIETY

Having identified some of the things addictions do for us, we can see that all addictive involvements—gambling, sex, shopping, drugging—help us temporarily to avoid isolation, insecurity, powerlessness, emotional deadness, painful self-scrutiny, despair, and lack of purpose, rather than address the underlying problems themselves.

The current explosion of addictive behaviors in our society is not occurring out of the blue. Nor is it solely attributable to the availability of "evil drugs." It is a product of our societal system—a system that models "quick-fix" solutions and offers little alternative gratification. Only by seeing the problem in this broader context can we even begin to understand it and do something about it.

The fact that we are seeking these payoffs from addiction tells us something about the societal context in which this is happening: collectively, *mood-changers are being sought to meet real, legitimate needs that are currently inadequately met* within the social, economic, and spiritual fabric of our culture.

Addiction has become so prevalent that we must consider that it may be a "normal" response to an abnormal situation—an attempt to adapt to an increasingly dysfunctional society. Addictive ways of thinking and behaving are actually *reinforced* by many aspects of our culture. And just as the child in an alcoholic or otherwise dysfunctional family seeks to adapt to this "sick" environment in order to survive emotionally, so may we be trying—in ways that work in the short run but are self-defeating in the long run—to adapt to our larger "sick" family, our society. Alexander Lowen writes in *Fear of Life* that "No one deliberately chooses a neurotic style of life, since it is a limitation of being. The armoring process is a means of survival, a way of avoiding intolerable pain."

Just what are we seeking through drug use and other compulsive activities? Having identified what the payoffs of our mood-changers are, we can deduce what we must be seeking:

1. A sense of belonging and intimacy—both on an interpersonal and a community level
2. A sense of meaning and purpose
3. Opportunities for fun and creative play
4. A sense of autonomy and personal potency
5. Vitality and aliveness
6. Predictability and consistency
7. Self-acceptance and self-worth

In today's society, these basic needs are simply not being met. At best they are met sporadically and sometimes not at all. Mood-changers, on the other hand, deliver in a very predictable and reliable way. The gambler knows what feelings to expect from his gambling routine and the drug addict knows what to expect from her chosen drugs. Although mood-changers are poor substitutes for genuine gratification—nurturing, soothing relief from insecurity—they are at least dependable.

It's not the money, food, sex, drugs, gambling, or work that is innately evil or bad or destructive—it's what people use them for. The source of the problem lies within us, because we are desperately seeking to meet legitimate needs that are going unmet. We are not actively trying to hurt ourselves; we are just trying to get by.

How we experience the effects of a drug is determined to a large extent by how we feel without it. A drug will have much more appeal to us if we feel bad to begin with and much better when we take it than if we are feeling pretty good in the first place. So if a drug—or any addictive activity—provides extraordinary relief, comfort, or pleasure, chances are that certain preconditions exist that make it so appealing.

We know, for instance, that when heroin—a drug with well-known addiction potential—was widely available to American soldiers in Vietnam, more than 50 percent of those who tried it became addicted. (Although even under more normal circumstances, heroin is a highly addictive drug, an inordinately high percentage of GIs who tried heroin in Vietnam found it extremely appealing.) These soldiers were living under extremely stressful conditions, far away from the support of friends and family, and had to forgo many of their emotional and social needs, so it is easy to understand how heroin, a superlative emotional pain-killer and stress-reliever, could have such a high reinforcement value.

The fact that addiction flourishes under conditions of deprivation and is counteracted by a supportive, gratifying environment was demonstrated in a laboratory experiment with rats: morphine-addicted animals were placed in a very stimulating environment, one that was spacious and contained spare tires, tin cans, and other things to romp in. In this environment, the majority of addicted rats *voluntarily* forwent their doses of morphine and went through withdrawal.

It seems that in this gratifying environment, the drug had less reinforcement value—because the rats' needs were being met so

well. Further, the discomfort of withdrawal could be better tolerated because it was offset by other available gratification. This
experiment tells us something about our current epidemic of addictions. Like the rats, we need a more supportive, gratifying environment in order to avoid or give up our addictions.

Looking at addictions as "adaptive" in a dysfunctional culture
may at first sound like more narcissistic preoccupation—"me and
my needs." But that's what addictions are, in a way: self-preoccupation. And that alone tells us something about ourselves. As a nation
with more and more addicts, we are preoccupied with ourselves,
not because we are overindulged in the ways that really count but
because we are in desperate need of *real* attention and gratification.

To say that society and our families are not adequately meeting our collective needs is not to make a plea for collective self-pity
and complaint. Recognizing our unmet needs can be a very positive
action, the first step out of our addictive vulnerability and narcissistic preoccupation. It's true, society isn't likely to change overnight,
and we can't wait for that before we begin our own personal recovery. But by recognizing what it is we really hunger for in our lives,
we can begin to find ways to satisfy and nurture ourselves and each
other in ways that will ultimately lead us out of self-preoccupation,
not further into it. And *society is us.* When enough of us change, it
changes.

Let us now look at what it is about ourselves, our family
systems, and our societal institutions that is creating this emo
tional, mental, and spiritual bankruptcy—our vulnerability to addiction. Only with *an understanding of where we are now* can
we—both individually and collectively—begin to find ways to recover that will actually work.

PART II

Why Are We So Vulnerable?

5

The Addictive Personality

WE HEAR A LOT THESE DAYS about the "addictive personality," and it is true that certain traits increase one's chances of becoming addicted to something. For instance, if you are painfully shy and self-conscious and a particular drug makes you feel more relaxed and sociable, chances are you're going to want to use it again and again—setting the addictive process in motion.

It's easy to think that the personality trait itself (painful self-consciousness, in this case) is what causes the addiction, but the problem actually goes much deeper than that. The inner dis-ease that makes us so vulnerable to addiction seems to originate in our *belief system,* for the beliefs we hold about ourselves, others, and the world around us determine to a large degree our feelings, personality, and outward behavior. In other words, if a person did not hold certain beliefs about himself, he would not be painfully self-conscious to begin with.

Unfortunately, the kinds of beliefs that make a person vulnerable to addiction are widely held today. Many of us were raised with these beliefs to some degree, since they became very common and flourished during the postwar era with the baby boom and the birth of the "American dream" (as we will see in chapter seven). The fact that these addiction-generating beliefs are now the norm makes it even harder to perceive the destructiveness in them.

For instance, if many people in a society believe that one's image is more important than being genuine, then the person who doesn't conform to the popular image (in the eighties, one who is achieving, successful, powerful) will feel that he's not measuring up. Instead of having a sense of intrinsic worth, he will come to believe that his real self is just not good enough. This painful belief then becomes a springboard to addiction.

Other addictive beliefs create a quick-fix mentality—an obsession with power, control, and immediate gratification. It is a mentality that drives people to habitually opt for the easy, fast, short-term fix to a problem—even when it's not really a solution but an escape (as a mood-changer is), even when it causes more problems than it fixes, and even when it means forgoing chances for more long-term gratification.

$$\frac{\text{THE ADDICTIVE}}{\text{BELIEF SYSTEM}} = \frac{\text{THE QUICK-FIX}}{\text{MENTALITY}} = \frac{\text{THE ROOT OF}}{\text{ADDICTION}}$$

THE ADDICTIVE BELIEF SYSTEM

Among the beliefs that contribute to addiction are "I should be perfect (and perfection is possible)"; "I should be all-powerful"; "I should always get what I want"; and "Life should be without pain and require no effort."

This, however, is just one set of beliefs, basically about how the world and oneself *should* be. Since these are all unattainable, the addict also comes to believe that he is falling short: "I am not enough"; "I am unable to have an impact on my world"; and "Externals (such as people, drugs and things) can give me the power I lack."

And to function in the world with such devastating beliefs about oneself, the addict develops these "operating principles": "Feelings are dangerous"; "Image is everything"; and "I should meet my needs indirectly (through those people, drugs, and things that have the power I lack)."

These beliefs are usually *not conscious*. People don't walk around saying these things to themselves. These are core beliefs that drive people to behave in certain ways, though they may not

60

even be aware of the underlying motivation. We shall now discuss each of these addictive beliefs individually.

"I Should Be Perfect (and Perfection Is Possible)"

Our increasing belief that perfection is attainable is at the core of our addictions explosion. If we truly believe that perfection is possible, then we can never measure up. Like hamsters on a treadmill, we keep running and running, even though we never get anywhere, because our goal of perfection is unattainable.

This quest for perfection—the perfect performance, perfect image, perfect body—fuels our addictions to compulsive exercise, compulsive shopping, workaholism, and drugs like cocaine. We are driven to chase the *illusion* of perfection offered by some of these mood-changers—even if it only lasts as long as the runner's euphoria, the first time wearing a new outfit, praise from the boss, or the freebase high. As Sheila, a teacher who is an anorectic, compulsive exerciser, and compulsive shopper, puts it: "I wanted to present the perfect picture—because things inside of me felt so imperfect."

"I Should Be All-Powerful"

Someone who is vulnerable to addiction also has severe delusions about the limits of his power, believing that he *should* be able to control not only himself but other people, too, and just about everything else. This drive for control catapults people into addiction because the most popular mood-changers today create the illusion of power and competence, of being "in control."

Steve, the sex addict mentioned earlier, cruised the streets for prostitutes whenever he was feeling not sufficiently "in control" in other areas of his life. When he had an argument with his wife, for instance, or was put down by his boss at work, the appeal of the "hunt" became irresistible. "While I was in the trance I felt a tremendous adrenaline rush—not so much from any sexual excitement but from the feeling that I was in control, unlike in my real life. That feeling was the bigger part of what I wanted—not the sexual stimulation."

"I Should Always Get What I Want"

Those headed for addiction believe, as children do, that there should be no limits placed on them. If a child wants a candy bar, she doesn't weigh long-term versus short-term benefits and costs to decide whether she should have it or not. Left to her own devices, she might even indulge herself to the point of getting sick.

Addicts act the same way. The compulsive shopper, for example, believes on some level that his resources *should* be unlimited; therefore, he acts as if they are. As he reaches for his credit card, he enters the world of fantasy where there are no limits and no ramifications of his behavior. The result is a lack of self-regulation.

Paradoxically, it is our rejection of limits that confines us to a life of relentless gratification-seeking. We cannot relax and accept ourselves because we continue to believe that we should *have* more, *get* more, *be* more. In a world without limits, there can never be "enough." Our belief in limitlessness makes addicts of us.

"Life Should Be Without Pain and Require No Effort"

The core of addictive thinking is inherent in this belief. If we insist on avoiding emotional pain, on being comfortable all the time, we will *have* to seek ways to avoid reality, to escape our mood. That is what the addictive person is saying through his behavior: "If reality is not what I want it to be, I will simply refuse to see it."

Ironically, it is through this *resistance* to pain that we suffer the most. For what is addiction but a way of resisting pain that causes far more suffering than the original problems or feelings could ever have. As children, we may have *needed* to find ways to avoid feeling intense emotional pain; we didn't have other means of coping. But the addictive person has *never* learned to face pain and deal with it effectively.

Refusing to deal with pain severely limits our freedom, because it means that we are controlled by circumstances outside ourselves. With this "modus operandi," or "m.o.," whenever uncomfortable feelings arise, we automatically seek to avoid them—by picking up a drink, picking up a charge card, or whatever else. To remain open to the real experiences and feelings that life brings us, and then apply skills to resolve them, is real freedom.

By insisting that life be without pain, we deaden ourselves. When we block out grief, fear, and other discomforts, we at the same time limit our capacity to experience pleasure, since all feelings are blocked, not just the negative ones.

These first four beliefs are the "shoulds" of the addictive belief system: I *should* be perfect, I *should* be all powerful, I *should* always get what I want, life *should* be without pain. Since these are all unattainable, the addict comes to believe that he—and life itself—is always falling short. He then formulates some other destructive beliefs based on these distortions.

"I Am Not Enough"

Perhaps no single belief is more painful and more central to the development of addiction than this one. It amounts to a total rejection of the self, to the destructive conclusion that "Who I am is unlovable, unworthy, and undeserving and if this is discovered I will be abandoned."

Most of the time, of course, the addictive person doesn't walk around saying this to himself. But this underlying belief gets expressed through various self-rejecting thoughts such as "I'm no good," "I'm bad," "I'm selfish," "I'm stupid." He then filters everything that happens to him through this core mistaken belief and bases his behavior on it. Steve, the sex addict, remembers having this "clear knowledge":

> I remember being head-over-heels about this girl in sixth grade, but having this clear knowledge that I could never have her like me back. It wasn't even a question, it was something I *knew* deep inside. And it had nothing to do with her, because I never even let her know I

63

liked her. I just acted upon my knowledge that I was not enough—and never would be. After all, I'd never had a winning experience with my mother, and if she didn't think I was good enough, why on earth would anyone else?

Tragically, the addictive person doesn't see that he is valuable, lovable, and a worthwhile human being. Lacking a sense of intrinsic worth, he is saddled with a profound insecurity and driven to prove that he is "enough" but in self-defeating ways. If being a big-shot gambler, a corporate executive (workaholic) or someone with a perfect body can help achieve this sense of adequacy, the addict will sacrifice almost anything—health, family, career, and money—to achieve it. Despite all of this, he never does feel adequate, but he is doomed to keep *trying*. He is caught in the vicious cycle of addiction.

"I Am Unable to Have an Impact on My World"

Even though the addiction-prone person believes she *should* be all-powerful, she experiences herself as being unable to meet her own needs or solve her own problems effectively (because she has never learned how). She believes that even if she tries, she will not be able to get what she needs. Consequently, feelings of helplessness and impotency prevail. That's why the illusion of power offered by many mood-changers is so intoxicating and so irresistible. The addict substitutes the illusion of power for the real thing—a dangerous trade-off.

"Externals Can Give Me the Power I Lack"

While addicts often believe deep down that they are impotent, they ascribe to people, substances, and other sources outside themselves the power they lack. They believe that these externals can magically supply what they cannot give to themselves. This belief is at the root of the quick-fix mentality.

Addicts often say that as children they relied very heavily on fantasy to meet their needs. By the time they were adults they had become very adept at projecting themselves into the world of make-believe and all but lost the ability to tell truth from fiction. The magic of the quick-fix is easy to "buy into." It is more immediately gratifying and less painful than facing the reality of life's problems.

When we use a mood-changer, we get an artificial sense of power and control. We can wipe out reality in an instant—go from misery to ecstasy at a moment's notice. Being able to exert such tight control over our mental state is itself intoxicating. Paul, the stock-market gambler, describes how he became enamored with the sense of power and control he got from playing the market:

> Even when I was losing, I'd keep sinking more money into the market, because I believed that I could make it back. The belief was that *I* had the power. I was making $10,000 in a single day sometimes. That gives you a sense of power. You feel invulnerable, that's the real trap. You identify with that feeling. You identify that as part of yourself, as some quality you actually have.

Mood-changers, then, help to deal with the terror that is sparked when we are confronted with our limitations and short-comings and propel us (if only temporarily) into a world where we can at least feel all-powerful, effective, and in control. So we think.

"Feelings Are Dangerous"

The fear of the addictive person is that if he admits his feelings something terrible will happen. Therefore, he concludes it is best not even to feel those feelings. The feelings don't go away just because he suppresses them. Instead they continue to influence behavior from the unconscious, as Seth, a recovering alcoholic and sex addict, describes:

> I learned from my parents (who are perfectionists and were terribly demanding of me when I was a child) that the world—and feelings especially—were essentially dangerous. I think I act out compulsively now because I feel I'll be overwhelmed by feelings if I don't.

My compulsive behavior "is" instead of feeling. Instead of feeling, I plug in the addiction. What I'm learning now is that there are other choices in between censoring a feeling and acting it out. You can simply *have* it. Somehow I never learned this before.

As long as the addicted person operates within the addictive belief system, the addict is in a no-win situation. The feelings that make her human become her enemy, capable of causing rejection by others, in whom she has placed too much power. Yet she can never get the sense of acceptance and connectedness that she yearns for because she has sent her true self into hiding.

"Image Is Everything"

The addictive person erects an image, a false self, that he hopes will be acceptable. In most cases, though, he doesn't even know that he has done this, for the image he projects has become second nature, an automatic reflex. He has merged with the mask.

Many of the most popular mood-changers help to prop up these false images. Cocaine, for instance, is widely sought for its performance-enhancing effects, promoting an image of someone who is sociable, energetic, competent, confident, a better lover. So too do other addictive involvements such as compulsive shopping, workaholism, anorexia and bulimia, compulsive exercising, and gambling promote a particular image.

The addiction-prone person will go to any lengths and risk almost any negative consequence to self and others to maintain this all-important image. It is his ticket to acceptance. Howie, a compulsive debtor, describes how desperately he tried to maintain his image through compulsive spending:

> Spending money—whether I had it or not—reinforced a view I wanted to have of myself. I was not able to live within limitations, because to do so would mean I might not be able to do the things I thought would make me acceptable: I might not have the money to take someone out to dinner, or buy the clothes I thought I had to have to achieve the "look" that would be appealing. I felt I *had* to do

those things, *had* to, no matter what—even if I had to bounce checks to do it.

The harder we try to maintain a false image, the more alienated we become from ourselves. It leaves us with a gnawing sense of emptiness, boredom, and futility. No wonder. We have made our (true) selves nonexistent, invisible. We no longer know who we are and must increasingly rely on externals—our "drugs"—just to feel alive.

Beth, a thirty-eight-year-old compulsive pot smoker, describes how a craving to "be herself" drove her to get high incessantly. Stuck in a perpetual struggle between who she was and who she thought she *should* be, she longed to break free of her image, which had become, she says, "a prison." "Pot removed the split between my real self and the artificial front I put up. In everyday life I felt that split constantly. I felt tortured by it. When I smoked pot, I felt 'there,' in touch with myself. The split was instantly gone."

"I Should Meet My Needs Indirectly"

If I can't be me (because doing so might get me rejected and abandoned) then I might as well just give up and meet my needs indirectly—through those people, substances, and other sources outside myself. This is a belief in the efficacy of the quick-fix.

The quick-fix takes many forms. For example, a teenager downs several beers in the school parking lot before going in to the dance in order to "fix" his nervousness and make it easier for him to approach girls and talk to them. It's quicker and easier than the long-term solution that would involve learning social skills to increase confidence and self-esteem. But because he doesn't know how to do this (and probably hasn't been helped to learn), he turns to the quick-fix instead.

But the quick-fix mentality involves more than always taking the short-cut to solving problems. It is a posture, an orientation toward life. It's a passive way of relating to the world. It stems from a belief that long-term gratification can't be found. It seems futile

WILLPOWER'S NOT ENOUGH: WHY ARE WE SO VULNERABLE?

even to try, so we opt to at least get something while we can and a quick-fix makes us feel better today, even if it causes misery tomorrow.

Changing the Addictive Belief System

Because addicts often display these "black-and-white" ways of thinking, they have difficulty thinking in the gray area. In reality, none of us is either perfect and all-powerful *or* worthless and totally impotent to affect our own lives. Once we allow ourselves to live in the gray area, we gain freedom because we no longer have to maintain the illusion of omnipotence and perfection. We become free to *risk* facing and coping with the real world, because making mistakes no longer makes us feel like failures.

Facing the gap between our false selves (dependent on the *illusion* of our omnipotence and perfection) and our real selves is what can give us the freedom to live our lives more fully, without reliance on mood-changers. And coming to terms with this gap, accepting and giving expression to our true selves, is what long-term recovery is all about. Because when we have closed that gap, we no longer have to go in search of an authentic experience. We live it.

THE ADDICTIVE PERSONALITY

People who operate according to these addictive beliefs typically develop certain personality traits to help them operate in the world. Most of these develop out of an impulse to protect themselves from the inevitable suffering inherent in these beliefs. Together, we call these traits the "addictive personality."

There is no one single personality profile that "guarantees" a person will become addicted. After all, there are as many different personalities among addicts as there are among the general population. Some addictive people appear passive and dependent, others confident, outgoing, and independent; some never show anger, some overreact with anger, and so on.

68

If addicts are so different from one another, how can we talk about an "addictive personality" at all? Because even though the "passive" addict and the "aggressive" addict *seem* very different from each other, these traits are often simply opposite sides of the same coin. In both cases, the *issue* is the same (for instance, trouble managing anger) even though it has manifested itself differently in their personalities.

There are a number of specific "themes" like these that characterize the addictive personality. Most addicts, for example, have power and control issues (as we have seen). Some come across as grandiose much of the time, others as having an inferiority complex. But whether they assume a top dog or underdog position, both are usually striving—in their own ways—to exert control. So too, most addicts have some kind of issue with responsibility. Commonly, addicts are thought of as irresponsible, but some (especially codependents) are *over*responsible for others. In reality, neither takes appropriate responsibility for his own life.

Few if any of us are free of addictive personality traits. Since these traits grow directly out of one's belief system, and since most of us have gotten at least partially inculcated with these beliefs, it could be said that *we all lie somewhere on the continuum.* But just as none of us is risk-free, neither are we inevitably doomed to addiction even if we have some of these traits. And by becoming aware of these traits, we are in a better position to examine the underlying beliefs that fuel them and begin transforming these.

There follow some of the most common high-risk personality traits and a brief exploration of how each one makes a person more vulnerable to addiction. Table 1 offers a summary. Since they have been discussed earlier, the first five traits from the table have been omitted from this section.

Self-obsessed

Preoccupation with one's self is probably the most predominant trait of the addiction-prone person. People who know little about addiction often assume that the addict is self-obsessed because he

69

TABLE 1. Addictive Personality Traits and the Fostering of Addiction

Personality Trait	How It Fosters Addiction
Feelings of shame	The drug props up feelings of adequacy and/or numbs from the pain of shame.
Perfectionism; harsh self-criticism	The drug makes a person feel more perfect, or in the case of, say, "downer" drugs, relieves him from striving to be perfect.
Hunger for power and control to compensate for feelings of powerlessness and shame	The drug provides the illusion of power and control and/or numbs the user from feelings of impotence.
Dishonest; self-deluding	With dishonesty "second nature," it's easy for denial about the drug use to take hold.
Thinking in black-and-white extremes	Black-and-white thinking causes addict to overreact to events; negative moods make drug use all the more appealing.
Self-obsessed	Addiction *is* self-obsession; an incessant "licking of one's wounds."
Self-less	Addiction provides a pseudoidentity—even if it's a negative one.
Inner emptiness	The drug is used to "fill the black hole" within.
Without meaning and purpose	Addiction provides something to do, a substitute "devotion."
Excessive approval-seeking; obsessed with image	The drug helps garner more approval from others and/or numb the user to rejection.
Self-censoring	The drug helps knock out the censor and let the user be "himself."
Guilt-ridden	Addiction provides an anchor for guilt, a way to act it out.
Trouble managing anger	Addictive behaviors provide an arena in which to act out anger or stay distracted from it. Either way, the addict doesn't have to take responsibility for it.

TABLE 1. *(Continued)*

Personality Trait	How It Fosters Addiction
Underlying depression	Stimulant mood-changers offset feelings of depression.
Emotional numbness	Mood-changers keep feelings at bay while simultaneously providing activity, crises, and sensations to counter feelings of "deadness."
Inner tension	Addiction provides constant activity or else reduces the tension.
Afraid of taking appropriate risks; inordinate fear of failure and rejection	Addiction covers up a person's fearfulness, providing "false courage."
Hidden dependency needs	The drug meets needs passively and magically, while providing a façade of independence.
Trouble with authority figures	Some addictions act out one's struggle against authority while others (like workaholism) seek to win approval from same.
Blaming; taking on passive/victim role	By blaming others, the addict avoids taking responsibility for himself and insures an excuse for turning to a mood-changer.
Poor coping skills	The addictive activity freezes time, puts life on hold, and provides distraction so the addict doesn't have to face problems.
Wishful thinking	Self-delusion is fertile soil in which the defense of denial takes root in addiction.
Never wanting to grow up	Addiction provides a never-never land where the addict's needs are met effortlessly, there are no ramifications for his behavior, and he doesn't have to take any risks.
Without boundaries	Compulsive behavior provides a way to avoid having to set boundaries.
Need for immediate gratification	Addiction provides a reliable quick-fix that the addict feels she "deserves."
No internalized "good parent"	The drug provides comfort and nurturing of a sort.

TABLE 1. *(Continued)*

Personality Trait	How It Fosters Addiction
Intimacy problems; feelings of isolation and lack of belonging	The drug substitutes for a relationship, relieves feelings of isolation, and sometimes provides a "pseudocommunity."
Trouble having real pleasure	Addiction provides "pseudopleasure.

is just selfish, caring more about himself than anything or anyone else. There is some truth in this when the addict's behavior is taken at face value: in the grips of addiction, he *is* driven to pursue the drug—with little regard for its effect on others. But the fact is, he is driven not because he cares so much about himself but because he is *self-rejecting.* And the pain of his alienation from himself (and others) leaves him hungry for the drug's effect. In reality, he is preoccupied with trying—futilely—to make himself feel better by incessantly licking his wounds.

Self-less

The addiction-prone person, far from being "selfish" in the literal sense, actually lacks an integrated sense of self, which is why she seeks the "pseudoidentity" that addiction provides—even if it's a negative one. She cannot express who she is—verbally or through her life-style—because she doesn't know herself.

As a result, the addict "lives" through the substance, person, or activity to which she is addicted. Tina, a relationship addict, describes how she desperately tries to find her "home" or identity through the men she goes out with:

> I keep looking for a man to live for me, who I can just hook into, because I don't know how to live. This last man had everything. He had the house, the sailboat, a full life with friends and family. When I was in his house I felt like I was home. I was home. Then I started to feel like he couldn't leave me, because if he did, I'd lose those things of his that I want to have as parts of me.

Inner Emptiness

Addiction-prone people often describe feeling "empty" inside. This is probably related to the alienation they feel because they are out of touch with their real feelings and lack a sense of identity. If you don't feel a sense of yourself, you are going to feel empty—as if there's literally nothing there.

Feelings of emptiness exert a powerful effect, driving a person to want to "fill herself up" with a drug, another person, sensations, and things. As Rachel, the compulsive overeater we met in chapter three, puts it, "When I'm on a binge, the first few bites are actually fun. After that, it's like a mission to fill up the hole inside of me."

Without Meaning and Purpose

Related to this inner emptiness, the person at high risk for addiction usually lacks a sense of meaning and purpose in his life. He is drifting without direction. This lack of devotion to anything else, this lack of commitment, makes addiction all the more appealing. Chasing after one's fix provides a "purpose" of sorts that makes the nagging sense of meaninglessness more tolerable. He knows what he is doing for that day, or that hour.

Excessive Approval-seeking

Because he lacks a sense of self, the addict must always think of himself according to other people's reactions and seek their approval. His good feelings about himself depend on doing so. Without approval, the addiction-prone person feels unworthy of existing, since it is only through the approval of others that he "is" at all. If he is criticized or rejected, he feels literally threatened with annihilation. This makes him excessively other-oriented, tuned into others' perceptions, rather than centered within himself. In a very real sense, he lives for others rather than for himself.

Unfortunately, because he also operates on a faulty belief system, the addict often misinterprets the signals coming to him, reading disapproval into people's reactions to him even where it does not exist.

Self-censoring

Fearing disapproval, criticism, and rejection, the addictive person constantly scrutinizes her appearance, behavior, remarks, performance, and is harshly self-critical. This is like having a critic constantly whispering in your ear, "You shouldn't have done that," or "Don't say that." Alice Miller, author of the acclaimed *Drama of the Gifted Child,* calls such an inner censor the "parents' heir," because it is usually the result of learning to quash one's true self in order to gratify the parents.

This constant self-scrutiny is one of the most painful traits of the addictive personality, as Joel, an alcoholic and heroin addict, tells us: "I'd give *anything* to get out of this self-consciousness. I feel like I'm in a prison, unable to move without being acutely aware of myself." The appeal of some addictive drugs (alcohol and heroin in particular) is to knock out the inner censor by depressing mental functioning.

Guilt-ridden

Most addictive and compulsive people have a lot of guilt, some of which is related to things they've done under the sway of the addiction. But there may be another reason why the addiction-prone person has so much guilt: guilt can be a smokescreen for repressed hostility. According to Alexander Lowen in *Pleasure,* when a child's real self is quashed (for instance, if he is punished for having normal aggressive, sexual, and other feelings), he is angry about this but doesn't feel he can afford to show it. So he covers the anger over with guilt.

Addiction thus provides a focal point or anchor for guilt, a *reason* to feel guilty, and a way to act it out. It keeps nagging, repressed hostility "in check" while simultaneously providing self-punishment for it. And the cycle is self-perpetuating. The more guilt the addict feels, the more he seeks relief in the drug—which only results in more guilt (and more need for relief).

Trouble Managing Anger

The addiction-prone person usually has little skill in expressing anger appropriately. She either banishes it to the unconscious and acts it out against herself or others, or she displaces it through blame or inappropriate outbursts or rage. Either way, she mismanages it.

Addictions become a way of discharging and therefore managing aggression. After all, addictions involve a sort of violence against the self, wreak havoc on those closest to us, and, in addictions like those to illicit drugs and sex, make a "screw you" statement to society as well. Other addictions, such as food and "downer" drugs like heroin, *numb* a person from her rage and render her passive. In this way she avoids taking responsibility for dealing with her anger appropriately.

Underlying Depression

Chronic depressed moods, either conscious or suppressed, also characterize the person at high risk for addiction. Internalized (and often repressed) reservoirs of guilt, shame, and anger contribute to this overriding sense of depression. As Anne Wilson Schaef points out in *When Society Becomes an Addict,* the addict's depression is also related to his belief that he *ought* to be able to control everything—a goal he will inevitably be unable to reach.

Addictions that are action-oriented tend to appeal most to those with underlying depression. The constant activity and excitement of the addiction serves as a distraction from the depressed feelings and provides some stimulation to offset it. As many as 75 percent of all compulsive gamblers, for instance, may suffer from depression, according to studies of this group.

Emotional Numbness

Most addicts have suffered plenty of losses in the past, not the least of which is abandonment—emotional and/or physical. If these feelings were too intense to cope with as a child, the addict may have learned to "stuff them" (the overeater quite literally so). If he has become so out of touch that he doesn't even know what he feels, he could be called "emotionally numb."

Unfortunately, without access to his feelings as a signal, he loses the opportunity to handle them productively, to problem-solve, grieve, or simply express and discharge his feelings. When he is feeling bad, he automatically seeks a mood-changer—often without even being aware of the feeling that is driving him.

And unexpressed feelings can "drive a person to drink"—quite literally. Lorraine, an alcoholic, prided herself in getting through her mother's funeral without crying. When her father died two years later, she again forged ahead with a flurry of activity, asserting that she was "strong." *And* she drank. Now recovering in AA, Lorraine looks back: "I didn't even know the words for feelings until after I got sober. There was no display of emotions in my family growing up—except rageful anger—and I didn't have the faintest idea about expressing or articulating them."

Addictions are tailor-made for those who are emotionally numb. They help keep feelings at bay while simultaneously providing enough activity, sensations, crisis, and excitement to counter the feeling of deadness inside and keep us at least feeling alive.

Inner Tension

Often, the person at high risk for addiction is driven by an inner tension or "restlessness" to seek constant activity. This is undoubtedly why many of the mood-changing experiences we're getting addicted to, in fact, involve a lot of action: gambling, shopping, compulsive sports, workaholism, and stimulant drugs. If you have a ritual to plug into, and a way to change your moods, you never have to sit still and do nothing long enough for unwanted feelings to surface.

Dana, the sex and relationship addict we met in chapter three, suffered severe abuse as a child. She describes how the resulting inner tension fuels her addictions: "I can't slow down, I can't stop, can't be alone, can't stay at home. I'm always searching for activity, action, excitement, to keep me away from getting back to my hurts. I'm always looking for the next distraction."

Afraid of Taking Appropriate Risks

People tend to think of the addict as someone who takes outrageous risks. This is certainly true on the surface, but appearances are deceiving. Fearing failure and rejection so intensely, the addict often hesitates to take *real* risks in his personal or career life. After all, if he reveals himself and is rejected, he is put in touch with his shame. But often the addict covers over his fearfulness with a false bravado that prompts him to take inappropriate—even danger-ous—risks.

Some aspects of an addictive life-style—buying drugs, for ex-ample *do* involve a substantial amount of risk to one's safety, health, or freedom. But what the addict *doesn't* risk is being *emo-tionally vulnerable.* The skills involved in addiction tend to be well defined: buy the drug and cook it up, call the bookie or broker, pick up the prostitute, complete the work project, run ten miles a day. There is little real risk of failure or rejection in these concrete steps. More important, the result is quite predictable—even down to the shame and guilt afterward.

This unwillingness to take risks often affects both the person's relationships and his career, where he prefers to "play it safe" by not putting himself in any position where he could be rejected. Remember Beverly, the compulsive overeater: "Taking risks has always been easy for me—so long as I felt confident that I would win. As far as relationships go, I've never fallen for a guy who hasn't fallen for me already. Otherwise, I might be humiliated."

Hidden Dependency Needs

Usually, the addiction-prone person has massive unmet dependency needs left over from childhood (as we will explore in the next chapter). As an adult, then, in spite of a common façade of independence, he relentlessly searches for something or someone to make him feel safe, secure, and whole. In *How to Break Your Addiction to a Person,* Howard Halpern calls this "attachment hunger."

Often, though, addicts are unaware of how dependent they are. While their neediness actually controls them and drives them to the addiction, it operates beneath conscious awareness. Many have even developed the outward persona of being "tough," outgoing, willing to take risks, and independent (an image the addiction helps to promote). But a profound inner "neediness" remains hidden behind this façade.

For the person with hidden dependency needs, addiction is perfect: it brings relief by meeting needs passively and "magically." The addictive drug or activity provides comfort, security, dependability, and soothing while insuring that the person will remain dependent on the drug as well as on those who take care of him in his addiction (pay his bills, take over his responsibilities, or whatever). The addict never has to acknowledge and address the needy feelings that don't fit his self-image.

Trouble with Authority Figures

The addictive person often has difficulty dealing with authority figures—bosses, parents, anyone in charge. This is related to the fact that *she* has to feel in control and omnipotent—or be plunged into feelings of impotence and humiliation.

Some addictions themselves are an acting out of one's struggle against authority: illicit drug use flouts the authorities, anorectics are not about to be told what they should weigh, and compulsive spenders will not be bound by credit lines or balances. In some other addictions, such as workaholism, the addictive person deals with his underlying fear of authority by seeking—compulsively—to please or even *be* the authority.

Blaming Others

Because the addict has trouble taking responsibility for himself, he often blames others and circumstances outside himself for whatever is wrong in his life. Says Lowell, a recovering alcoholic, "I'd get a traffic ticket and blame the police for it. The fact that I'd gone through a stop sign was irrelevant, as far as I was concerned. The problem was that this guy gave me a ticket!"

The person who blames others rather than take responsibility for himself is particularly prone to addiction because his posture makes it nearly impossible for him to resolve his problems. If he assumes no responsibility for his problems, he also forfeits the power to change them. That's why in recovery it becomes so important to take an inventory of one's mistakes and accept responsibility for them. In recovery, one gives up the victim stance in exchange for a greater sense of one's own potency.

Poor Coping Skills

As Stanton Peele writes in *The Meaning of Addiction,* "Those who rely on drug-induced moods want simply to modify their feelings, since they don't genuinely believe they can influence the situations that cause those feelings . . ." There is some truth to this helplessness, because much of the time the addiction-prone person has never learned problem-solving and coping skills and has only learned to blame others.

Among the tools she lacks are the abilities to (1) pause and take stock of a problem, (2) evaluate options, (3) tolerate ambiguity and frustration, (4) self-observe without being harsh (the addict knows only how to either blame and judge others or herself), (5) communicate directly and honestly, setting clear boundaries, (6) take direct, constructive actions to resolve problems, and (7) resolve conflicts through negotiation and cooperation. (Note that as a society we also lack these skills—an important reason why we've become a "quick-fix society.")

As we've seen, while he's escaping the need to problem-solve by using a mood-changer, the addictive person develops *more* problems than he had in the first place—and the addictive escape looks better and better.

Wishful Thinking

The person at risk for addiction is prone to "if only" thinking: "If only I could ____ [fill in the blank: get a boyfriend, reach a certain weight, buy the right stocks, win the athletic award], I'd be happy."

The addicts' insistence on living in fantasy means he must ignore all feedback from the environment that runs counter to the fantasy. The compulsive debtor, for example, in order to maintain the fantasy that his resources are unlimited, might ignore bounced check notices from the bank—blocking out fact because it doesn't fit with what he wants to believe. Likewise, the gambler in the throes of his compulsion might ignore the fact that he's losing a lot and that the mortgage is due—and keep throwing good money after bad. And the love addict might stay in a relationship despite clear evidence that it's a "dry well," thinking, "If only he changes, he's going to be wonderful (and I'm going to be happy)."

Such self-delusion is the fertile soil in which the addictive defense of denial takes root.

Never Wanting to Grow Up

Related to this magical thinking, the addiction-prone person often harbors a wish that he will never have to grow up, never have to take responsibility for himself, never have to exert the kind of effort and follow-through that comes with taking on an adult role in life. He fears that he will be inadequate at fulfilling adult roles, so he would just as soon not try. As long as he stays in the illusion of addiction, he can be whoever he wants to be and live in a sort of never-never land where there are no ramifications to his behavior, where his needs will always be met effortlessly, and where he won't have to take any responsibility or risk.

Without Boundaries

Because the addiction-prone person is not "behind himself," he cannot take positive, assertive actions on his own behalf to set appropriate boundaries in relationships, financial dealings, and other aspects of his life. By "setting boundaries" we mean establishing and sticking to standards by which the addict wishes to be treated.

One way the addict deals with her discomfort about setting boundaries is simply to *avoid* situations where she would have to—such as intimate relationships or positions of authority. She would rather sacrifice the gratification that would come with these roles than to suffer the discomfort of setting limits, as Marie, a sex and relationship addict, tells us:

> I learned from my parents that I was in this world to please other people, not for myself. So I went through my life never setting any limits with people. I wouldn't say, "This is O.K., this is not O.K.," because I thought if I did they wouldn't like me. And if even one person didn't like me, I thought I was a worthless piece of junk. So, rather than feel that, it was a lot easier just to avoid any situations where I'd have to risk setting limits. I look back now and can see where I passed up promotions at work and settled for one-night-stands in my love life—both because if I had taken on those challenges, I would have had to set boundaries—and that was too threatening to me.

Need for Immediate Gratification

As we have seen, the addictive person has many unmet needs that she doesn't believe she can meet. It's no wonder, then, that she has difficulty postponing present gratification in favor of some long-term benefits. She doesn't believe that better things *will* await her

81

in the long run. Addictive involvements offer a sure thing—now. With a drug, the addict doesn't have to endure any ambiguity or frustration but can count on fast, predictable relief.

Playing a part in this is the addict's sense of "entitlement." Because she often has so little real, substantial gratification in her life (having given so much of her power over to other people to approve or reject her), she often harbors a sense that she "deserves" the indulgence of her addiction. Rachel, the compulsive overeater, grew up with an abusive, alcoholic father and recalls having these feelings of entitlement even as a child, when her overeating was just getting underway:

> I'd get up in the middle of the night and sneak to the frig, then back to my room . . . praying all the way I wouldn't get caught. What did I feel? That I was only taking what was *mine,* that it was what I *deserved,* that I couldn't have it in regular life, but I could sneak it and have what I deserved this way.

No Internalized "Good Parent"

As we've seen, the addiction-prone person often has internalized a critical—even abusive—parental voice ("You shouldn't have done that; you better do this.") as well as that of a rebellious child ("I'll do what I want and you can't stop me!"). What he is missing is an *adult* voice—one of compassion, reason, and mediation—something like an internalized "good parent."

Without this, a person is unable to nurture himself and is more likely to compulsively seek soothing and nurturing outside himself. And many drugs or activities provide this sense of soothing. Bruce, the sex addict who frequents peep shows and compulsively masturbates, describes how his inability to nurture himself plays a part in his addiction:

> When I'm feeling agitated, I just don't know how to calm myself down and relax. I just push myself and feel very exhausted. I get really spent, emotionally and physically. I feel very weary. I feel like

I just want to lie down, have someone cradle me, say it's O.K., and just be taken care of.

That's what I get from masturbating. I feel so relaxed afterward, like the edge is taken off my neediness. And a lot of times when I see a prostitute, I just want her to hold me. It's almost like I want a rapport with these women.

Related to having no internalized good parent, the addict often neglects his basic needs. He indulges himself in his drug use, but often neglects his needs for rest, good nutrition, regular meals, medical and dental care, financial security. Far from caring too much about his own needs (as many think), the addict doesn't care enough! Addiction feels "right" because it is itself a form of self-neglect and self-deprivation—though it looks like self-indulgence.

Intimacy Problems

The person at high risk for addiction suffers from a gnawing sense of loneliness deep within. Out of touch with her self, unable to set boundaries, needing to control, she cannot be authentic with others and cannot form lasting, gratifying bonds.

This trait is not always apparent, however, because the addictive person may *appear* outgoing, have a lot of friends, and even be married. Generally, though, the level of intimacy in his relationships is limited—based on superficials or on mutual dependency rather than mutual sharing. So while addicts may have the outer appearance of connectedness, most describe having profound feelings of isolation deep within.

The addictive involvement, then, comes to *substitute* for intimacy—because in many ways addiction *is* a relationship. The addict is often as preoccupied with his drug as a lover is with the object of his dreams; he may seem to love, honor, and protect the supply of his drug more than he does the people in his household. That's because the drug provides feelings of connectedness with others—without the demands of real intimacy. Or, in the case of a downer drug like food, heroin, and sometimes alcohol, it can numb a person from his isolation, as Beverly, the compulsive overeater, now recovering in Overeaters Anonymous, attests:

> For me, food *is* a relationship. And when I was an active overeater, it was my primary relationship. In my twenties, if I didn't have plans for the weekend by the middle of the week, I would start planning an eating binge. Come Friday and Saturday night, I would binge and go to sleep. It was an absolute drug. I'd wake up from it around 10 at night, binge some more, and go back to sleep. The eating made me feel like I wasn't alone. It numbed me from the gut-wrenching pain of my isolation.

Another facet of the addict's isolation is that she often lacks a sense of belonging to a supportive "community" of others— whether immediate family, extended family, or some other group. Deprived of such a "safety net" of acceptance and support (as many are in our hectic, "each-man-for-himself" modern culture), the addict comes to *crave* this sense of belonging and will be all the more attracted to the "pseudocommunity" (the crack-house community, the barroom community, the racetrack community) available in many addictions.

Trouble Having Real Pleasure

Far from having too much of a good time from overindulging in pleasure, the person at highest risk for addiction may actually have a *lack* of substantial gratification in her life. Starved for genuine pleasure or just plain "fun for fun's sake," (she is too self-conscious and self-preoccupied to "lose herself" in an activity and tends to deprive herself of many simple pleasures), the addict is compulsively drawn to addiction as a sort of pseudopleasure. But it is a substitute that never really provides the refreshment and rejuvenation she seeks, so (once again) she can never get enough.

WHY ARE ADDICTIVE PERSONALITIES SO COMMON?

As we have seen, many of the addict's beliefs and personality traits "set him up" to find mood-altering drugs and activities extremely appealing. After all, if he doesn't believe in himself and his own ability to cope with everyday life, is overburdened by intense feelings, believes he *should* be perfect and is ashamed that he isn't, and thinks that people, substances, and other externals can *make* him feel better, it's a perfect match.

But, as you've probably noticed, many of these traits can be found in almost anyone. It's often a matter of degree that determines whether or not these traits drive us to seek relief through a drug of one sort of another.

The question then becomes, *Why* are these beliefs and traits, which are the cause of so much suffering, so prevalent today? The fact is, the addictive belief system and the personalities that emanate from it are to some extent generated in our own families. Unwittingly, many parents are conveying addictive values—image over genuineness, delusion over reality, power over personal potency, the quick-fix over problem-solving—that put their children at risk for becoming addicts. We have already mentioned examples of addicts whose addictive beliefs were acquired at home.

This is not to say that we should blame our families (or society) for all of our problems. To do so would only further our addictive thinking by blaming externals. To the contrary, recovery means taking responsibility for our own lives. Yet before we can free ourselves from the influence of these addictive beliefs, it does help to examine the past, to root out any messages received as children that are now making us vulnerable to addiction. As always, the more we understand the past, the less likely we are to repeat it.

85

6

The Addictive Family

WHILE IT'S TRUE THAT THE PHYSIOLOGICAL component of some chemical addictions can be created simply by repeated exposure to a drug later in life, the *emotional* component of addiction—addictive "dis-ease"—usually develops during childhood. It grows directly out of the experiences we have in our families.

What type of family *is* it that fosters addiction—however inadvertently? We've often heard that "broken" families, with divorced or separated parents, pose the greatest threat to children's emotional well-being. But actually, it's the overall way that family members relate to each other, *the family "climate"*—intact or not—that determines whether a person grows up vulnerable to addiction.

A vital function of any family is to serve as a buffer between the individual and society, to protect family members from outside dangers and pressures. It is also the training ground for acquiring the coping skills to deal with life, the place where one can go to get refueled. Kids need to count on their family to bolster their self-esteem, not break it down. Tragically for many addiction-prone people, home was not a place to get refueled but a place where their self-esteem came under attack.

Our epidemic of compulsive behaviors is, in a sense, an epidemic of child-rearing practices that lead children to believe they are "not enough." The fact that addiction is considered a "family disease," handed down generation after generation, probably has more to do with transmitting this and other addictive beliefs than it has with genetic predisposition (although that exists too, especially with chemical addictions).

And the addiction-generating family is not always one that is so obviously dysfunctional. To the contrary, the majority of families in which addictive people have grown up *appear* quite typical. The dysfunction shows up only in the outcome—in the compulsive, dependent behavior of the "adult-children" who emerge.

Some of the difficulty in identifying addictive family traits is that such behavior has become so common in our society as to actually be the norm. Much family dysfunction is even fostered by conditions in our culture. In a society where so much emphasis is placed on image, performance, success, and power over others, the needs of the children are pushed aside by parents who are themselves struggling to survive emotionally or economically. When parents must expend so much emotional and physical energy just to maintain their *own* life-style and self-esteem, there is little left over to emotionally support, guide, and nurture the children.

In a way, we are a nation of families who have abandoned their own children. It's this abandonment that is the core family problem underlying our addiction epidemic today.

The single most distinguishing trait of the addiction-generating family is that *it fails to meet the dependency needs of its children,* not necessarily by outright neglect and abandonment but, much more often, simply by failing to acknowledge the child's *emotional reality.* Families do this, as we shall see, by conveying to the child that it is "not O.K." to have certain feelings and perceptions. The result for the child is that she learns to repress her true self (her emotional integrity and vitality), and erects in its place a false self.

John Bradshaw, author of *Bradshaw On: The Family,* uses Morton Schatzman's term "soul-murder" for this squelching of the child's true self: "Soul-murder" is the basic problem in the world today; it is the crisis in the family. . . . Once a person loses contact with his own feelings, he loses contact with his body. . . . To lose one's self is to have one's soul murdered."

Because we as a society have come to value image more than substance, delusion more than honesty, "having" more than

87

"being," we are increasingly unable to "be there" for our children in the ways that count. As a result, more and more kids are growing physically into adults and taking on adult roles without being inwardly prepared and capable of coping with life's challenges, and they are therefore susceptible to the allure of the quick-fix. They become "adult-children."

The term "adult-child" was first coined to describe adult-children of alcoholics (ACOAs), but it's not just ACOAs who qualify as adult-children. Children of any parent who was not able to be there—physically or emotionally—are prone to become adult-children in the sense that they enter adulthood with many unmet dependency (or nurturing) needs. Many aspects of the addictive personality discussed in chapter five develop, in fact, out of this type of emotional abandonment. For to have one's true feelings, perceptions, and thoughts negated in favor of upholding the family myths and public image leaves a child feeling as if he is not enough. His true self is experienced as "invisible," and therefore impotent.

Many of us are puzzled when we hear news stories about successful stockbrokers, attorneys, and other seemingly "well-functioning" people who've become addicted to a drug like cocaine. "What happened," we wonder, "that they let their lives unravel like that?" What's usually not evident from the superficial facts of the story is that beneath the well-functioning exterior of the "professional" persona, there is an adult-child with hidden, unmet dependency needs.

It may be hard to believe, but *most* of us today may be adult-children. Sharon Wegscheider-Cruse, a pioneer in the treatment of children of alcoholics and codependents, claims that fully 96 percent of all Americans are codependents (we would say adult-children) because they come from one of three family situations that foster this condition: "(1) are in a love or marriage relationships with an alcoholic, (2) have one or more alcoholic parents or grandparents, or (3) grew up in an emotionally repressive family."

How could growing up in a family where emotions are not allowed to be freely expressed have the same devastating effects that growing up with an alcoholic parent has? If feelings are not allowed to be expressed in a family, the child's true self—her emotional reality—is *by definition* rejected. This rejection of her self is experienced as a profound abandonment—just as if she had been rejected by overtly hostile, unstable parents.

The family is where we receive virtually all information about ourselves in the first couple of years. The beliefs we form about ourselves, others, and the world around us grow out of the feedback, or "mirroring," we receive from our parents. If they smile warmly at us, we conclude that what we are doing is "good"; if they become stern, angry or violent, we get the clear message that what we are doing is "bad."

Contrast the positive feedback that a healthy family provides with the ways the addictive family abandons its children. Because the parents in an addictive family are often themselves adult-children (by the broad definition given above), they are still preoccupied with trying to fill their *own* emotional needs, though most of the time they are not aware of this. Without realizing it, they relate to their children as objects, as extensions of themselves, rather than as separate individuals with separate needs. They are unable, then, to provide the acceptance children need to grow successfully into separate, truly independent people.

The child in such a family may receive a constant barrage of messages about what he must do to please Mommy or Daddy: "Don't be angry," "Don't be selfish," "Be nice," "Don't cry," and so on. The message to the child is, "Don't be yourself . . . Be someone who will make me feel better about myself (or I'll be angry at you)."

The parent believes that it is for the child's own sake that this "molding" is taking place, this breaking down and rebuilding of the child's "will" (self). But to the infant or little child on the receiving end, this is terrifying. He senses that someone so angry at him may not meet his nurturing needs—physical or emotional. Since he is totally dependent on the parent for survival, the threat of such psychic abandonment is as threatening as death. Of course, the child does not think any of this through. These are simply *associations* that get made automatically—deep within the unconscious. He adapts, squelches his genuine emotions and perceptions, and erects a false self—something we have seen to be a key feature of the addictive personality.

Parents who are seeking to fill their own emotional needs through their children are using their children as a mood-changer, the way an addict uses a drug. They are trying to fill themselves up with the feeling that they are "enough" as parents. Like any addict, they want to maintain whatever illusions are necessary to keep this fix going; otherwise, they will be put in contact with their own inner reality and have to face their own unresolved feelings of abandonment and despair. Again, this is not conscious exploitation. Using the child to fill their own needs occurs automatically because dependent people seek (compulsively) to meet their unmet needs.

But like any other addiction, using a child in this way ultimately doesn't work. What the parent really wants is to undo his own abandonment—something he can never accomplish through his kids. Try as he may to control behavior, the child will still be angry sometimes, fearful sometimes, needy much of the time, and seek autonomy. Any of these threatens to strain the parents' precarious equilibrium—especially if they feel inadequate to begin with and have come to count on the child to make them feel adequate.

Perhaps that is how the child develops the belief "I am not enough." The child never *is* "enough" to fill up the needy parent. (For it is only by gaining a conscious awareness of the losses and abandonment *they* suffered in their childhood—and finally mourning them—that such parents can resolve their own inner neediness and break this cycle.)

The child in this situation comes to believe, "There must be something wrong with me; I am flawed; I am not enough." Now the *child* comes to hunger for something to make *him* "whole." As he comes to believe that sources outside of himself (drugs, other people, certain activities) can do that, he becomes vulnerable to addiction.

The roles have been reversed. The child has been "parentified." Because he has had to take care of Mommy's or Daddy's dependency needs, he has not been able to climb up into the lap of parental love and let himself be vulnerable, weak, passive, and needy, as a child may be. He has had instead to rally a false self that meets his parents' needs rather than his own.

The result of this emotional rejection for many children is premature "independence." They cannot afford to show their own dependency needs—or even to feel them—because they have no chance of being met. So they typically pretend they don't *need* nurturing and grow into adulthood never having had their child-hood feelings of dependency met. Later they will be prime candidates for seeking a substitute "object" to be dependent on—in another equally futile attempt to get their needs met.

Lana is a relationship and sex addict whose parents subjected her to frequent ridicule, beatings, and sexual abuse. In such a constantly threatening climate, it is unlikely that she could have gotten what she needed to become an independent adult. And indeed she has not. Today, at age thirty, Lana has yet to have a lasting intimate relationship of any kind. Instead, she frequently picks men up in bars, seduces them into "wanting her," and then drops them (usually before there's been any sex).

It's easy to see how Lana's craving for power (left over from her own feelings of helplessness as a child), so integral in the addictive personality, gets played out in her compulsion. When Lana seduces, then drops the men she pursues, she is recreating a pattern from her unhappy childhood. Only this time *she* gets to do the rejecting; *she* is the powerful one. But inside, Lana is undoubtedly still a very needy, hurting child.

But what about the addict who comes from a "good" family, an intact "normal" family, one that functions appropriately and is well regarded in the community? We wonder, "How can this happen?" It happens because even in a family that by all appearances *seems* caring, the child's individuality may be just as ignored as it is in an overtly chaotic family—only here it is hidden behind a veneer of social propriety. In such a family, what the child receives may be a kind of smothering "pseudolove."

And when emotional rejection, abuse, or neglect is present but covert, it may be even more difficult for the child—and later the adult-child—to come to grips with. This person *feels* deeply wounded but has no evidence of it. Caught in a dilemma where rejection remains hidden and even denied, she develops a great deal of guilt. Because the parent is fulfilling the external role of a "good parent," the child can only conclude that she, the child, is wrong for feeling angry and resentful. The child senses that "who she is" has some destructive effect on the parent, and she strives to keep her true self in check.

Doreen, a thirty-seven-year-old teacher, compulsive debtor and overeater, grew up in such a family: intact and by all appearances well functioning. But behind the scenes was a great deal of emotional repression. While Doreen's mother, Erma, often talked about what a "happy" and "close" family they were, this was not evident. There was little playfulness, communication, or spontaneity—in short, little life.

Erma was the adult-child of an alcoholic father and a stern, distant mother, and she was determined to make it different for her children. She was perpetuating a myth—"We are a happy family"—because it was very important to *her* that she produce a happy family. Her motivation was a good one—to give her children a better home than she had had. But what she failed to realize is that you can't *control* people's experiences. You can't *make* people "be happy" because you tell them to. Having an agenda for how people *must be* makes it literally impossible for genuine intimacy to develop.

Denying a child's reality, in fact, is one of the most damaging, addiction-generating behaviors a parent can engage in. Rollo May, in *The Courage to Create,* cites a study of women suffering from severe anxiety (often a springboard to addiction). He found that the original trauma and source of anxiety is not solely rejection by the mother or other primary nurturer but *rejection that is lied about.* "Anxiety," concludes May, "comes from not being able to know the world you're in, not being able to orient yourself in your own existence."

In Ann Smith's study, *Grandchildren of Alcoholics,* of people who grew up with parents who were themselves adult-children of alcoholics, 80 percent were *told* they were loved, but only 20 percent say they *felt loved*. Seventy-five percent were never told there was alcoholism in the family, and 80 percent were told *repeatedly*, "We have a good family." This is not surprising; the dysfunctional, addictive family often tries hardest of all to convey this image, while a healthier family permits a full range of emotions and experiences to be expressed.

In both kinds of families, then, those where there is overt neglect and abuse and those where the abandonment is more subtle and hidden, the child grows into adulthood with her own dependency needs unmet. She becomes prematurely "independent," which is not true independence at all but "pseudo-independence," a show of independence that is not genuine. It is this core of dependency, covered up by pseudo-independence, that later becomes the fertile soil for addictive behavior.

THE ADDICTIVE FAMILY "RULES"

Stemming from the parents' difficulty in subordinating their own needs for ego gratification to those of their children, a number of family "rules" often evolve—all of which are in the service of meeting the parents' needs rather than the children's.* The most common of these are

1. "Be perfect"
2. "Play it safe"
3. "Don't be selfish"
4. "Stick to the script"
5. "Don't express your (true) feelings"

Except for "Don't be selfish," these rules are usually unspoken. But while they remain largely out of conscious awareness, they exert a very strong influence on family members' behavior—long after a child is grown up and out of the house. Many of the addictive

*The idea of family rules discussed here is further discussed in the booklet *Co-dependency and Family Rules*, Robert Subby and John Friel (Deerfield Beach, FL: Health Communications, Inc., 1984).

beliefs that predispose a person to addiction grow directly out of these rules.

Rule #1: "Be Perfect"

Remember from chapter five that addictive people often believe they should be perfect. This belief is not internalized by the child for no reason, picked up out of the blue. Usually, the child got messages at home that she should "perform" in certain ways—ways, as we have seen, that make the parents feel better about themselves. Again, this is not because the parents consciously want to be unreasonable or overtly demanding but because of their own internal deficits.

Deirdre, a compulsive marijuana smoker, grew up in New York City with parents who had thriving careers in the theater: her father was a director, her mother an actress (and alcoholic). Following her father's death when Deirdre was thirteen, her mother remarried. Deirdre didn't get along with her stepfather and was sent to live with an older sister and her husband in a neighboring state. Deirdre says she got the message that if she wasn't perfect, she was nothing:

> I always felt like a prop in my mother's life. I never experienced myself as an entity separate from her. And I felt like a stone around her neck, that if I wasn't perfect, I was just an inconvenience to her.
>
> She usually did one of two things to me. She would either put me down totally, tear me apart and tell me I was worthless and would never amount to a row of beans, or she would pump me up, say that I took after my father and that I should be this great TV director, that I was talented, wonderful, beautiful, funny, musical, and could do anything I wanted to do. Then the next minute she'd be tearing me apart again.

Of course, when a parent's strong approval is won only for performing or behaving well, it fails to nurture the child anyway, because she senses she is not loved for who she *is* but for what she does. And this further increases her craving to be loved and accepted. Since the closest she can come to this craving is getting approval for her performance, she may learn to compulsively perform. The fact that so many of our addictions "enhance performance" (at least temporarily) illustrates the crucial role this "training" plays in our current explosion of addictions.

Such children typically become "people-pleasers," in desperate search of approval. What they yearn for is to be accepted for who they really are. But since that's not forthcoming, in its place they seek approval, a poor substitute. Hungering for approval, they develop a strong self-censor to make sure they don't do anything that could incur disapproval and they become hypersensitive to criticism and rejection—all traits, as we have seen, of the addictive personality.

Certainly not all addictive families are achievement- and performance-oriented. In a family that has little reputation to uphold because its overt problems (addiction, alcoholism, legal problems) are already known to the community, the emphasis may not be on turning out perfect children but simply on blaming its children for the family's problems. They are the scapegoats. Nothing they do is right. They may be called "stupid," "bad," "selfish," and so on. Members of the family then focus on that child (or children) as the identified "problem" and are distracted from their own uncomfortable feelings and problems.

But whether a family is outwardly or inwardly demanding—or both—the result is the same: the child experiences a constant sense of failure. His deep-down reservoir of shame is fed. In a nonaddictive family, children learn that to make mistakes is human. But in an addiction-generating family, the child feels *bad* and different from others for making mistakes. It is this sense of being *uniquely* bad that is the core of haunting inner isolation.

Rule #2: "Play It Safe"

Because members of the addictive family tend to be so fearful of criticism and rejection due to the perfectionism rule, few risk trying anything new. Instead, they tend to play it safe and avoid taking

95

risks. As a result, there are few "heroes" in the family for a child to emulate; few members have the courage to move outside of the predictable, to try new things, or to take on challenges.

That means spontaneity is out too, because being spontaneous means taking a chance that you'll be wrong, look foolish, or fail—all "imperfect" things to do.

Rule #3: "Don't Be Selfish"

One of the most destructive features of the addictive family system is the injunction "Don't be selfish." It usually gets applied to those who try to meet their own needs directly, by asking for what they want or saying what they really mean. Most addicts remember hearing this rule a lot as children, as Amy did:

> I'd hear, "You are selfish," all the time, over and over as a kid. They told me I was selfish to think of myself and what I wanted. So I went through a period of trying to be giving and doing the "right thing," which basically seemed to mean doing what other people wanted. By the time I was a teenager, that's exactly what I was doing.

While the word "selfish" is usually meant to convey acting without regard for others, in our normative (but unhealthy) family systems, it may simply mean that the child is acting as a separate "self" instead of as an enmeshed extension of others. The addictive family's balance is threatened by "self-ish" people because someone acting as an independent self cannot be manipulated so easily into doing what others want.

The message is, "If you act on your own behalf, you are bad." This trains the child not to meet her own needs directly and honestly but indirectly—by taking care of others' needs. "Don't be self-ish" means don't be your own person, be the person *I* want you to be; then I will reward you with (conditional) love and approval.

Ironically, the child never allowed to be "full of herself" often becomes incapable of giving to others as an adult, becomes truly selfish. If her own dependency needs remain unmet—sacrificed to the rule "Don't be selfish"—she will always be looking to get nurturing from others and will have little to give to others.

People in this system become less and less attuned to their own needs and desires and learn instead to anticipate what others want, give it to them, and reap whatever "rewards" they can that indirect way. They learn to react to others rather than to act directly from their own "center," or self. No wonder addiction-prone people develop the belief "I must meet my own needs indirectly."

When people in recovery from addiction begin to identify what they want and feel and state it to others (set boundaries), they often experience a great deal of guilt. Guilt, as said earlier, serves to keep us in check to make sure we don't exert too much of our personal power, our *self*. It keeps us from being "selfish."

Rule #4: "Stick to the Script"

Members of the addictive family have an unspoken agreement to maintain and promote certain myths or delusions, to "stick to the script." This is the family version of denial.

The reason family members collude in this way is simple: they're afraid to see things as they really are because to do so threatens them with loss. If they acknowledge to themselves what is really going on in the family, they lose the comfort of their own illusions. They also stand to lose acceptance by other family members, and whatever sense of belonging they do have. It's just too much to lose—especially if they don't have other sources of emotional support.

Several "roles" that children of alcoholics play in the family have been identified: the "scapegoat" or "rebel" who acts out the family's problems by getting in trouble, the "achiever" who gains approval by performing well and making the family "look good," the family "clown" who distracts family members from their feelings, and the "lost child" who fades into the woodwork and causes problems for no one. These roles can be found in most addiction-generating families, not only in alcoholic families.

These rigid roles have some (short-term) adaptive value. They allow family members to act out or otherwise manage their over-whelming feelings through their roles without rocking the boat and breaking the secrecy that surrounds the primary problems in the family; they provide some sense of identity—even if it's negative; and they often have some secondary payoffs (the rebel gets to feel powerful; the achiever gets praise; the clown gets attention; and the lost child often develops an active imagination).

Over the long haul, though, these rigid roles have a number of very negative effects. For one thing, people playing roles can't be themselves. They're stuck filling some particular needs of the family system. If you are playing the role of the "tough" kid (the rebel), you have to bury such vulnerable feelings as weakness and sadness because they are "out of character." If you're playing the role of the achiever, you have to forgo your anger and rebelliousness, since that role is already being played by someone else. Members of this family, as a result, feel a great sense of futility, frustration, hope-lessness—of being stuck.

The roles are also deadening. The same kinds of interactions get played out over and over and over again—the same accusations, the same arguments, the same outcomes. There is little opportunity for personal growth and change because everyone sticks to the script. If one person starts to recover and change, in fact, other family members may react negatively, perhaps even sabotage the recovering person's efforts to protect the precarious dysfunctional balance. The recovering person often feels guilty about changing as if he is being disloyal.

It takes tremendous courage to break out of prescribed roles and begin communicating honestly. But most addicts in recovery begin to do so—one small step at a time.

Rule #5: "Don't Express Your (True) Feelings"

In virtually all addictive families, the full range of feelings is not permitted to be expressed. When parents are repressing their own spontaneous feelings, they can't afford to have the kids freely ex-press theirs. The family needs to maintain control over what gets expressed and by whom to avoid the dangers of spontaneous expression.

What is feared most is a family member "blowing the system wide open." This would happen if someone stopped playing his role, stopped denying the underlying painful feelings and problems, and started being honest about them. To be emotionally honest could blow the cover of the entire family and disrupt the fragile balance.

In the addictive family, members are often seen as "strong" if they don't show vulnerable feelings and "weak" if they do. Kids who grow up to be addicts were often told as children, "You're too sensitive," and so they learned to squelch their feelings. The real question is, too sensitive for whom? Unfortunately, too sensitive for the parents' comfort is often the answer.

Spontaneity in the addictive family gets squelched, because spontaneous expression can lead family members dangerously close to their real selves. Along with this, creativity—by definition a form of spontaneous, uncensored expression—is often discouraged, either overtly or by lack of support, for the same reason. Children's artistic and other creative talents can be experienced as threatening to the addictive family. In an emotionally repressive atmosphere, parents are most comfortable if they are *in control* of what gets expressed, and an overtly artistic, creative child can be experienced as a threat to this kind of control. Creative expression is too spontaneous, too real.

Amy, a compulsive marijuana smoker, describes how she lost access to her creativity over the years:

> As a child, I was very creative. It was who I was. I danced, made up stories, drew, painted, would lie in bed singing. But it was never encouraged. In fact, I seem to remember some teasing about it and self-consciousness that I developed, like I was being foolish somehow.
>
> Gradually, I moved away from it. By college, I was trying to be as conventional as I could. My goal then was to be like everyone else, because that seemed more acceptable. I had cut off my inner life, was removed from who I was and what my real interests were. It took me

the next twenty years—and a couple of addictions—to finally get back to where I had been as a child, in touch with my inner self.

ADDICTIVE FAMILY TRAITS

Out of these rules, addictive families often develop certain traits, and ways of interacting with each other. The presence of some of these traits in a family does not mean that all members will develop addictions or compulsive behavior for certain. Some addicted people, in fact, come from families that do not fit this general picture, though their numbers are admittedly small. A brief discussion of the most common of these traits follows.

Dysfunctional Communication

In the addiction-generating family, people rarely say what they really mean. Instead, communication tends to be indirect and full of seduction, manipulation, and intimidation. That's because in order to communicate directly and clearly, you need a sense of *identity*—who you are, how you feel, what you think, what you want, and what you don't want; *boundaries*—where you end and someone else begins; and *willingness to take responsibility* for your communications—not altering what you say to get someone else's approval or to maintain a "precarious peace."

Members of the addictive family have trouble with all three of these traits. First, they're largely out of touch with their feelings, perceptions, and desires, having buried them long ago as children—and you simply can't communicate to someone else what you don't know yourself.

Second, they lack boundaries and tend to relate to others as extensions of themselves, as we have seen. The addictive family fails to teach their children to be assertive, to speak up firmly and take an active posture in meeting their own needs. Instead, they teach them (directly or indirectly through example) to be passive (say nothing directly but manipulate people to get them to do what you want) or aggressive (seek power over others through intimidation). Often a person who is passive most of the time has outbursts of anger when she can't hold it in any longer.

And finally, no one wants to take responsibility for saying what he really means. As we have seen, in the addictive family, people often put more priority on maintaining the family image than on being genuine. They are unwilling to be themselves and break the code of conformity because they lack the internal supports needed to withstand the "heat" they would receive from others who want them to stick to the script. As a result, communication tends to take the following self-defeating forms.

Silent violence. Because the repressed type of addictive family doesn't tolerate healthy confrontation, feelings often get expressed through moodiness, or what has been called "silent violence." People *know* something is bothering Mom or Dad or Sister but have to guess at what it is. The person who is upset doesn't take responsibility for it or for resolving it and instead manipulates others through guilt. "Look what you're doing to me" is a cop-out on responsibility.

Intimidation. In the explosive type of addictive family, intimidation through ridicule, back-stabbing, and outright threats is commonplace. Members are talked about frequently behind their backs, so everyone feels that he too may be cut down—even if people are nice to him face to face. Though home is supposed to be a safe place, a place for emotional "refueling," people in the addictive family are often on guard all the time against the next psychological blow. The person who has grown up with intimidation is at a great handicap in forming adult intimate relationships because his hyperalertness often causes him to experience putdowns and threats even where they don't exist.

Triangulation. Addictive families tend to communicate *through* each other rather than *to* each other. This is called "triangulation." If Mom has a gripe with her son, she might tell her daughter or husband, knowing it will reach the son. This way, the two people who are having the problem get to maintain the illusion that there are no problems, because in the repressed addictive family, face-to-face confrontation is unthinkable. This makes true intimacy—a sharing of selves—unattainable.

The end result of all this unhealthy communication is that family members (1) learn not to trust what people say, (2) develop overly sensitive "antennae," the ability to read people's nonverbal cues in order to try and figure out what's going on, (3) experience high levels of confusion and stress because they can't count on communication being honest, (4) feel vulnerable to seduction, manipulation, and domination on an ongoing basis, with no relief, and (5) fail to learn healthy communication patterns themselves.

No Models for Problem-solving

As we have seen, many addictive families *deny* that problems exist to begin with. Trying to maintain an image of a good family precludes being a *real* family. To maintain the myth, as addiction specialist Robert Subby has pointed out, there is often an unspoken rule against talking about problems, such as marital conflict, physical, sexual, or emotional abuse, a member's addiction or psychological problems. And you can't resolve problems if you're not willing to even talk about them.

Children in the addictive family end up feeling inadequate to meet the challenges of life, in part because they *are* inadequate to meet them. They haven't been taught how to resolve conflicts or take constructive action. As a result, when problems arise that the young person must cope with (which happens particularly in adolescence), he feels helpless to solve them. He begins avoiding problems as much as possible.

Then, somewhere along the line, the young person is exposed to a drug, to alcohol, to gambling or to another mood-changer—abracadabra! While high, he doesn't have to feel that tension inside and can forget about the problems with his courses, his teacher, his girlfriend. And if the teen has seen a parent "cope" this way already, this way out will be all the more convincing.

102

Trauma

Children from addictive families often have been subjected to overt trauma of some sort. Trauma is defined as a negative experience, or shock, that has lasting and profound psychological effect.

One of the most common traumas is living in a family where a parent is an addict. Sixty-five percent of teens dependent on drugs or alcohol have at least one substance-abusing parent. Serious illness or death in the family is another common trauma, especially if the child is not given emotional support and clear information about what is going on.

Physical violence is, of course, a blatant trauma that is also related to the later development of addiction. Of 250 families seen at one adolescent addiction-treatment center, most had experienced some form of family violence. Such trauma may be overt and obvious, as when a child is beaten in public, or it may be very well hidden. A child also is traumatized when she witnesses violence against another family member.

Finally, children who are sexually abused have an extraordinarily high rate of addiction as adults. One half of all sex addicts, for example, were sexually abused as children. And women who were victims of either rape or incest as children are far more likely to later become addicts of one sort or another than are women who were not subjected to this particular trauma.

When children are exposed to trauma at home, they often come to exhibit the same "posttraumatic stress symptoms" that combat veterans suffer: depression, nightmares, a numbing of emotions, a withdrawal into passivity, and uncontrolled aggressiveness. Experiencing trauma in childhood literally sets the child up for addiction, because to cope with the shame, helplessness, and rage that trauma elicits, the person develops a natural inclination to want to "numb" her feelings—as addictive drugs and activities do quite well.

A Lack of Playfulness

There is little joy or spontaneity in the addictive system. Often, it has *forced* versions of playfulness, such as ritualized family gatherings intended to promote the myth of the happy family, or compulsive "partying," which is dependent on a lot of drinking and eating. True playfulness requires letting go of control, risking being seen as "foolish"—something the addictive family avoids.

Recreation is often centered around the adults' interests rather than the children's. Marie, now recovering from an addiction to sex and from alcoholism, used to go fishing with her father as a child, since that's what he liked to do. Afterward, they'd stop at the local bar and spend a lot of time there. Marie says she tried not to complain too much, because then he might not take her anywhere at all.

IT'S CLEAR FROM OUR DISCUSSION that a person doesn't develop an addictive personality out of nowhere, that certain experiences as a child set him up for addiction later by introducing and reinforcing addictive beliefs and ways of being in the world.

Unless we begin to interrupt these addiction-generating family patterns, we are destined to pass our addiction problems on to the next generation. For as long as we keep giving our children the message that they are not enough, it matters not how much we teach them about the dangers of drugs or how much we admonish them to "just say no." We truly protect our children from addiction when we embrace and support them as separate individuals and not try to mold them into objects to enhance our own sagging self-esteem.

Just as the individual addict has been influenced by his experiences within the family, so too are our families influenced by the society in which we exist. Because the family is the chief vehicle through which the values of our larger culture are transmitted, we must look now at what societal influences are perpetuating our addiction epidemic.

7

The Addictive Society

IT'S NOW WIDELY KNOWN THAT CHILDREN growing up with chemically-dependent parents are at high risk for developing addictions themselves. But what we are just starting to realize is that growing up in an addictive society affects us all too—in many of the same ways.

In fact, it may be all but impossible to grow up in our present culture and not acquire at least some vulnerability to addiction. That's because the addictive personality traits (an emphasis on image, cravings for power and control, denial, dishonesty, just to name a few) are increasingly reflected in society's values and trends. And it's a self-perpetuating process. Certain trends create the conditions in which addiction thrives, and growing numbers of addictive people reinforce these trends.

Our society, in a sense, is becoming a large dysfunctional family. And just as children in dysfunctional families become prone to addiction as they try to adapt to their troubled family, so too are we becoming more addiction-prone as we try to adapt to the larger dysfunctional system in which we live.

That's why our government's well-publicized War on Drugs has met with little success and is doomed to repeated failure. It does not address the underlying cultural factors that help to create the insatiable demand for drugs. Many people are getting addicted not because they lack information about drugs, but because they are attempting (in the self-defeating manner of an addict) to meet basic, normal emotional, social, and spiritual needs for intimacy, community, acceptance, and relief from stress. Of course, mood-changers cannot provide these comforts, but they do offer the *illusion* that they can—and a desperate person will settle for the illusion.

Our addiction epidemic actually makes sense, given the cultural context in which it occurs. In a society where image is everything, for instance, people can be expected to use mood-changers to help create or maintain a certain image, or to numb themselves from feeling inadequate. Likewise, as more and more people feel a lack of control in their lives, we can expect them to crave mood-changers that provide intoxicating feelings of competence, power, and control. As life becomes more stressful and complicated, we can expect mood-changers—which deliver their effects simply and predictably (at least, at first)—to have all the more appeal.

Although we are all strongly influenced by societal forces, we also have personal choice. Addiction-generating values and trends can only make us vulnerable to addiction if we buy into them. That's where our individual responsibility comes in—and where our hope lies. The more aware we become of how cultural forces shape our addictions, the more likely we are to work on creating a healthier culture in our own lives.

THE IMAGE SOCIETY

"Certain advertisements and pictures in magazines make him suspect that he is basically unattractive."
— Wendell Berry, *The Unsettling of America*

In a society based largely on projecting an image that is acceptable to others, on the quest for a perfect body and perfect performance, addictions help us feel more acceptable, masking fears that we are not enough as we are. As Sheila, the multiply addicted teacher, noted, "I wanted to present a perfect picture, because things inside of me felt so imperfect."

That so many people in our society, like Sheila, are haunted by feelings of inadequacy is perhaps the biggest tragedy of our

106

time—and a key to why our addiction epidemic is so massive. We have lost touch with the fact that we are valuable and worthy just because we exist. Without this basic sense of intrinsic worth, we've become obsessed with putting forth an image that we think will make us more acceptable.

This obsession with image draws us to drugs and activities that either prop up our image (make us thinner, more sociable, more productive, a "winner") or numb us (as overeating and "downer" drugs do) from constant self-scrutiny.

Belief in the supremacy of image—an addiction unto itself and part of the underlying "dis-ease" of our culture—is perpetuated by denial. Rejection of our true self and reliance on a projected image is often so complete that we do not even know that this mask is not us. It becomes impossible to separate illusion from reality. We start to believe that we really *can* be a superperson, that perfection is possible, and that if we're not reaching it, we must be falling short.

We have already seen how families unknowingly reinforce this rejection of self and striving for image. But why are these self-destructive beliefs so prevalent in our culture today? How is society reinforcing and even helping to create the addict's belief "I am not enough"? Becoming aware of how the self-rejecting "tapes" (critical thoughts we have about ourselves) are reinforced daily in the media and other aspects of our culture is a first step. With awareness, we can begin replacing the tapes with messages of self-acceptance. This will be a big step toward becoming less vulnerable to addictions.

We are—as a group—particularly obsessed with how we look. We grow up bombarded with messages in the media that tell us appearance is of the utmost importance, and we come to believe it. In a national survey, one of every two teenage boys and one in five adult men rated appearance as the most important thing to them about a female. Not surprisingly, the same survey found that only one in three females feels satisfied with how she looks.

Weight is a particular preoccupation in our society. When men in this same survey were asked, "What turns you off about a woman?" 52 percent put "overweight" at the top of their list. Certainly, anorexia and bulimia have evolved in tandem with society's increasing insistence on thinness as a measure of one's attractiveness. In *Hunger Strike: The Anorectic's Struggle as a Metaphor for Our Age*, Susan Orbach suggests that the anorectic stands as a caricature of this demand for slimness, at once conforming to it and—by going to such an extreme—demonstrating its absurdity.

A look at some of the advertisements for exercise spas reveals more about our preoccupation with the perfect body and how seriously we take it. The models in these ads are suntanned, muscular, without an ounce of body fat. But what is most striking is that they almost always look quite grim and joyless; what they are doing there is obviously not intended to be fun but serious goal-attainment, acquiring a certain body image.

Trying to put together the body, build, face, and clothes of an "ideal" person is an enormous task. This preoccupation with achieving a perfect image siphons energy, time, money, and attention away from other more productive, creative, and gratifying pursuits. It is ironic that while we are preoccupied with our physical appearance and worried about aging, our lives—our youth—pass us by. In denying who we really are (ever-aging people like all those who passed before us), we forfeit the one feeling that is perhaps most associated with youth: joy.

Another area in which we strive to conform to images rather than just be ourselves is that of stereotypical sex roles. The male and female roles transmitted through our culture have tended to be very polarized: to be considered "masculine," a man has had to be aggressive, in control, active, analytical; to be considered "feminine," women have been expected to be the complement: receptive, emotional, nurturing, and passive.

Since to conform to these polarized ideals means to negate whole aspects of one's self, our human nature fights against it. A man *feels* vulnerable at times, even if he doesn't show it, and a woman *wants* to express her power and take action at times, even though she may hide this impulse. Since these polarized sex-role expectations still persist—despite our growing awareness of them—the feelings and desires that conflict with our role often cause us inner confusion and fears that we are "unacceptable" to others. The drugs and activities we get addicted to often help us shore up our sense of "gender competence" (for the moment), and this is another part of their reinforcement value.

That both women alcoholics and women cocaine addicts often suffer profound feelings of shame and humiliation about their drug-related sexual behavior testifies to the double bind of the feminine role in our society. The message for women is "Be accommodating; to be self-defining and assertive is not feminine." Yet to accommodate, to give in, strips the woman of power. She is debased in a no-win situation.

Likewise, the man who feels he must always be in control, powerful, aggressive, and invulnerable, is trapped in a prison that can make a drug escape or other high an enormously welcome effect, especially if it aids his feelings of powerfulness, competence, and performance.

People who are relationship addicts also struggle to project a certain image. They strive to be "seen" as part of a happy couple—at any cost—even if it means staying in a relationship that does not meet their needs or subjects them to abuse, even if it means living a lie. The message "You're Nobody 'til Somebody Loves You" can be heard in our popular music, films, and other media. Sadly, we often get this message from our own families as well.

Brenda is a woman in her early thirties who has had considerable difficulty forming lasting relationships with men. She always seems to wind up with men who feel overwhelmed by her hunger for a relationship, and they inevitably back away. Brenda concedes that her intense craving for a relationship seems to keep her from having one. Yet, she refuses to accept not being in a relationship, because it makes her feel like a loser, a societal "reject." As with other addictions, using a relationship as a way to feel accepted brings exactly the opposite: a string of broken affairs and excruciating loneliness.

People who are vulnerable to addiction usually crave attention. They describe a sense of being "invisible," unseen. It is easy to understand why, since their true self—with its inevitable "flaws"—has been banished and an false image substituted for it. The result is a craving for any type of attention, a craving to be seen *at all.*

Out of this sense of invisibility has grown our modern-day celebrity worship. Since collectively we share a hunger to be seen, the people who succeed in getting all eyes on them, regardless of how it's done, are considered successful. They need not have accomplished anything significant or displayed any unusual courage; just to have been recognized, to be singled out for attention is enough. The celebrity is our modern-day "hero."*

We tend to think in absolutes in our addictive society, just as in the addictive family: you're everything or you're nothing. To be someone who matters, *somehow* you must get attention, rise above the masses. Or we try to live *through* our hero/celebrities, devouring every bit of trivia we can about their lives. To be ordinary, to be average, to be "regular" means you don't matter.

No wonder so many of our addictions—to dieting, running, cocaine, alcohol, or work—represent efforts to become worthy of attention, to help us stand out from the crowd, feel like a winner, or improve our performance. The person who succeeds in being seen, even if what is seen is merely one's image, is rescued from the haunting tyranny of insignificance. The need here is to differentiate between the healthy drive to fulfill one's potential and the unhealthy addiction to perfection.

Unfortunately, we also use celebrities as the models against which to measure ourselves. We see them interviewed on talk shows, and they do not appear to be fearful or anxious or unhappy. They banter easily with the host, laugh readily, and dress with flair. They *appear* flawless, and so our shame over our own perceived flaws is heightened. After all, if these celebrities are so important and so perfect, where does that leave us?

It's easy to forget that images in the media are carefully orchestrated, set up to achieve certain effects, not to honestly reflect

*We are grateful to Alexander Lowen for his analysis in *Pleasure: A Creative Approach to Life* (New York: Penguin, 1980).

reality. The only explanation we see for not being as happy, self-confident, and as worthy of attention as those celebrities is that *we* are not enough—once again. We want so much to be able to project an image of self-assurance that we will snort cocaine or have a few drinks in order to better do so.

To become free of the compulsive desire to make ourselves more acceptable, we must gain a solid measure of true self accept ance, to know that we are intrinsically valuable, that we need not earn that value by measuring up to arbitrary, external perfectionistic standards.

MARKETING TO OUR ADDICTIONS

"The most powerful, all-consuming market in this country is compulsive eaters, and while everybody else is talking about bean-sprout sundaes and sugarless ice creams and everything else, there are 120 to 140 million people out there who can't help themselves to various degrees.... It's an incredible sickness, and all I'm doing, on the evil side, is exploiting the sickness."
—David Liederman,
founder and president of David's Cookies

Most of us know that it's important for a parent to give consistent messages to children, not to say one thing with words and another with actions. For example, if a father punishes his teenage daughter for drinking beer on one occasion and gives her a beer mug as a gift on another, which message is she to believe? If a mother in structs her children not to use drugs "because they're bad for you" but has to be carried to bed every night after passing out from vodka, what are the children learning? Actions, as the saying goes, speak louder than words—always.

Yet throughout society, we too are transmitting double messages about drugs, gambling, sex, and other mood-changers. Alcohol and tobacco, our legal drugs, are openly marketed, despite the fact that they together contribute to an astounding 450,000 American deaths each year. Sugar too is pushed, despite growing numbers of people who, as Liederman puts it, "can't help themselves."

111

Children are urged by Nancy Reagan and others to "just say no" to drugs, yet thousands of advertisements each year promote the notion of a quick-fix—pills for sleeplessness, drinks for more fun, remedies for stress headaches, food products for resolving family disagreements.

Major magazines run feature articles regularly on compulsive overeating, obesity, and dieting. Yet as Liederman's statement suggests, certain segments of the food industry actively promote overeating and exploit people who have the problem. Liederman is probably not much different from other effective marketing strategists—or from ourselves for that matter. It's not a matter of "good" guys versus "bad" guys; we are all in this together. But when healthy foods are dismissed with disdain because there are millions of compulsive eaters who "can't help themselves," we are blatantly promoting addiction.

Compulsive shoppers and spenders have not gone unnoticed by marketing strategists either. Shoppers in department stores are barraged with displays aimed to stimulate impulse buying. Sexy lighting, carefully coordinated colors, and "mood" music all blend together to create an "experience" for shoppers that ultimately leads them right to the cash register.

Like most addicts, compulsive shoppers can't accept limits. They often block from their minds the bottom-line reality of their financial resources and make impulsive purchases (to satisfy that insatiable sense of need) even when drowned in debt from previous shopping sprees. This excessive consumerism has been encouraged deliberately by marketing strategists.

Witness the designer jeans commercial aired several years ago in which the young superstar model Brooke Shields says that she is saving her money to buy a pair of these jeans—"and if there's any left over, I'll pay the rent." Sounds amusing, but considering the humiliation and stress of those severely in debt who come off the high of their last purchase and have to face their creditors, pushing this attitude is hardly different from pushing drugs. Says Brian, the compulsive debtor and spender whom we met in chapter one, "That's exactly how I used to live; eating out in fancy restaurants seven nights a week was my priority. I put it before paying the rent."

Government officials decry compulsive gambling, yet more than $2 billion a year is spent in the United States promoting legal forms of gambling. OTB (off-track betting) and lottery ads play to the fantasy of "if only" thinking, and the compulsive gambler—with his insatiable need for illusion—can hardly resist. Those who operate gambling casinos know too that feeling like a "big shot" is one of the payoffs for the compulsive gambler—and they seek to stimulate this fantasy by surrounding him with blinking lights, free alcohol, glitz, and glamour.

Advertising practices render us more vulnerable to addiction by promoting the addictive belief "I am not enough." It is a common marketing strategy to bring out (or even create) a *perceived need* which only the advertised product can fill. An advertisement cannot imply that we are already lovable, worthy, and attractive just as we are; if it did, we wouldn't need what they are selling. In a sense, we are "set up" every day to feel in want so that we keep buying.

Marketing analysts know what we need to believe about ourselves—are *desperate* to believe about ourselves—and they market to those needs. Magazine and newspaper ads reveal to any interested observer exactly what images we desire to achieve and how the ads promise to deliver. Common words and phrases in the large-type copy include "the best," "winning," "sexy," "perfect," "flawless," "unforgettable," "alive," "action," "privileged," "master," "manly," "you've arrived," and "performance." These words and phrases, among many others, sell products. They reinforce that it is "the best," "the winner," "perfect," "unforgettable," and "alive" that we are compulsively trying to be because we don't feel that being ordinary and average is good enough. We are striving to stand out from the crowd, and any product (or mood-altering drug, activity, or person) that can help us to do it is likely to be appealing.

In addition to having the image of a winner, of someone worthy of attention, we also want to look like we're having fun. Alcohol ads often show groups of friends having laughs around the piano or at the beach, or a couple strolling arm in arm into the sunset, bottle of liquor in hand. The message, of course, is that by drinking this brand of beverage, you too can have all this: romance, sex, adventure, fun. We all know *rationally* that drinking a certain brand of alcohol cannot possibly guarantee us fun, adventure, or love, but because these satisfactions are paired with the brand name over and over, they come to be associated in our minds.

Marketing strategies aimed at conveying the message "You're not O.K. now—but can be with this product" aren't likely to change as long as we respond to this approach. Our hope in overcoming addictions lies in changing *ourselves,* in becoming more accepting of our own imperfect selves, more honest about who we are, and less dependent on false images.

OUR LIVES HAVE BECOME UNMANAGEABLE

If many people in a society feel a substantial lack of control over their lives, rates of addiction in that society will jump. This observation by Stanton Peele in *How Much Is Too Much?* holds another, implicit, observation to why addiction is widespread now: in a society in which people feel less and less control over their lives— from work conditions to crime, foreign policy, and even survival in a nuclear age—our mood-changers provide at least the illusion of being powerful, competent, in control of *some*thing.

A 1986 survey published by *USA Today* asked respondents open-ended questions about what they liked and didn't like about their lives. The desire to gain more control was mentioned again and again. This was confirmed in a follow-up survey of more than 15,000 respondents who again stated that a desire for more control over their own lives as one of the primary concerns.

The first suggested step in Alcoholics Anonymous's 12-step recovery program states: "We admitted we were *powerless* over alcohol and that our lives had become *unmanageable* [emphasis added]." We have in our society today an epidemic of unmanageability, powerlessness, of having lost control over many aspects of our own lives.

Exactly what we lack control over covers a wide range. On a global level, we all experience some sense of powerlessness over issues of war and peace, life and death, over a destiny that is increasingly controlled by people and circumstances outside our immediate and direct influence. The fact that surveys show one in four American teens expects to wake up one day within the next decade and find the United States engaged in global nuclear war points up how little control teenagers feel over their future. On the neighborhood level, a rising crime rate—particularly since the escalation of the cocaine epidemic—contributes further to feelings of helplessness. We feel the need to be on guard more and more against unpredictable, irrational crime.

In the workplace, too, people report feeling a lack of control over conditions, workload, stress levels, rewards, hours, and security. In the survey cited earlier, work emerged as the greatest source of stress in our lives. A recent Harris poll found that the majority of workers don't feel they have enough input into the decision making process and they desire more autonomy. In the area of personal relationships, we are also feeling a lack of control and predictability. Men may be experiencing this as a result of shifting male-female roles that have changed the rules of the past. Instead of unquestionably assuming the dominant role, men are increasingly being required to share their previously unchallenged power with women. Yet the addiction-prone person (or society) is extremely reluctant to give up power over others, since to do so plunges him into his own feelings of shame, helplessness, and dependency.

Experiencing demands that we cannot directly change—and feeling that we *should* be able to change them—is what drives us to seek escape through the illusion of power and the magical solution of the addictive experience. Through addictive drugs and activities we play out our struggle for control over ourselves, over the addiction, and over others.

Studies of gamblers, for example, have shown that those most frustrated on the job by a lack of control are those most likely to gamble compulsively and be addicted in other ways too. Perhaps gamblers use the stimulating high of gambling to avoid this nagging sense of impotence and to enter a world where they experience themselves as powerful, influential, and competent, if only for a few hours.

A strong connection between a sense of helplessness and the appeal of mood-changers is dramatically revealed in the experience of people chronically exposed to certain conditions. Groups whose security and control have been undermined either by invasion (the American Indian), poverty (the innercity poor), or war (American soldiers in Vietnam) have shown high rates of addiction. Each of these groups has been subjected to traumatic conditions that its members feel powerless to change. And feelings of powerlessness in the face of unmitigated stress render otherwise healthy people far more vulnerable to addiction.

While today's society promotes the belief that we *should* be all-powerful, the reality of our lives—at home, at work, in the environment, and in international affairs—makes it clear that we actually have little impact. We are but tiny cogs in an increasingly technologically powered wheel. It's one thing to feel powerless and know that that's O.K.; it's something else again to expect omnipotence of oneself in the face of insurmountable challenges.

Lacking the sense of empowerment that comes from having the skills to manage one's affairs, we crave the *illusion* of power and try to get it from sources outside ourselves or through power *over* others. Neither of these ultimately works, since what we really want is to feel that we *can* make a difference in our own life and the lives of others. It is this sense of genuine effectiveness—personal empowerment—that must be acquired for a lasting recovery.

THE NORMALIZATION OF DISHONESTY

"Ours is the lying society."
—Leon Wurmser, *The Hidden Dimension*

From cheating on taxes and buying off officials to breaking international agreements, dishonesty has become so common as to be seen as normal. There are few role models for unwavering honesty, and this lays the groundwork for denial.

Addiction thrives on dishonesty. Because the addict lies to herself about the consequences of her drug use, she is unable to evaluate it and stop it. If and when she eventually enters treatment or a self-help group, she will be told that only by becoming honest with herself and others can she recover and only by continuing to practice honesty in all her affairs can she remain so.

Most of us remember getting firm messages as children about the virtue of honesty. We learned not to steal and to always tell the truth, no matter how painful or embarrassing. Unfortunately, though, these admonitions lost effectiveness as soon as we were old enough to observe our adult models and realize that they often relied on the maxim "Do as I say, not as I do."

We have also seen how emotional honesty is "trained out" of children who grow up in an addictive family. They learn not to be honest about their feelings and perceptions, because to do so leads to emotional abandonment. Relationships necessarily become dishonest because you can't share yourself honestly (the basis of intimacy) if you don't know what you honestly feel.

Within the culture at large, dishonesty is promoted and modeled. Advertising relies on dishonesty to a large degree: products are promoted by associating them with qualities they cannot possibly deliver (the toothpaste that will give you sex appeal) and that are totally unrelated to the product (the car that gets "forty laughs per mile"). Other ads lie to us about how bodies "normally" look, the aging process, and countless other issues.

We practice dishonesty with each other in our everyday interactions. We get the impression from social mores that to communicate honestly and straightforwardly is either impolite or naive. We are encouraged to communicate in ways that will "get us over" (one is reminded of the book titled *Winning Through Intimidation*). Controlling and manipulating are seen as legitimate and even preferred ways to get what we want.

Perhaps this is because work values have carried over into our private relations. We are encouraged to use strategy, remain "one

117

up," to manipulate situations and people to get what we want. These strategies have questionable value even in business and no place in intimate relations. This kind of rampant dishonesty only furthers our isolation. There is the growing sense of not being able to trust what anyone says, whether it is a coworker, salesperson, or even a friend or family member.

Dishonesty is all but expected in financial matters. Cheating on taxes, lying on credit card applications, and other such dishonesty is seen as normal and adaptive. The person who chooses to be scrupulously honest in these affairs is usually considered naive, a "chump." Barbara, a recovering addict interviewed for this book, was encouraged by a realtor to draw up a set of false tax returns reflecting greater income so she could qualify for a mortgage. When she refused saying it would be an act of fraud, he pressured her: "Oh, come on. It's done all the time! This is how the real world operates!"

These types of expressions pepper our language; "Good guys don't win ball games," "You might as well, everyone else does it," and "Nice guys finish last" are just a few. It is common while being dishonest in our society to minimize or even deny that there's anything wrong with it, as the realtor did.

Polls show too that while Americans want to be able to look up to their employers as models of honesty, often they cannot. A recent Harris poll of over a thousand workers found that only 41 percent considers the management where they work to be "honest and ethical in their dealings with employees and the community."

Among public officials, examples of corruption and dishonesty are too numerous to even cite. In a recent "sting" operation led by the FBI, an astounding 105 out of 106 bribes offered public officials in New York State were accepted. And the only official who turned down a bribe did so not because he was being honest but because the payoff offered was "too little."

When public officials say one thing and do another, we cannot expect our children not to grow cynical. A blatant example is the hypocritical stance against drugs of the former county prosecutor and mayor of Charleston, West Virginia, James Roark. Nicknamed

"Mad Dog" for his tough antidrug stance, Roark spearheaded an aggressive, citywide campaign against drugs until one day he himself was arrested and charged with possessing and distributing cocaine—during his crusade. Eventually Roark pleaded guilty to cocaine possession and agreed to resign.

Then there's the dishonest message given by former President Reagan, who, after signing a 1986 bill to pump an additional $1.7 billion into the War on Drugs (a move that won considerable applause during the height of the media coverage of the cocaine epidemic), later called for cutbacks of over half of it—a behind-the-scenes action that went largely unnoticed by the public.

There are other inconsistencies in the way our officials have behaved regarding worldwide drug dealing. At the same time that the War on Drugs is being pursued fervently, a number of federal officials have been drawn into controversies regarding the alleged drug-smuggling operations of the U.S.-backed Contras in Nicaragua as well as of General Manuel Noriega of Panama.

Even on the highest level, the executive branch of our national government, laws are broken with mind-boggling frequency. Only one cabinet member of the original Reagan administration remained at the close of the president's eight-year term; nearly all had resigned under accusation of some dishonest or unethical dealings. Yet, oddly enough, we persist in thinking of our government and our culture as morally superior (another parallel to the grandiose self-delusion of the addict).

Living in a society in which the highest leaders give double messages about their values is no different from living in a family in which parents behave inconsistently. And just as children in a family with contradictory rules tend to act out their confusion, so do we.

Of course there are many public officials, policemen, law enforcement agents, and government leaders committed to honest dealings. But sadly, we have more publicized examples of those in positions of power who don't take honesty too seriously.

Still, the dishonesty is not the worst of it, for none of us can claim to lead perfectly honest lives. The worst is that we have so few role models in positions of authority who are willing to *admit* their mistakes openly and honestly. The only time a public figure admits a mistake, it seems, is when it is politically expedient to do so, when he has no other recourse.

How refreshing and inspiring it would be to see someone have the courage to admit his mistakes publicly and promptly. Imagine what it could do for our young people to see a president take inventory of where he was wrong and promptly admit it, as one of the twelve steps of recovery in Alcoholics Anonymous suggests!

This tendency to espouse honesty but practice dishonesty—with ourselves, in interpersonal relations, in our work, in our everyday affairs—permeates life in America and creates the fertile soil in which addiction thrives. Becoming inured to dishonesty, accepting it as normal, makes it that much easier for denial to take hold.

Since we no longer see honesty as its own reward, we cannot use this value system as a way of regulating our behavior. More and more, we rely on *external* controls rather than self-restraint, and this too contributes to the addiction epidemic. Instead of living by shared and agreed-upon values, we increasingly accept the notion that the only reason not to do something is the possibility of getting caught.

Dishonesty is ultimately self-defeating, and to the extent that it makes us more vulnerable to addiction, it is a downright threat to us. As dishonesty becomes second nature we become increasingly an addiction-prone society. Dishonesty to self and others is the soil in which denial grows best, and denial makes addiction possible.

RELIANCE ON THE "QUICK-FIX"

"The avoiding tendency lies at the very root of American character."
                                      —Philip Slater, *The Pursuit of Loneliness*

Just as the addictive family fails to model effective problem-solving skills, so does the addictive society. Lacking the skills needed—the ability to pause, self-observe, honestly admit problems, resolve conflicts—we rely heavily on short-term solutions, perpetuating the illusion that the world (and our power) is without limits. Whatever the problem—acid rain, unsafe nuclear weapons plants, the budget deficit, ocean dumping—positive action is rarely taken to address it until it reaches crisis level.

Our nation's sense of omnipotence contributes to the denial we have about our problems, including our addiction problems. That's because our addictive belief system holds that we should be invulnerable, always in control, and that to be unable to control something is shameful.

Anne Wilson Schaef, in *When Society Becomes an Addict,* brilliantly exposes the power addiction of some political leaders within our addictive system. With the illusion of control, she writes, "Reagan has not only convinced himself that he can control what happens on this planet, he also thinks that he can control outer space."

A 1987 Gallup poll found that 68 percent of Americans believe that the United States has a "boundless ability to solve its problems." To believe that our power is "boundless" is addictive thinking. It denies that we have limitations like everybody else and ignores the need to periodically take inventory of where we could be wrong.

Interestingly, 56 percent of the same group of over 4,000 people surveyed believes, "Communists are responsible for a lot of the unrest in the U.S. today." This too smacks of the kind of thinking characteristic of addicts: "I am perfect and limitless. If it wasn't for *them* I would be O.K. *They* are the problem."

Also like the addictive family, we as a nation are becoming more isolated from the "community" of other nations. Our compulsive pursuit of power over others, our attempts to control, our dishonesty, lack of humility, blaming, and willingness to break agreements are all addictive traits. If other nations do not support our addictive ways, we blame them and withdraw further into our own self-justified, defiant stance—just as the addict does. We are unwilling to examine our own behavior and are convinced others are betraying us. It's as if our society at large is operating according

121

to distorted beliefs "I should be perfect," "I should be all-powerful," "the world should be without limits," "feelings are dangerous," and "the image I present to others is most important."

Perhaps the best example of the ways in which our problem-solving skills are lacking is our approach to the drug-addiction epidemic. Hardly a day passes that our newspapers and TV news shows don't bring more proclamations about the War on Drugs, about the dragon we are about to slay with this next initiative. Yet over the period that this war has been waged, the problem of drug use in America has grown much worse. While expenditures have increased sixfold in two years—to a whopping $6.6 billion allocated for 1989—the amount of drugs on the street has skyrocketed pro-portionately. Americans now consume 60 percent of all illicit drugs produced in the world and more drugs per capita than any other industrialized nation.

Yet we are still largely in denial about the conditions in our culture that contribute to making so many of us vulnerable to drug addiction. This too parallels the addictive family, in which the member who dares to speak out and acknowledge the family's addictive problems is accused of being disloyal, of displaying the family's dirty laundry to outsiders.

But to reassess our approach to the drug problem would re-quire a temporary cease-fire, a pause in our frenzied antidrug activ-ity and a period of national self-observation and analysis. It would mean taking the focus off "them" (the drug dealers, the coca farm-ers, the South American governments) and taking an honest look at ourselves as a society. And just as the addict cannot bear to look within and accept the truth of conflicting and uncomfortable feel-ings but instead projects them outward, so we as a society cannot seem to look honestly at ourselves and accept the disconcerting truth of our collective discontent.

We much prefer to look for the "evil" in the drugs themselves and in those who sell them than to look at the question of why *we* want them. As long as we blame the farmers in Bolivia or the government in Colombia for our drug epidemic, we don't have to look at ourselves. To paraphrase Freud, it's much easier to deal with an outer threat than an inner danger.

To many Americans, doing nothing or taking the time to consider a problem tread dangerously close to "passivity" and "intellectualizing"—both of which are abhorred. The American way is to "get tough," to take "firm action." To be passive—even while devising a plan that might actually work—is equated with being helpless, powerless, weak. It is to be a "wimp," perhaps the most despised character in America.

Paradoxically, our inability to surrender, to admit we are not in control of it all renders our flurry of antidrug activity ineffective, impotent. Our insistence on trying to *control* the problem renders us powerless over it. This is the same thing that happens to the individual addict: he tries to cure his addiction by trying ever harder to control it. Though effort after effort fails, he still believes "this time" he's going to conquer it. He doesn't realize that willpower's not enough.

It is a form of collective insanity, collective delusion, to believe that if all illicit drugs were somehow removed from this country overnight, we would become a society of noncompulsive, life-embracing people. The fact that so many other types of compulsive behaviors besides addiction to illegal drugs are erupting among us should start to pierce our denial about that.

To recover from the drug-addiction epidemic will require the same searching and fearless honesty required of the addict in recovery. Just as the individual addict must admit being powerless over addiction before recovery can begin, so we as a society will not substantially reduce our addiction problems until enough of us become aware and acknowledge that we are an addiction-generating society.

Most important, we must stop promoting the addictive belief that we as a nation are infallible and all-powerful, for this omnipotent posture only impedes our ability to solve our problems—just as it does the addict's. We must admit that we *don't* have all the answers and begin looking to a higher value system than that of greed and power over others for our direction.

YEARNING FOR COMMUNITY

*"[C]ommunities in the true sense barely exist anymore. . . . In-
dividuals and families, who share common basic values and
goals, who partake in each other's joy and griefs, where each
knows the other by name, history, weakness and strength."*
—Leon Wurmser, *The Hidden Dimension*

In a highly individualistic society, we increasingly lack the support
and security of extended family and community. Many addictions
provide nonthreatening contact with others and numb our feelings
of insecurity.

It's no coincidence that the self-help movement has been so
successful in fostering the recovery of countless addicts. A crucial
aspect of self-help programs like Alcoholics Anonymous, Gamblers
Anonymous, and Sex and Love Addicts Anonymous is the *fellowship* they offer. The camaraderie is something for which many
people in modern-day American society seem to yearn.

The desire for "community," as Philip Slater wrote in *The
Pursuit of Loneliness,* is one of several basic human desires deeply
frustrated by modern American culture. This drive for community,
he writes, is "the wish to live in trust and fraternal cooperation with
one's fellows in a total and visible collective entity."

So it is not only that we lack the skills (and sometimes the
courage) to face our problems but also that our families, social
institutions, and communities are failing to provide us with the
emotional and social support necessary to muster courage. Having
sufficient emotional, physical, and social support in our lives brings
out the best—the heroic—in any of us. Knowing that we are not
alone as we take a courageous step to confront a problem and that
if we fail to successfully resolve it we won't be abandoned undoubtedly gives us greater access to our courage.

Increasing individualism is another factor that frustrates our
desire for community and leaves us more vulnerable to addiction.
Our economic system rewards individual performance rather than
cooperative effort. As a result, writes Charles Derber in *The Pursuit
of Attention,* "each person functions as an independent, isolated

'self' whose survival and success depend on his own resources."

Consequently, we are set against each other, our trust and mutual reliance eroded. We feel we cannot count on anyone else but ourselves, and this creates profound feelings of alienation and insecurity. We are led to feel that if we don't make good, we will be ostracized, seen as unworthy, and left to flounder on our own.

This "each man for himself" orientation is often called "rugged individualism" or "survival of the fittest," and it is the philosophy upon which American society was founded. If each of us is expected to "pull ourselves up by our own bootstraps," the implication is that we should not expect any help from others. To be in a position of weakness or neediness is, as we have seen, to be scorned. The connection between our growing insecurity, our yearning for community, and our growing vulnerability to addictions becomes clear.

One of the secondary payoffs of addictions—an underlying attraction—is that we get membership in the "club" with other addicts. The gambler enjoys the camaraderie of the "game" with other gamblers. The drug addict usually interacts with a steady flow of people with whom he gets high, buys from, or sells to. Many an alcoholic remembers enjoying—in the beginning—the sense of belonging she felt in the bar or at parties with other drinkers. For the workaholic, office relationships often provide community.

Leon Wurmser, writing about addiction, calls this a "pseudo-community" and notes that it is unable to fulfill the addict's need for real community. One's "drug buddies," he contends, are not so very different from the rat race they substitute for, chasing largely superficial goals and equating happiness with acquisitive success of one sort or another. Whether your goal is acquiring goods or acquiring drugs, you are looking to something outside of yourself to make you whole.

Within such a "club," there is little sense of unconditional acceptance or trust; one's mask or image must be maintained. People are still usually judged according to quite superficial criteria, and the shared goal of getting high (or gambling or shopping) can hardly be expected to sustain one with a sense of meaning and purpose over the long haul. For a community to be supportive, it must provide a shared value system of a higher order (some sense of purpose and meaning) and provide a sense of security to its members.

As stated earlier, a major reason for the success of self-help groups is that they also provide fellowship, the security of a community of supporters. What these groups provide that the pseudo-community of other active addicts cannot is unconditional acceptance of the real person on the other side of the mask, the person with weaknesses and vulnerabilities.

This sense of acceptance by a community of others provides for many the first true sense of connectedness, of belonging—securely—based on one's intrinsic worth. The power of that support—that sense of community—cannot be underestimated. It is the atmosphere in which we can begin to let down our masks and allow our wounds to heal. As one recovering addict put it, referring to the self-help group he attends, "They know who I am, and they still accept me."

ADDICTION AND THE (SECRET) SEARCH FOR MEANING

"All addictions are forms of idolatry."
—M. Scott Peck, interview, *Changes,* March–April 1988

Our society's obsession with acquiring money and possessions is yet another factor that makes us addiction-prone. If we look to things to fill us up, we pay for this magical solution with our freedom, our soul. As long as we think we must protect our supply of things, we are impeded in making career and other life decisions that will truly gratify us. Then we look for something else (our mood-changer) to fill the emptiness. In fact, the word "addiction" derives from the Latin word *addere,* which means "to devote." In the absence of anything greater, we *devote* ourselves to our addictions.

Workaholism, another addictive behavior, is fueled by the striving for material success. People stay at jobs ill suited for them, commute long distances, put in ever-increasing hours, bring work home, and work weekends. A 1987 Harris poll found the typical American's work week has increased to 46 hours, up from 35 in 1973. Correspondingly, the amount of time left for leisure has dropped from 26.2 hours a week in 1973 down to 16.6 in 1987.

But this increasing work involvement isn't leading to increasing satisfaction; later, only 42 percent of men and 56 percent of women said that they are "very satisfied" with their work, and a majority said it is the most stressful part of their lives. We measure ourselves and others by what we do, what we have, and how much we accomplish rather than by how we feel about what we do and whether or not we are truly enjoying life. We label people who contemplate the meaning and purpose of life as "too idealistic." We hide our fear of just "being" behind the self-righteous condemnation of those who "aren't going anywhere."

Student concerns and interests reflect this leaning toward the pragmatic over the philosophical, with the decline in enrollment in the humanities and liberal arts courses in favor of highly specialized training for high-paying careers, mostly in business. More and more students believe that if they are better able to accumulate material goods and comforts, they will be happier. We have come to believe that *having* is the prerequisite to happiness and that questioning this formula is just a case of sour grapes.

Ultimately, though, the addictive pursuit of things—like any other addiction—cannot fill us up. We feel empty, bored, tired from overworking, guilty about neglecting ourselves and our children in the process, and we ask, "Is this all there is?" Once again, there is a paradox: the compulsive pursuit of material success keeps us from the only kind of success that actually can gratify us, the success of just *being* and knowing that we are enough.

NOT ENOUGH FUN

"Modern man is drinking and drugging himself out of awareness, or he spends his time shopping, which is the same thing."
—Ernest Becker, *The Denial of Death*

127

Despite our materialism we are nonetheless a society that places high value on having fun—so it seems if the amount of money we spend on it is any measure. We spend billions of dollars each year on everything from running shoes and golf sets to health club memberships. But here too work values have invaded our leisure time—making it more goal-oriented than creative and playful. We indulge not just for the fun of it in many cases but to accomplish or win something: to surpass our last performance; to surpass someone else's, to improve our technique, to make business contacts, or to lose weight. There's nothing wrong with these goals, but they don't substitute for the refreshment that fun for fun's sake provides. This too plays a part in our susceptibility to addiction.

To be goal-oriented in a leisure pursuit makes it impossible to lose ourselves in the activity just for the fun of it. We stay too self-conscious of how we're doing, of how we look doing it, of what time it is, of how others are perceiving us, of who we can meet. We remain in a state of self-consciousness rather than become engaged and absorbed in the activity.

But it is only by losing ourselves that we can emerge rejuvenated and refreshed, according to Geoffrey Godbey, author of *Leisure in Your Life*. We must be fully engaged in an activity, doing it because it is *compelling* and *fun for its own sake* for this to occur. By immersing ourselves in an enjoyable activity, losing track of time, and suspending self-consciousness and awareness, we emerge refreshed and rejuvenated—"re-created!" In this way, leisure activities that refresh are similar to single-point meditation: for the moment all rational concerns and worries are set aside; all that matters is the moment.

Mood-changers provide this opportunity for "single-point focus." They allow us to temporarily escape self-consciousness by becoming wholly absorbed in the experience. The ritual of the addiction, the high, and the aftereffects of guilt and shame all consume our awareness for the time being and remove all other problems from our minds. For the time being nothing else matters but which blouse to buy, which horse to bet on, or where to get the drug. Total submersion in an addictive activity allows us to be in the here and now, and we crave this loss of time-consciousness. At the same time, the pseudopleasure our drugs provide keeps us from seeing how little joy we actually have in our lives.

Having fun has become part of our image rather than part of our genuine experience of life. We are bombarded daily with images in the media that make it appear that everyone else is having a blast. Celebrities on talk shows chatter gaily, models in commercials are "alive with pleasure," and groups of beer-drinking friends enjoy conviviality on the beach. People who are not tripping gaily through life cannot help but think that everyone else is, so they feel even more isolated. Part of being a successful person, it seems, is to be always having fun. If you're not, then something's wrong with *you.*

But our compulsive chasing after what looks like pleasure belies a kind of desperation. Rather than an excessive pleasure-seeking society, we may be a people desperately seeking a respite from the relentless doing, accomplishing, measuring, and self-monitoring required by our demanding, fast-paced, schedule-laden life-styles. What looks like recreation may be more like recuperation. What lies at the heart of the issue is not too much indulgence but too little surrender to our inner selves.

SO A DEEPLY ENTRENCHED DESIRE for the quick-fix underlies the addiction epidemic in America—a belief that took root and flourished to a large extent during the postwar fifties and sixties, when the baby-boom generation was growing up. It's no coincidence that we are seeing a proliferation of addictions now, as this generation approaches middle age. Before we leave our discussion of the addictive society, let's explore how the baby-boom generation—perhaps more than any generation before it—was raised with the types of values and beliefs most likely to foster addiction.

Baby Boomers:
The Trendsetters of Our Addictions

THE BABY BOOMERS ARE THE largest generation ever to move through our society. As they progressed through each stage of life, from childhood in the fifties and adolescence in the sixties to early middle-age in the eighties, their changing tastes and values have had tremendous impact on American society. They have been the trend-setters, the barometer of our culture for the past three decades whether in fashion, life-style, or drugs of choice.

It was not by chance that marijuana became the popular drug of the sixties. This drug fit the needs of then teenage baby boomers almost perfectly. Being laid-back, reflective, and inwardly focused, all qualities that marijuana enhances, were deemed highly desirable at that time. Likewise, cocaine became the drug of the eighties because it fit the needs of the now middle-age baby boomer. Cocaine makes you feel in charge, outgoing, productive, and energetic. What could be better suited to hard-driving people trying to move up the career ladder and achieve material success?

In other words, as the developmental task of the baby boomers changed, so did their drug of choice. Their appetite for drugs did not remain permanently fixed on one specific chemical; but they had internalized a quick-fix mentality, a belief that some kind of mood-changer can do for them what they can't do for themselves.

Operating from this mentality has made it difficult for many baby boomers to confront the responsibilities and challenges of middle age—relationships, commitments, careers, and aging. Facing these realities has been more difficult for many baby boomers than they ever expected, especially against the background of their stimulating—indeed "intoxicating"—youth.

Many have become disillusioned and even despairing. Like an army of Peter Pans banished to the world of bill-paying and baby strollers, they have been trying to do what they thought they'd never have to do: grow up. Annie Gottlieb, in her critique on the sixties generation, *Do You Believe in Magic?*, eloquently describes the problem:

> It is drugs' most bittersweet legacy to our generation: the desire "to stay up there" in a life made of ups and downs. Drugs were like a helicopter that dropped us off on a peak in the Himalayas to enjoy the view without the climb. That experience . . . gave us, for years after, a greed for ecstasy, an impatience with the mundane, a mistrust of the efficacy of effort. For those who took a shortcut to magic, it's been hard to learn patience, persistence, discipline, to endure exile in the ordinary.

Indeed, many baby boomers are profoundly dissatisfied with their lives. Asked in a *USA Today* survey if they were "happy," those ages 25 to 34 were at the bottom of the list. Baby boomers were also most likely to report dissatisfaction with their work, say their lives were "getting harder," report intimacy problems, be divorced or separated, and to say they were not having enough fun in their lives.

Baby boomers are also the most likely to be addicted. It's not just drug addiction but all types of addictions that are widespread among them, including those involving achievement, power, material things, and image. And they are well-represented among compulsive spenders, sex addicts, compulsive exercisers, anorectics and bulimics, and workaholics.

THE "AMERICAN DREAM": A WORLD WITHOUT LIMITS

During the fifties and sixties, when the baby-boom generation was growing up, a number of factors converged to create the climate in which their quick fix mentality took hold on a widespread basis.

In the early fifties, the "American dream" was hatched. From the conveniences of canned food and sliced bread to the miracle of television and the mobility provided by the family car, there emerged the promise of a world without limits. More children than in any previous generation were growing up in middle-class homes, where material needs were routinely met.

Parents had just lived through an economic depression and a world war. They had experienced much deprivation and insecurity and wanted things to be different for their kids. Many were also first- or second-generation immigrants or had worked their way up from working-class status. They had struggled and worked hard to "make it." They believed that "good" parents should be self-sacrificing and self-denying so that their children could have a better life. In their enthusiasm they failed to realize that kids need acceptance of their real selves much more than they need their own TV set.

The pendulum swung too far in the other direction. Children raised in the relatively easy, affluent atmosphere of the late fifties and early sixties were often materially indulged but emotionally deprived, forced to live up to an image their parents had and were fed daily by images in the mass media.

Wanting so badly to create the good life for their children, parents often bailed their children out of financial, legal, and emotional difficulties. They provided their kids with more spending money and leisure time than any previous generation had. This material indulgence and overprotectiveness sent the message, however inadvertently, that life would be made easy, that problems would be taken care of by someone else, that there would always be a way out.

But this is merely the socioeconomic stage against which this scenario is set. There were other influences of the times too.

Television

The baby boomers were also the first generation to be raised on television. Unlike previous generations reared in a slower-paced

132

culture where reading required a certain amount of effort and perseverance, TV provided instant distraction and entertainment for virtually no effort. With easy distraction at hand, one doesn't have to feel one's feelings—which worked out well, since baby-boom families often discouraged their expression anyway.

TV also fed the belief that problems could be solved in easy, magical ways—within half-hour segments. Sound anything like a drug experience? There is another parallel to drugs: while TV distracts us from our feelings, it simultaneously stimulates. *And* it gave this generation a shared culture. For the first time, virtually all kids had been exposed to the same messages, advertising lingo, songs, themes, and role models. This too would later play its part in the emergence of a youth culture in the late sixties.

Consumerism

With the end of the Second World War and the introduction of TV and mass advertising, consumerism became a dominant force in this country overshadowing the preexisting emphasis on values of democracy, ethics, and freedom that had been unifying forces throughout the war effort. The consumer mentality *is* the quick-fix mentality.

These children were the first to be exposed—through TV—to hundreds of thousands of advertisements, which promised that buying a certain gadget, using a certain toothpaste, washing with a certain detergent, eating a certain cereal, swallowing a certain medicine, and so on, would make the consumer happier, sexier, stronger, more competent, or more attractive. The success of advertising depends on convincing us that (a) we are "not O.K." as we are but (b) will be if we buy this product. The belief that "I am not enough" is one of the most destructive, inaccurate beliefs this generation was raised on—and a predisposing factor for addiction.

The "Father Knows Best" Family

With the growing influence of mass media, we became a culture increasingly based on image. It was in this context, amidst a growing belief in the American dream, that the image of the ideal family—the "Father Knows Best" family—began finding its way into the collective American consciousness. Parents of the baby boomers may have taken for reality the perfect families depicted on such TV programs as "Father Knows Best," "The Donna Reed Show," and "Leave It to Beaver."

TV viewers were brought right into the private lives of these "model" families and what they saw looked quite good. There were relatively few arguments, and those that did occur didn't seem very ugly and were quickly (and humorously) resolved; the kids got into a few scrapes here and there but did nothing horrible to shame the entire family. Mom and Dad displayed a cozy (albeit nonsexual) intimacy. Confrontation was rare, nobody rocked the boat, and the show always ended with everyone being close and loving.

Middle-class parents of the sixties generation may have tried to duplicate these perfect families. Conflict and aggression were repressed, denied, or—if allowed—carried out behind closed doors. Such "negative" feelings as anger, sadness, loss, and depression were unofficially not allowed in many families. The image of the happy, close family was promoted and the reality of human nature with its full range of human emotions suppressed. Problems couldn't be solved (and kids weren't given a chance to learn problem-solving skills) because the family wasn't supposed to have problems in the first place.

But to live an image is to deny one's true self, as we have seen, and that is shame-inducing. So a generation of kids grew up angry at this denial of their real selves, alienated from their feelings, and unable to express or deal with conflicts or solve problems. All of these traits contributed to making this group more vulnerable to addiction than any before it.

A Stressful, Rapidly Changing Society

Stress has been a staple of every generation. Whether it is the stress of war, economic depression, poverty, famine, or some other hardship, there has always been some type of problem with which to contend. While it's hard to compare stresses with each other and weigh relative impact, one cannot help but think that some of those faced by the baby boomers have contributed to their addictive vulnerability.

The baby boomers are the first generation, for instance, to grow up under the threat of nuclear war and annihilation of the human race. Of course, there is no way of precisely measuring what effects this threat has had on this and subsequent generations, but its impact been probably been profound. Baby boomers were also the first generation to grow up with a substantial number of working mothers and a loosening of community and religious ties.

Rapid technological advances and cultural changes have pushed many people's coping skills to the limit, and beyond. Whenever a culture changes faster than its people and institutions can adjust to—psychologically and socially—there results a breakdown in that culture's shared value system and the result is widespread dysfunctional behavior, such as addiction.

Easy Access to Drugs

The baby boomers were also the first generation to grow up amidst the widespread availability of mood-altering drugs and the social encouragement to use them. Prior to this, pot and other drug use (outside of legal alcohol and nicotine) were associated only with a fringe group of society's "outsiders." Now, recreational drug use burst onto the American scene for the first time in the twentieth century.

Marijuana fit the sixties perfectly: young people wanted to break free of the image-consciousness of their parents, reject the materialistic value of hard work for acquisition, and expand their consciousness. Pot's mellow, laid-back high was just what was called for.

As growing numbers of college students joined in opposition to the U.S. involvement in Vietnam, marijuana served another purpose: it became a source of shared identity. To a group of kids with hidden feelings of isolation (the natural result of growing up in emotionally repressive families) the craving to belong was strong. This yearning for community, combined with access to spending money, more leisure time than previous generations, a quick-fix mentality, and the normal rebelliousness of youth, led to the creation of the drug culture.

This was the largest group of adolescents the country had ever seen. Since youth is by its very nature rebellious and narcissistic, the culture itself became dominated by these forces in the sixties. Altering one's moods with drugs fit with what this generation had already learned as children: that things should—and can—be easy, painless, and require little effort.

But though they were "dropping out" in some ways, members of the sixties generation were simultaneously internalizing some of their parents' expectations. They went to college in unprecedented numbers and were expected to someday achieve a measure of material success and a "good life" beyond that which their parents had. While rejecting these expectations on the surface, somewhere deep within, most internalized a belief in achievement as a measure of one's worth. This belief, buried in the sixties, would come into full bloom later, in the eighties.

The Seventies: The Party's Over

If the sixties were a period of expansion and growth—a "high" of sorts in both consciousness and economy—the seventies were the start of the "crash" and found society pulling in, constricting. Economic recessions and high inflation dampened material expectations; Watergate and other scandals led to increasing cynicism about government and a further loss of models of honesty and integrity.

The stimulation and excitement of student strikes and rock concerts faded into memory as baby boomers began facing the demands of adult life—jobs, rent, and intimacy (not to mention the repayment of all those student loans). High expectations ran head-on into stark reality. Illusions—that the world was without limits, that drugs were like magic and had no drawbacks—were challenged.

From feeling powerful—indeed omnipotent—in the sixties, this generation had to face the reality that they hadn't really been able to revolutionize society, that society's march toward ever-increasing materialism was continuing without them, and that the choice was either to join the fold, at least to some degree, or remain societal outcasts (and suffer more painful isolation).

Never provided with the necessary problem-solving skills in childhood, and entrenched in a belief system that encouraged immediate gratification, the first quick-fix generation tried to grow up but found themselves in search of never-never land.

The Eighties: "Things Go Better with Coke"

As baby boomers began settling into the work force, marijuana lost its appeal. It made people too laid back, passive, lethargic, and did nothing to boost performance. In short, it made you the *opposite* of a "good business person." Beginning in 1979, marijuana use began to decline for the first time since its popularity began in the early sixties.

At about the same time, cocaine use began to rise. Too expensive for them as teens, coke now became more readily available and at cheaper prices that the baby boomers, now earning some money, could afford. Just as pot had seemed perfect for the sixties, cocaine—which most people then believed to be harmless and nonaddicting—seemed perfect for the eighties. Instead of making you laid back (no longer a desirable state, given their new goal-directedness), cocaine gave you energy, a sense of power, and self-confidence. For busy people trying to manage increasingly demanding careers, relationships, marriage, and children, cocaine seemed to be a made-to-order drug.

Unsuspecting baby boomers, whose previous experience with pot led them to believe they could control any drug, and who had never become addicted before, fell into the cocaine trap. What they didn't know was that cocaine's performance-boosting effects only occur at the beginning of use, during the honeymoon period. With continued use, increasing tolerance forces the user to take larger and larger doses just to get the same effects.

In the eighties, the addiction shifted to *achieving*—more money, more things, better orgasms, a perfect body. A drug that seems to fit in with achieving these goals is likely to become very popular. Perhaps cocaine is the secondary addiction of this generation; achieving is the first.

With all addictions, it's not the money or the achievements themselves that are the problem, for those can be appropriate goals. It's what the money, things, and achievements are used for. When anything is used to try to fill oneself up and get something other than what it really can give, there can never be enough. Just as the baby boomers couldn't satisfy their parents' needs, drugs— and now power, success, relationships, the perfect body—cannot fill *them* up.

Chasing the carrot of success with this addictive orientation is like trying to recapture the original drug high. It's a perpetuation of the belief (stemming from consumerism) "If I just take this drug (or accomplish this, or make this amount of money), I'll finally be happy." The person gets on that treadmill, chasing that illusive fix, and gets trapped in a vicious cycle. But it doesn't work, the high cannot be maintained. The work, the orgasm, the relationship, the success feel empty. It doesn't do what the person expected it to do.

But the person keeps going back to get more anyway, still believing that (magically) she will be able to recapture that high. The result is despair and disillusionment, but the addict knows no other way, doesn't *believe* she can achieve happiness and solve her problems on her own, so she keeps compulsively going back to that quick-fix—or another one. For members of a generation who don't believe they can cope or that effort will pay off, and who still hold out the hope that something or someone outside of themselves will bail them out, addictions are a natural development.

The Nineties: Age of Recovery?

One of the paradoxes of addiction is that by bottoming out and reaching despair, addicts finally surrender their addictive life-style and in the process discover ways of living that are far more gratifying.

It is this hope for recovery that the nineties hold for both the baby-boom generation and for the larger society. Since we can't successfully arrest out addictions without giving up unrealistic expectations and goals and opening ourselves up to receiving help from others, the more people that bottom out in our addictive society, the more society itself will change for the better. But in the meantime, all we can do is change ourselves.

We can stop embracing and reinforcing self-defeating beliefs in perfection, image, and omnipotence. We can learn to accept ourselves and others as we are and stop trying to control everything. We can practice honesty, stop blaming everyone else for what's wrong in our lives, and start changing what we can. In this way, the *real* War on Drugs will be fought by each one of us, through our own personal recovery.

PART III

Recovery

8

Getting Off

RECOVERY FROM ADDICTION IS NOT ONLY possible, it can be one of the most exciting journeys of discovery a person can make. Far from being just a grim struggle, it can open the door to a way of life more gratifying than any drug could ever provide: the chance to know and reclaim aspects of yourself long abandoned for others' approval; to regain a sense of meaning and purpose in life; to form deeper, more satisfying relationships than ever before; and to learn how to respect and honor yourself—perhaps for the first time.

But breaking free of addiction requires more than simply plugging in self-help tips. It means fundamentally changing how you live. It means dismantling the addictive framework of your life—how you see yourself, what you believe, how you take care of yourself, and how you relate to others—creating a healthy structure in its place.

In choosing the addictive path, you took what looked like the easier route and turned away from the one that forced you to deal with the feelings and problems you wanted to avoid. That's pretty natural; who among us would want to face obstacles if we didn't have to? The problem is, as we've seen, that the addictive path is a vicious cycle. It has some pretty treacherous terrain of its own.

Now, to recover, you have to stop going around in circles—avoiding and anesthetizing—and face those feelings and beliefs that made you so vulnerable to addiction in the first place. But what's the first thing you have to do when you're going in circles

143

before you can find a new way? Interrupt the cycle. Stop doing the same old thing.

So your first goal in recovery is to break the cycle; stop using drugs, activities, or people to anesthetize your feelings. To do this, you have to get out of the addictive loop that leads you round and round, from addictive thought to negative mood to addictive urge and addictive behavior. It's impossible to recover from addiction without breaking the cycle first. The road to recovery starts with total abstinence.

Until recently, many psychotherapists, especially those unfamiliar with addiction, thought that addicts had to first resolve their underlying psychological problems in order to break the addictive cycle. The belief was that they had to acquire enough self-esteem, insight, and relief from inner conflicts to be "cured" of the addiction problem.

But most professionals now know that abstinence is a *prerequisite* for recovery, not its end point. Continuing to flirt with an addictive activity only keeps the cravings alive and makes relapse inevitable. The only thing that will eventually extinguish cravings is total and complete abstinence from the addictive behavior. If you continue to use even occasionally, you'll be so preoccupied with that process and its consequences that you'll be unable to make the kinds of changes that lead to real recovery.

Let's go back to the allergy model to better understand this point. The first thing someone with an allergy needs to do is learn to avoid the irritant. If he's allergic to feathers, for example, he can't keep sleeping on feather pillows and expect his symptoms to go away. Once he learns to avoid the irritant and is relieved of symptoms, he can then work on building his resistance and reducing his allergic vulnerability. But unless he first avoids the irritant, his energy will go into dealing with his symptoms, not to building long-term recovery.

Abstinence doesn't have to be a grim, grit-your-teeth-and-bear-it process either. If it is, you're probably "white-knuckling" it— straining to stay abstinent, holding on so tight that your knuckles turn white. If abstinence is that stressful and difficult, you'll have a hard time resisting your mood-changer, and you'll remain extremely vulnerable to relapse.

To stay abstinent then, you'll have to do the opposite of white-knuckling: you'll have to build enough predictable and reliable comfort and relief into your new life so that you won't *need* to resort to your old route, the mood-changer. This means, among other things, letting a support system of other people become your mood-changer for now—a point we'll come back to.

A word of caution: addiction-prone people tend to want perfect results, and want them *now.* In early recovery, this can mean expecting too much too soon; you may want to get off your drug without a hitch, have everything in your life that's gone wrong for several years fall instantly back into place, never suffer a craving or a slip (a return to use), and live happily ever after.

Recovery is a process, like learning to ride a bicycle, ice skate, or ski. You might have to try several times to break an addiction before you finally succeed. Even then, you may have a slip, especially in the beginning. But if you don't give up, you will eventually see progress and even start enjoying the recovery process. So practice just letting yourself "be." If you fall down in the first stage of abstinence, simply get back up, brush yourself off, and try again—but this time make sure you get more help and support.

GETTING READY

Breaking Through Denial

The first step in recovery is to admit to yourself that you are addicted—to booze, cigarettes, money, people, sex, whatever *your* drug is. As we explained in chapter two, the most reliable sign of addiction is continued involvement in the addictive activity despite negative, life-damaging consequences.

A major stumbling block to breaking through denial is the self-recrimination and guilt that addicts feel about their problem. They *can't* accept themselves as they are: addicted. As long as you believe horrible things about addicts, as Lorraine did, you'll have trouble facing up to your problem: "I couldn't admit I was an alcoholic, because to me that meant being a totally worthless, horrible person. I felt it was especially unacceptable as a woman."

The belief that an addict is a "bad person" perpetuates the problem. That's why it's so important to reframe addiction in a nonjudgmental light, to separate who you are from the addiction problem you've developed. Remember, *you are not your addiction!* You are something much greater than that. Doing this should be easier now that you know you were vulnerable to addiction for some very "good" reasons and that you are not alone in that.

Wallowing in guilt about misdeeds of the past is often a cop-out that prevents you from taking responsibility for yourself right now. As long as you remain immersed in guilt, you keep yourself in the addictive cycle. Taking responsibility means not wasting any more energy on "would haves," "should haves," or "could haves" and putting your efforts into starting recovery today.

Some people are "invested" in feeling like failures and have trouble letting go of this identity. Being accepting and positive about themselves is foreign to them. If this is so in your case, when you try to get abstinent, you might hear old, self-critical tapes play in your mind: "Who are you kidding, this will never last; you can't function like everyone else." These tapes are not easily changed right away; they've probably been playing for a very long time. But becoming aware of them is a first step toward eliminating their negative influence on you.

It helps to have compassion toward yourself for being so wounded as to compulsively seek mood-changers and become vulnerable to addiction. Compassion is not the same as self-pity. Self-pity keeps a person stuck in the addictive cycle, whereas compassion is the impetus for self-loving action. Once you can see that your addiction *began* as a positive impulse (seeking relief and comfort), you will be better able to accept having the dis-ease and to begin recovering from it. Recovering addicts often word the shift in perspective this way: "I'm not a bad person getting good, but a sick person getting better."

146

Tell someone. Once you've admitted to yourself that you're hooked, tell someone else. Why? Because in sharing this secret you lighten your burden. People at AA and other self-help meetings routinely introduce themselves by saying: "My name is _____ and I'm an alcoholic (and/or a drug addict)." Sharing the secret dilutes the power that addiction wields when it is kept hidden. Saying it out loud also helps to counteract denial. To admit that you have a disease is to acknowledge that something is significantly wrong with your life, and this sets the stage for making recovery-oriented decisions.

Choose someone to tell whom you think will be supportive, not judgmental. If possible, contact someone who you know is a recovering addict and tell that person. He will be in the best position to receive your admission without having a negative, emotionally charged reaction.

Deciding to Quit

In *Cocaine: Seduction and Solution,* Nannette Stone and her coauthors suggest drawing up a "balance sheet." On one side of a sheet of paper list the pros—what positive effects you get from your drug (excitement, sympathy from others, relief) and on the other side the cons—what it costs you. In order to benefit from this exercise, it's important to let go of being right and try instead to simply be truthful.

On the cost side, consider how your drug of choice has affected your family relationships, friendships, work and career, physical health, mental health, self-esteem, family responsibilities, hobbies, and dreams. List everything you can think of, large and small, from "affecting my liver" to "causing me to get to work late." Make sure the costs you list are things that are of concern to *you,* not just the reasons other people think you should quit.

How have the benefits changed over time? Have the costs increased? At some point in an addictive "career," the scales tip. The costs exceed the benefits. That's what leads addicts to seek help. Their self-loathing becomes more than they can tolerate; they suf-

147

fer depression, anxiety, and other serious negative moods; they run into medical, social, and financial problems. Life becomes unmanageable and chaotic.

Equally as important as admitting the costs of your addiction is listing what you think you get out of it. Does it help you relax? Socialize? Erase your loneliness? Remove anxiety? Make you less self-conscious? Eliminate boredom?

Now, look at whether your addictive involvement is really giving you what you think it is or just giving you the *illusion* of it. For example, if your reason for staying in an addictive relationship is that it keeps you from being lonely, look closer. Is it really providing the comfort and companionship of intimacy or just the illusion of it? Chances are, if it's addictive, you're actually becoming more isolated and more lonely—if you look below the surface.

It's hard to face the truth about any addiction. It's like admitting that a marriage has failed. You may have been trying to keep up a front for a long time, but if you're ever going to really get what you want, you're going to have to stop living a lie and admit it.

Now is also the time to consider what you truly want out of life. Make another list—this one of your dreams and goals, from the biggest to the smallest. Is your addictive involvement interfering with reaching your dreams and goals? If so, how? Can you imagine how stopping your addiction might help you get what you want out of life? Is what you're getting from your drug what you want in life, or is it what you're settling for?

Expect to feel ambivalent. It is normal to feel ambivalent about quitting; you wouldn't be addicted in the first place if there weren't things you wanted to get out of your drug. In order to make a commitment to recovery, you *have* to recognize your ambivalence; otherwise you can't be honest with yourself. The person who says "I have no desire to do it ever again" is more likely to relapse than the person who recognizes her ambivalence and decides to quit anyway, who says, "I *want* to use this drug, but just for today I'm not going to."

148

Your mood-changer has probably been a primary relationship in your life. You may be married to it, in a sense. Getting it, using it, and recuperating from it may have become your occupation. It may be your primary leisure activity. If you spend lots of time with other users, it is probably also your primary source of friendship. Who would find it easy to let go of something that had become such a major part of their life?

When should you quit?   At one time it was believed that an addict couldn't quit until she "hit bottom," lost everything, and had no other recourse. That's true for many people but, it turns out, not for everybody.

Some people are able to see themselves headed on a downward spiral and get help before falling all the way down. They are said to have a "high bottom," meaning that they enter recovery while still at a higher level of functioning than a "low-bottom" person. Basically, if you can see what your use is doing to you, and if you *want* something more out of life, then begin now. In the words of one recovering alcoholic, "You don't have to have a 'better bottom.' "

How committed are you?   You need to be clear about your motivation. Is your commitment genuine or superficial? Are you giving lip service to the idea of stopping your drug, or do you mean it? Are you saying things like "I'll quit as soon as ____" (fill in the blank: I have my birthday, the holidays are over, I'm married, I'm divorced)? Are you considering quitting only because other people want you to and you're trying to please them or get them off your back, or is the decision mainly yours?

Watch out for discrepancies between what you say and what you do. Do you (the compulsive spender) say you're going to stop accumulating debts but apply for a new charge card "just in case"? Do you (the cocaine addict) say you're going to stop using cocaine but keep your coke spoons, freebase pipe or other paraphernalia around the house "as souvenirs"? Do you (the compulsive overeater) say you're going to eat less, but keep your cupboards stocked with high-calorie junk food?

Your recovery has to come first—before *all* other commitments (even family and friends). There's a sound reason for this: without recovery, nothing else will work in your life. This means if someone asks you to make social plans on the evening of your self-help meeting, the meeting takes priority. If you start making exceptions to this rule, you will find yourself losing ground and slipping back into addictive thinking.

Actions speak louder than words—always. If and when your commitment to recovery wavers, it will show up in your actions sooner than in your words. "Talking the talk"—repeating recovery slogans, making grand promises about how it's going to be—does not substitute for "walking the walk," the hard work of changing the addictive beliefs and attitudes that made you vulnerable in the first place.

This may be the first time you've considered making a real commitment to yourself (even though you may be responsible for other people). This is recovery: learning to successfully take care of your own needs and deal with your own problems, so that you don't crave a mood-changer, an instant escape. It's making a commitment to take care of the child within that you abandoned so long ago. And this care is needed in order to recover from the serious, life-threatening disease of addiction.

Once you're clear about your intention to recover and committed to that child within, taking the concrete steps described in this chapter will be much easier. There's a saying, "If a man does not know what harbor he is sailing for, no wind is the right one." Making a commitment to recovery is like choosing a harbor. Now it's just a matter of taking the actions necessary to catch the winds, of harnessing the power that can get you there.

A leap of faith.   Once you quit your drug, there's no guarantee that you'll feel "good as new" right away. You will probably have to enter what feels like a void, where you don't have the drug anymore but don't have new inner resources yet either. Sandra,

150

recovering from compulsive pot smoking and relationship addiction, talks about how difficult it is to enter that "space" between active addiction and recovery, that period of time when you must "float."

> Now every illusion I had has been dashed to pieces, and it's painful as hell. So I'm floating, but I don't float well. I'm a good compulsive swimmer. Give me a goal, give me an objective, give me a point to go toward, and I'm great. But this thing of floating . . . talk about emptiness, it's terrifying.

While quitting an addiction does require letting go of all the baggage that once accompanied you through life—illusions, mistaken beliefs, survival mechanisms—it also holds the potential for attaining meaningful, lasting gratification.

One cannot say that spiritual faith, a belief in a power greater than oneself, is *necessary* to enter this space between addiction and self-actualization, but many who have successfully recovered tell us that this is what made it possible for them to get beyond short-term abstinence. In fact, the second step of recovery in Alcoholics Anonymous is "Came to believe that a Power greater than ourselves could restore us to sanity" (see Table 2 on page 152), and step three is "Made a decision to turn our will and our lives over to the care of God *as we understood Him.*" This is that leap of faith.

Some people who attend 12-step programs for the first time are put off by the spiritual underpinning of the program and references to a "higher power." Some have had negative or unpleasant experiences with religion while growing up or are disillusioned with organized religion. Often, though, they find that cultivating a belief in a "higher consciousness"—a spiritual "energy" that is everywhere—works for them. Craig, recovering from compulsive pot smoking, describes this concept:" "I don't believe in God, per se, but I believe in a higher power that is everywhere present in the universe, including within me. I believe that my higher power is very strongly connected to my unconscious, and that it *wants* to heal—just as there is a force inside us that wants to heal when we get physically ill—if we don't interfere with it."

TABLE 2.　The Twelve Steps of Alcoholics Anonymous

1. We admitted we were powerless over alcohol—that our lives had become unmanageable.

2. Came to believe that a Power greater than ourselves could restore us to sanity.

3. Made a decision to turn our will and our lives over to the care of God *as we understood Him.*

4. Made a searching and fearless moral inventory of ourselves.

5. Admitted to God, to ourselves, and to another human being the exact nature of our wrongs.

6. Were entirely ready to have God remove all these defects of character.

7. Humbly asked Him to remove our shortcomings.

8. Made a list of all persons we had harmed and became willing to make amends to them all.

9. Made direct amends to such people wherever possible, except when to do so would injure them or others.

10. Continued to take personal inventory and when we were wrong promptly admitted it.

11. Sought through prayer and meditation to improve our conscious contact with God *as we understood Him,* praying only for knowledge of His will for us and the power to carry that out.

12. Having had a spiritual awakening as the result of these steps, we tried to carry this message to alcoholics, and to practice these principles in all our affairs.

The Twelve Steps reprinted with permission of Alcoholics Anonymous World Services, Inc.

Surrender: From Admission to Acceptance

To arrest an addiction, you must go beyond the intellectual admission of "Yes, I have a problem" to acceptance of it on a deep or emotional level. This means accepting (1) that you are addicted, (2) that recovery will not result from exercising your willpower, and (3) that to recover you will have to substantially change how you think and how you live.

Out of this acceptance comes the openness required to begin recovery. You give up your own way of doing things and make a deeper commitment to give some other approach a try (second-order change). Barbara was able to stop overeating for the first time in her life while in a treatment program. The only thing that was different from past attempts to stop overeating, she says, was that she admitted to herself she didn't know how to handle the problem and was tired of trying. Then she put herself in the hands of the program:

> I told myself I would do everything they said, no matter if I thought it was stupid or not. All of a sudden I found that I had the power I never had before to stop compulsive eating. But I had to surrender first. I don't know how else to explain it to other people.

The idea that willpower is enough to overcome an addiction grows out of the addictive belief system, as we have seen. If we believe we are omnipotent, then we think we should be able to control ourselves too. Yet even if we succeed in controlling our mood-changer with sheer determination and willpower, we will probably relapse or begin a new addiction.

Each of us *does* have a lot of power but only if we first acknowledge our own limitations and become receptive to outside help. So again, there is a paradox, a contradiction. Admitting I am hooked, that I don't have control over my behavior, gives me access to the power I *do* have: the power that comes from *telling the truth and facing reality.* Pouring attention and energy into maintaining the illusion of control saps our power. The minute we say, "I am an addict" or "I can't handle it," we reclaim the wasted attention, energy, and time spent maintaining the façade that everything's O.K.

To take this first step, you must let go of the belief that you should be all-powerful and perfect. When the addict comes to know that to be limited is not shameful but human, his humiliation is transformed into humility: "I am just like everybody else. I am human, I have human limitations." Humility and honesty, then, are the two antidotes to feelings of powerlessness. By humbly and honestly admitting powerlessness over your addiction, you tap into your true power.

The addict is caught between a rock and a hard place. To give up hope of controlling one's addiction is contrary to his modus operandi. He's used to trying to control *everything*. Yet letting go of control is precisely what is required to recover. If he continues using, he suffers additional and mounting negative consequences; if he admits defeat, he renders invalid the belief system upon which he has based his whole life. No wonder he so often has to hit bottom before he can get himself to make this critical leap! At that point, he has no choice but to surrender, because he is defeated.

Addicts who don't recover are those who fail to surrender this control. Joyce, a cocaine addict, called a treatment center recently asking for help, and her approach was typical of those stuck in addictive thinking. She stated that she had tried to stop using cocaine "dozens of times" but always relapsed. She asked the counselor on the phone for help but warned him that she "can't stand being in a structured program" and "can't handle having people tell her what to do."

The problem is that Joyce hasn't given up control. She wants a solution to addiction that allows her to maintain her addictive thinking, the illusion that she's in control. She wants help but on her terms, which are addiction-generating. Her attempts to stop using cocaine are what we earlier described as first-order change. Her solution (that she control conditions of treatment) is framed within the same context (that she can recover by exerting self-control) that made her sick in the first place, and so she is doomed to failure.

Many who attempt to stop their addictive behavior get only to that first step, to an intellectual admission and superficial attempt to break the cycle. Even if they become abstinent for a short while, their addictive thinking leads them to conclude that they're cured and don't have to put in any more effort. Then they repeat the cycle all over again. Surrendering to a lack of control is second-order change, because it moves a person—perhaps for the first time—out of the framework "I am in control" and into that transformative space she has dreaded for so long.

Sometimes acceptance occurs in the way we think of a religious conversion, in one dramatic moment of insight, as it did for Richard, a recovering compulsive gambler:

On October 19, 1985, at about 3:30 A.M., I had just come back from the racetrack and a bookie joint. I found myself trying to scheme how I could get out of taking my kid to the beach the next day like I'd promised him so I could go back to the track. I was also trying to figure out what I would tell my wife about the money for the bills this month—since I'd promised her (again) I was not going to gamble again. I leaned up against this building and suddenly it hit me that this was not how I wanted to live my life. The revelation was even more specific than that: it hit me that *I had a choice,* that I did not have to do what I was doing.

Suddenly, a pure, strong knowledge filled me that I did not have to gamble, and that gambling had put me where I was—scheming about how to let my kid down this time. It was alienating me from anyone who'd ever loved me. So the revelation was a dual one: gambling was ruining my life and I did not have to have a ruined life. I did not have to do this to myself. Surrender came to me in that one, clear moment, absolute surrender to my powerlessness over what gambling did to me. It was very simple. I knew that if I gambled I would be ruined; if I did not, at least there was a chance I'd have a real life. It was a glorious revelation—it still is.

More often the realization is less dramatic. It may even slip in quietly, on the heels of yet another failed attempt at controlled use. Lorraine, the recovering alcoholic we met in chapter five, describes how she came to acceptance:

My "Ah-ha" moment was kind of a quiet one. There were no lightning bolts of insight, just resignation that came over me. For me it followed an eleven-week period when I was doing surreptitious "controlled" drinking. I mean, I was out of control because I couldn't keep from drinking, but I wouldn't get high or drunk, because I wanted to show everyone how I could control it. But I was sneaking. I had this jug of wine hidden in the basement that I convinced myself I would finish rather than let it go to waste.

As I saw it going down and down, I suddenly realized that when that bottle was gone I was going to go out and get another one and that I had been fooling myself. Suddenly, all the pieces just fell into place, very quietly, but solidly. It was no big, explosive thing, just like

"Oh, O.K." I threw the rest of the wine away and went to my first AA meeting that night. I haven't had a drop since.

With acceptance, superficial, half-hearted compliance is replaced by a willingness and even eagerness to do the work of recovery. The person lets go of the need to control, the defiance and grandiosity associated with addiction, and starts accepting help with gratitude rather than resentment. In short, the person accepts the identity of being an addict—of having the disease of addiction—and no longer fights it. He becomes willing to do whatever he has to do to get better and to trust that he doesn't know what that is and will have to rely on the recovery program in which he has put his trust. Now the energy that he put into resisting his fate as an addict becomes fully available for recovery.

There is little anyone else can do to help an addict reach acceptance. The reason why lots of self-help books don't work is that unless the addict admits that willpower alone isn't working, all the self-help tips in the world can't help.

In this book, we can't give you acceptance either, but can suggest some ways to help the process along. By participating in a recovery group, for instance, you will meet others who have given up their own way of doing things, accepted the recommended route to recovery, and can testify to the positive results. Usually, the results are apparent anyway. People in recovery (not just abstinent) often appear confident, calm, centered, peaceful, and (paradoxically) in control of their lives.

About Abstinence

If you are not willing to agree to an initial target period of abstinence, recovery cannot begin. Successful recovery is not flexible about the goal of abstinence.

Depending on the addiction, the word "abstinence" means different things. Some addictive substances and activities—like alcohol, illicit drugs, and gambling—must be avoided totally if you're addicted to them. But obviously, one cannot avoid food, sex, money, work, or relationships altogether. So with these addictions, it is essential to differentiate between appropriate and inappropriate or self-destructive use. Compulsive overeaters can't totally abstain from eating, for example, but they can abstain from *over*eating.

With these addictions, then, abstinence means not using the substance to a degree or in any situation where it serves as a mood-changer. As Julian, a sex addict recovering in Sex and Love Addicts Anonymous, puts it: "Becoming abstinent for me means I have to abstain from *acting out,* from using sexual behavior to anesthetize or escape from painful or uncomfortable feelings."

It is virtually impossible to define the bottom line by yourself, since distorted thinking is what got you into trouble in the first place. That's why outside help is so essential, as Patti, a recovering alcoholic, anorectic, and compulsive exerciser, found:

> It was easy to know what to do to recover from alcoholism. In AA they tell you: "Don't drink, and go to meetings." With food and exercise, though, the only way I was able to draw my boundaries was with food and exercise plans given to me in the hospital rehab.
>
> Basically, the plan calls for abstaining from any inappropriate behaviors with my food or my body: no starving, no bingeing, no abusive exercising, no purging with laxatives, and no overeating.
>
> Now I only eat the quantities and foods outlined in this plan. I eat to maintain the weight *they* think I should weigh, not what *I* would like to weigh. Theirs is based on body-fat percentage; mine is based on distorted thinking.

Some sex addicts find an initial period of abstinence from *all* sexual activity helps them avoid relapse triggers and concentrate on recovery. Marie, the sex and relationship addict we first met in chapter five, determined along with her "sponsor" (a mentor, who guides another person through a 12-step recovery program and who is also in recovery) that her recovery could benefit greatly from a period of abstinence from *all* dating and sex for several months:

We agreed I wouldn't pursue a relationship or sex for a period of four months. I limited myself to going to work and coming home and working the program. And the amazing part was that I was able to do it.

At first, I'd said to my sponsor, "What am I going to do with all my free time?" And my sponsor, who's very wise, said, "I think that will take care of itself." In the beginning, the way it took care of itself was that I just went to every self-help meeting available, which is just what I needed. And the next thing I knew I was making friends for the first time in my whole life.

Another thing that happened was as soon as I got abstinent from my compulsive pursuit of relationships and sex, with the humiliation and embarrassment and everything else that comes with it, a flood of self-love came over me. I was finally doing something for myself. I was finally accepting myself just as I was. That was a great feeling. I can't tell you all that has happened in my recovery because of going forward into that "black hole" of abstinence.

Set a Manageable Goal

Up to now, you may not have been able to go a week (or in many cases a day) without engaging in your addiction. To aspire now to a lifetime or even a year of abstinence is unrealistic. Set a goal that you feel is within reach—one day, one week, one month.

If your goal seems within reach, you'll be less likely to give up when you hit a rough spot. And the sense of accomplishment you'll get from reaching your short-term goal will reinforce your motivation. Unrealistic goals are a setup for failure. You get overwhelmed, you relapse, you feel defeated and hopeless once again, which only makes continued relapse even more likely.

Cultivate a Positive View of Abstinence

People tend to equate abstinence with deprivation, loss, and restrictions. But, as the sex addict Bruce points out, in reality it is just the opposite:

There's a part of me that looks at abstinence as something very painful, because now I have to face these feelings that I've been hiding from. But more and more, I see how it is actually *liberating*. I have been controlled, held in prison, by my addiction. Abstinence is my way to freedom.

It's the *addiction* that deprives you of what you want in life: good health, good relationships, the ability to do your best work, and so much more. It's the addiction that restricts you, that robs you of personal freedom. We all *need* to have internal limits in order to be free. The inability to freely choose and self-limit your behavior *is* the bondage of addiction.

So begin, as Bruce has, to look upon abstinence not as self imposed deprivation but as liberation from something abusive, and restrictive.

Try always to remind yourself of personal gains you are moving *toward* by becoming abstinent. Formulate some long-range plans. People less vulnerable to addiction are those with clear direction and goals (not just material ones), because they have more reason to want to function as well as they can so they can achieve their dreams. Start *expecting* life to be good!

Don't Taper Off Gradually

Most addictions can—and should—be stopped all at once, "cold turkey." Exceptions include stopping chronic heavy use of alcohol, sleeping pills, tranquilizers, and other drugs associated with dangerous withdrawal syndromes. These substances require gradual weaning under medical supervision, because stopping them abruptly can cause convulsions and other life-threatening physiological reactions.

With most other addictions, including cocaine, tapering off slowly simply doesn't work. That's because trying to cut down your intake is like trying to control it, which by definition an addict cannot do. *Any* use at all just triggers the addictive cycle all over again. As long as the cravings are being reinforced—even occasionally—they will continue to exert an irresistible pull back to compulsive use.

Paul, the compulsive stock-market gambler described in chapter one, found he couldn't taper off on his investing, because every time he tried to, he kept getting pulled back into his former level and beyond by the thrill he experienced. He finally got out altogether, all at once, and *that* worked.

How long it takes to establish abstinence depends on your pattern of use. If you're a "binge" user who goes a week or two without using, then the first couple weeks of abstinence may be easy. The danger is that you might assume you're on safer ground than you really are. Bingers are highly vulnerable to relapse right around the time that their next binge would ordinarily have occurred. Make sure you exert special caution and carefully plan your activities right around that time.

"Keep It Clean"

Once you've become abstinent, you may start to wonder if you're sticking too rigidly to your abstinence plan. Thoughts might start creeping into your head that "my addiction wasn't such a big deal after all" or "other people seem able to control it, why not me?" or "I'll do it just once more."

The best policy is to stick to your abstinence plan *completely.* Other people might be able to do the things you can't do, and they suffer no negative effects, but for *you,* cheating on your plan pulls you back into the addictive cycle. It blurs the edges of abstinence. And once these boundaries become blurred, it's all too easy to slip into denial again. Before long, you're way off track, back to making excuses, and well on your way to relapse.

Abstinence from All Other Mood-Changers

To recover from any single addiction, you must stop using not only your drug of choice, but *all* drugs and activities that serve as mood-

160

changers for you. If you use something to anesthetize your feelings, it falls into the category of a mood-changer.

This step can be harder for you to accept than abstinence from your drug of choice. A cocaine addict, for example, may see no reason why she can't continue social drinking while recovering from cocaine addiction, especially if she's never had problems with alcohol before. Similarly, an alcoholic may resist giving up occasional pot smoking, thinking, "I have to be able to do *something*."

There are several reasons why abstinence from all mood-changers is important to you:

- You may not have a problem with these other substances or activities right now, but you *do* have a problem with addiction, and your addiction can be triggered by any mood-changer. If you want to recover, you will have to address the dis-ease within or it will surface again and again in different forms.
- Most relapses to a person's primary addiction are preceded by use of other mood-changers that have been previously associated with your primary drug. For example, cocaine addicts whose cocaine use had been associated with seeing prostitutes find that even thoughts and fantasies about these sexual encounters will elicit strong cravings for cocaine.
- When you're under the influence of any mood-changer, it is much more difficult to say "no" to your drug of choice. Your resolve is weakened when you're intoxicated.
- To recover, you must learn how to cope with feelings, face problems, and socialize without artificial mood alteration. This can't happen as long as you're substituting one mood-changer for another.
- With total abstinence, the energy, time, and attention that went into chasing mood-altering experiences becomes available for making the personal changes required for a lasting recovery. You'll need all the time and energy you can get.

If, after reviewing these reasons for total abstinence, you're still resistant to the idea, just try it for one month—despite your objections. Take it on blind faith, in light of two important facts: total abstinence has worked for countless others; and you apparently haven't succeeded in breaking your addiction by doing it *your* way.

TAKING ACTION

Now your decision to stop must be translated into specific, concrete actions. The sum of these actions must be to restructure your daily life—a vital component of breaking any addictive cycle. Our lives are structured according to certain routines, the rituals of our daily life. Through this structure, we eliminate many smaller decisions; our choices are determined by the structure.

In order to stop an addictive behavior, you have to create for yourself a whole new structure for your life. The rituals of seeking, using, and recuperating from your drug must be replaced with healthier rituals and actions. This section provides a substitute framework that you can use. The six steps are

1. Identify and make use of a support network.
2. Get professional help.
3. Remove all sources of access to your drug and its reminders.
4. Break off with people who make it available to you.
5. Structure your time.
6. Put major problems on hold for right now, where possible.

Some of these steps may appear to be difficult, even daunting. You might rationalize that they are unnecessary in your case and try to cut corners. Perhaps you'll see yourself as an exception to the rule and conclude that you don't need to take the same extreme measures as others do to stop your addiction.

If you hear these destructive tapes running in your head, be aware that it's your addictive thinking. Remember that if you want to set the conditions of recovery yourself, you will be attempting

162

first-order change, which is just setting yourself up for failure. Try to trust that since these steps have worked for many others, there's a good chance they'll work for you too.

You will be most likely to carry these actions through if you have already accepted that you have the disease of addiction, and that recovery will require considerable time and effort and must come first—before everything else.

Identify and Make Use of a Support Network

"My biggest mistake was trying to quit on my own for twenty-two years. It never, ever, worked, and I wasted a lot of time."
—Carl, recovering heroin addict and alcoholic

Don't try to go it alone. Your tendency to isolate under stress is probably one of the factors that made you vulnerable to addiction in the first place. Isolating now only feeds self-pity and loneliness, both of which spark cravings and precipitate relapse. You're much more likely to succeed if you become part of a support system.

Make a list of people you can call on for guidance and encouragement throughout this early stage of recovery. This support network should consist of people who are not actively addicted and whom you can call on if you get an urge to use. They might include nonusing, supportive friends and family members, a therapist or counselor, or fellow members of a therapy or self-help group.

Write down the names and telephone numbers of at least five such people. *Memorize their phone numbers,* or keep the list with you at all times. Calling someone from your "team" should become an automatic reflex whenever a craving or other stressful situation arises. It's a good idea to call at least one person every day during this early stage.

Let the people on your team know what you will need from them. Basically, this is to (a) listen, not judge, (b) provide support and encouragement, and (c) remind you that negative moods or cravings will pass. Let them know that you don't expect or even want them to actually solve your problems for you although their

163

suggestions are welcomed. Part of recovery is learning to take responsibility for yourself. You simply need them to be part of a support network that will make it possible for you to do this.

By establishing this network you create a healthier support system around you—perhaps for the first time. This is a powerful antidote to the isolating aspects of our modern culture.

The most effective support network is usually a self-help program such as AA. Some 14 million Americans already attend one of a half-million such groups. The rapid growth of self-help programs in recent years is a testimony to their value.

Getting into the routine of attending a self-help meeting as often as possible, every day if you can, is a great replacement ritual. This new, positive routine helps break the cycle of your former addictive routines. It pulls you away from addiction rather than toward it.

"Self-help" programs, as contrasted with addiction-treatment programs, are led by peers rather than professional counselors. They are attended by people with a common problem who share their experiences with each other. The most popular self-help groups are those based on the 12-step model of Alcoholics Anonymous. Founded in 1935 by two alcoholics in desperate need of a support network themselves, by 1986, AA had a worldwide membership of 1.5 million. Since 1935, groups to help people recover from many types of addiction have sprung up around the country: Narcotics Anonymous, Cocaine Anonymous, Smokers Anonymous, Gamblers Anonymous, Workaholics Anonymous, Overeaters Anonymous, Debtors Anonymous, Sex and Love Addicts Anonymous, Codependents Anonymous, and many more.

The original 12 steps developed by the founders of AA are given in table 2 on page 152. While there is no time frame for completing these steps, most people take at least a few years. The results are often astounding. Many addicts who start out emotionally, physically, and spiritually bankrupt proceed through these steps and attend meetings regularly over a period of time to gain the skills they need to enjoy satisfying lives.

Twelve-step programs provide the recovering person with:

1.   *Hope.* Seeing others who are successfully dealing with their addiction means that recovery is indeed possible.

2.   *A nonjudgmental support system.* Writes a member of Sex and Love Addicts Anonymous: "I feel so safe there, because I know I'm not being judged."

3.   *Feedback.* As one recovering amphetamine addict put it, "Two heads are better than one, providing they're not on the same set of shoulders."

4.   *A spiritual foundation.* Since addiction is fueled by a lack of meaning and purpose in life, the spiritual aspect of self-help programs can be an antidote.

5.   *A chance to help others.* Helping others is rewarding. Contact with beginners in the program is an excellent reminder of every addict's continual vulnerability.

6.   *A sense of belonging.* Since isolation fosters addiction, this is another antidote.

7.   *A new framework for looking at the problem.* By admitting powerlessness, one makes the leap to second-order change.

8.   *Round-the-clock support.* Self-help groups provide a telephone network twenty-four hours a day (unlike most professional programs).

9.   *Ongoing membership.* People can continue attending self-help meetings for as long as they wish (whereas professional treatment is usually time-limited).

10. *Free of charge membership.* Self-help groups charge no membership dues, so they are financially accessible to everyone.

11.   *Structure.* The addictive rituals are replaced with healthy ones such as meetings and phoning, which provide needed structure.

Of course, the benefits of joining a self-help program are not instantaneous, and many addicts, still searching for the quick-fix, get discouraged when attending a few meetings doesn't "fix" them. That's why it's a good idea to attend for several weeks before deciding whether it's right for you. If you measure it by the addictive standard, "Is it magically taking away all my pain and discomfort—right now?", it will not measure up. But if you stick around long enough to pierce your addictive thinking and measure it by the promise of long-term reward, it undoubtedly will.

Lowell, a recovering alcoholic whom we met in chapter five, resisted joining a support group because he thought he'd lose his individuality. Much to his surprise, the opposite occurred—he *found* it:

> I had no idea that I would become *more* myself if I was part of a group. But that's what happened. Becoming part of a support group gave me back my individuality. I never would have expected that. I thought by drinking I was asserting my independence and individuality, and I looked at people who joined groups like AA as "weak" and dependent. Turns out to be just the opposite. It's another one of those paradoxes: By letting go, you gain.

There are those who claim that involvement with self-help groups merely replaces dependency on one's drug with a dependency on going to meetings. That may be true, but dependency is not always a bad thing. Dependency is part of normal functioning; it's only unhealthy if it becomes exaggerated and causes negative consequences. Going to meetings that help a person become *less* dependent on a destructive drug can hardly be considered negative.

Get Professional Help

You can increase your chances of success by enrolling in a professional treatment program designed for people with your particular type of addiction. In fact, the most effective recovery program includes both 12-step self-help and professional guidance. Professional programs now exist not only for drug addicts and alcoholics but also for gamblers, codependents, overeaters, sex addicts, anorectics, and bulimics. There are also private therapists who specialize in various addictions, including workaholism and relationships.

Some qualities to look for in professional treatment include:

Treatment based on the disease model. The program should subscribe to the view that addiction is a permanent disease and primary disorder and must be treated as such.

Requirement of total abstinence. Achieving abstinence must be seen as a prerequisite for treatment, not the end goal.

Expertise in treating addiction. Don't always assume that the higher a professional's degree, the more qualified she is to treat addiction. Most medical and graduate schools still offer little or no training in this specialized area.

Emphasis on relapse prevention. Rather than simply helping you to get off your drug (detoxification), the program should focus very specifically and intensively on preventing relapse. Getting off is the easy part; you'll need more help with staying off in the long run.

Group counseling. A group experience is vital to recovery from addiction. The professional program that does not help patients build a peer support network is not doing its job.

Frequent individual counseling sessions. Individual counseling sessions provide a chance to review the events of the preceding days, identify triggers for cravings, establish a structure for the coming days, and discuss sensitive or intimate issues not well-suited for group discussion.

Self-help endorsement and referrals. In the past, many professional programs viewed self-help groups as competing and interfering with professional treatment. It has been our experience, however, that patients in a professional program who *also* attend self-help groups have the best prognosis of all.

Get Rid of Supplies and Reminders

Once you've pulled together a support network, build in as much distance as possible between you and your mood-changer. This means getting rid of all drug supplies and paraphernalia that are part of your addictive ritual. Reminders of your mood-changer can cause cravings as powerful as those elicited by the actual sight of the drug itself. Of course, you can always get more, but the point here is to eliminate all easy, ready access to your drug so that you can't drift back to use without having to think about it first.

Because this is so important, here are some specific examples:

Drug and Alcohol Addiction

Alcohol, marijuana, cocaine, and all other mood-altering drugs should be flushed down the toilet. Any substances used to process your drug, such as baking soda used to make cocaine freebase, should also be discarded.

Spoons, mirrors, freebase pipes, syringes—*all* drug paraphernalia—should be broken and disposed of immediately. These items should *not* be given or sold to friends, who might readily give them back to you later on. You don't need to be tempted.

Alcoholics should throw out not only their alcohol supply but any nonalcoholic beers or wines. Even though the alcohol content in these is supposedly negligible, the taste and even the sight of the bottles can serve as triggers.

Cigarette smokers should throw out all cigarettes and other tobacco supplies and all ashtrays. Don't worry about keeping them for visitors. For now, it's best if you ask people not to smoke in your home.

If possible, seek the cooperation of others users you live with who might be maintaining a supply of drugs or paraphernalia. To be exposed to anything that triggers cravings is to make it that much harder to break the addictive cycle.

Don't test yourself by keeping a few reminders around as mementos or souvenirs of past times. Inadvertently coming across these items in a closet or drawer could set off intense cravings. If you feel vulnerable, you may even want to ask a nonaddicted friend or relative to complete this "search and destroy" mission for you. It can be a tremendous relief to walk into the house and know there is nothing tempting there.

Relationship Addiction

Get rid of any mementos you use to maintain the illusion that this relationship was really meeting your needs. For instance, if the person you are addicted to once treated you to a wonderful evening at the theater but most of the time is not emotionally available, why save the ticket stubs from the play? Such reminders only reinforce the illusions you have about this relationship, illusions that keep you coming back for more.

Compulsive Gambling

Compulsive gamblers should stay out of OTB parlors and Atlantic City, Las Vegas, and Lake Tahoe. You can't shut down these places, but you can choose to stay away from them. Discard all racing forms, track tickets, and other betting reminders.

Compulsive Shopping and Spending

Compulsive spenders should cut up their charge cards. If you compulsively draw money out of an automatic cash machine, ask the bank to cancel that service for you. Close checking accounts with overdraft privileges. Refuse offers of credit.

Compulsive Sex

If you frequent prostitutes or call girls, throw out their phone numbers. Get rid of collections of sex toys or lingerie. If X-rated cable TV shows are a relapse trigger for you, discontinue your cable service. If you compulsively masturbate to pornographic magazines, discard these materials. Of course you can easily replace these magazines at the newsstand, but the point is to eliminate all *easy, ready* access in your own home.

Workaholism

You must start planning a reasonable work schedule for yourself and stick to it—with the help of a family member or friend. It may be necessary to change positions at your workplace, remove yourself from an overly demanding job, or even leave a job if it supports your workaholism by demanding exceedingly long hours and unreasonable sacrifices.

Compulsive Overeating/Food Disorders

Clear out any food stashed in your bedroom or any place where you binge. Throw out or give to charity all foods that are not on your abstinent food plan. If you live with others who eat these foods, this may not be possible, but you may want to store your food in a separate cupboard. Anorectics and bulimics must get rid of scales, laxatives, purgatives, and related paraphernalia.

Break Off with People Who Make the Mood-Changer Available

It is all but impossible to stop using a mood-changer while continuing to have contact with people associated with it. If there's someone with whom you usually get high, tell him you won't be doing that anymore. Ask him not to offer you any, do it around you, or otherwise bring it into contact with you. This may seem extreme, but you are especially vulnerable right now and this step is absolutely necessary to become abstinent.

Extremely tough decisions arise when the people who are your users and dealers include a mate, sexual partner, coworker, or family member. In extreme cases, you may have to change jobs, temporarily separate from a spouse or lover, or permanently end relationships with people who refuse to stop using. You may have to ask anyone who is a coaddict to stop her use or seek help as a condition for continuing your relationship.

A situation which severely threatens your early abstinence is continued contact with any "pushers" of your drug. For a drug addict it's the dealer; for a gambler, the bet-maker or stockbroker; for the overeater, a person who relentlessly pushes food on you that is not on your food plan. Other examples:

Drug Addiction

The best way to break contact with people associated with your addiction is to get a new, unpublished phone number. If you owe money to a dealer, repay it in full as soon as possible—preferably through a third party—otherwise, he will keep contacting you and your abstinence will be threatened.

If your addictive behavior took place at work or with people from work, you may have to change jobs. If drug users continue to drop by your home, you may even have to move, as Jeff did:

> At first I just stopped hanging out with a couple of people, but that didn't do it. There was always that third person I hadn't thought about who rang the doorbell. It took a while—and a slip—but eventually I broke off with everybody by changing my phone number and moving. I just had to do it.

These more involved steps don't take place overnight, but you should explore and address them with members of your support network and take appropriate action.

If someone you can't avoid altogether right now (a parent, child, coworker) is still an active addict or alcoholic, you can establish conditions (she should not get high in front of you or offer you anything). If possible, limit the amount of time you spend together.

When an active addict *lives* with you, the issue is even more critical, because your abstinence is in immediate danger. One option is to ask that the other person go for help too. If he refuses, and you are committed to stopping your own drug use, you may want to explore with people in your support system whether to separate from this person for right now.

171

Alcoholism

You will have to break off contact with all drinking buddies. This may seem impossible to you because they may be a major part of your social life. But if you continue to see them, it will become impossible to maintain your sobriety. Still, some people have to discover this for themselves—firsthand—before they accept the inevitability of taking this type of action. Lowell looks back at his early recovery from alcoholism:

> For the first nine months of my recovery, I insisted I could still hang out with my friends. I went to the bars with them daily and drank club soda. I defended my right to do this and saw myself as a loyal friend. "They're good people," I'd say; "they're still my friends." Well, eventually I drank, and this time I barely made it back alive. That was a tough learning experience.

Relationship Addiction

Break off all compulsive involvements for now and devote the necessary attention to your recovery without the constant distraction of an addictive relationship. If you are married and/or have children with the person you are addicted to however, breaking all contact may not be desirable. It *is* possible to transform the addictive patterns of a relationship while still involved with each other, as has been done by many spouses of addicts. It requires a strong commitment to your own recovery and a strong support system.

Compulsive Gambling

A gambler has to break off contact with all bookies, bet-makers, stockbrokers, and gambling buddies. Paul, the stock-market gambler, after withdrawing all investments (getting abstinent), broke off all contact with his former brokers and fellow investors with whom he had discussed investment strategies. "Brokers are like drug dealers," he says, "they *always* tell you they have good stuff" (in this case, good investments). He admits he missed the "intellectual stimulation" but found ways to replace that in his life.

172

Workaholism

If you are a workaholic, your boss may be a "pusher" of over-work to whom you can't say no. If so, you may have to change positions or even jobs.

Compulsive Overeating/Food Disorders

Compulsive overeaters sometimes have a particular person with whom they overeat, often a spouse. For the time being it may be necessary to avoid sharing meals with this person.

Structure Your Time

During early abstinence, all of your free time should be structured, especially times of the day or week when you usually used your mood-changer. Keeping busy with positive, recovery-enhancing activities reduces time available for fantasizing about your drug and avoids the common tendency to gravitate (however unconsciously) to high-risk situations.

Schedule at least one "safe" and enjoyable activity for every evening or other period of free time each week, especially during this early period of recovery. Barbara, a recovering compulsive overeater, knew that evenings would be high-risk for her since she used to spend all evening eating, so she signed up for a number of interesting night courses that kept her busy during the first few months of recovery. Have a substitute activity in mind for a time when plans fall through. Review your daily plan with a member of your support system.

Plan each day *in advance.* Don't wait until Saturday morning to start thinking about what you'll do on the weekend. By that time, you may already be feeling bored or full of self-pity and can easily drift into "isolating." Plan your weekend by Wednesday or Thursday, and plan holidays one to two weeks in advance.

Continue working right now, if possible. This builds in structure automatically. Exceptions are if you're so distracted as to be a hazard on the job or if work presents access to your drug.

Whenever possible, plan to do things *with another person.*

Line up "safe" people who aren't actively addicted. As important as it is for everyone to spend time alone at least once in a while, right now it's best to be with other people. Try to have a backup person to spend time with if plans with the first person fall through.

Do things you've always wanted to do but never did. Go to a dance performance, a play, camping, traveling, or have a group of friends over. Sign up for a course in something you've always wanted to learn. Volunteer your time to a cause, or provide some service for others. The possibilities are endless. In short, allow yourself to be the person you've always wanted to be. Stretch your identity. Why not sing, dance, or learn an instrument or an art, if that's what you've always been drawn to? Watch out for inner voices that say, "That's for others, not for me." Realize how you've stopped yourself all these years. It's time to start giving yourself these pleasures.

Structuring time has been compared to putting a cast on a broken leg: it gives it time to heal. One certainly wouldn't want to wear a cast forever. But the structure is necessary now to keep you from falling out of "alignment" while the healing of early recovery is taking place.

Put Major Problems On Hold Where Possible

Most addicts have accumulated some pretty serious problems by the time they try to stop using their drug: creditors may be hounding them, spouses threatening divorce, and problems piling up at work. Having a crisis-ridden life right now makes it very difficult to give up your drug. Being surrounded by turmoil will cause you to lose what motivation you have, and the mounting stress will supply you with an excuse for relapse: "My life is so hard, I deserve to get high," or "Is this what I got straight for? Forget it!"

There are two dangers in coping with crisis in early abstinence: one is ignoring problems, so that they fester and build up stress; the other is trying to do *too* much about them—right away. As soon as you're abstinent, you may feel as if you have to jump in and resolve problems that have existed for a long time: start divorce

174

proceedings, find a new career, file for custody of children, and so on. But this is exactly the opposite of what you should do. First you must establish stable sobriety.

Make no radical changes in your life right now other than those needed to get off the drug. Major life changes inevitably create uncomfortable feelings that you aren't equipped to cope with yet. Keep focused on your top priority right now—getting abstinent. It's unrealistic to try to give up a deeply ingrained behavior like addiction in the midst of crisis and turmoil.

It is important, however, to *make a commitment* to address these problems as soon as your recovery allows. If you are in debt, for instance, remain committed to debt repayment—but work out a payment schedule that is realistic and that puts your recovery first. Let's face it, if you go back to using, you will not be able to meet your obligations anyway. The most responsible thing you can do right now is to focus on your recovery.

To assure yourself that you will address these problems as soon as possible, *make a list of them now* and acknowledge to yourself and others that you will begin dealing with them within a certain time period, say, in six to twelve months. Just making this commitment will relieve a good deal of anxiety and allow you to focus more intensively right now on getting abstinent.

WHAT TO EXPECT IN EARLY ABSTINENCE

Many people fail to establish abstinence and return to full-blown use within the first thirty days. That's because there are some common stumbling blocks at this early stage which, if you're not prepared for them, can lead you to become discouraged and give up. If you know to expect them, however, you can take appropriate action to protect your abstinence and recovery.

Withdrawal

Some people experience aftereffects (physical and emotional withdrawal) when they stop using. These include insomnia, irritability, mood swings, emotional overreactivity (or its reverse, numbness), low energy, short attention span, an inability to experience pleasure, lack of sexual desire, and extreme sensitivity to stress. The withdrawal syndrome can also include mild, temporary impairments in mental functioning, such as memory lapses, clouded thinking, difficulty concentrating, and a shortened attention span.

These syndromes can occur when you quit *any* addiction, not just chemical addictions. Overeaters, sex addicts, gamblers, spenders all have reported aftereffects of quitting to one degree or another.

Without being forewarned, a person can become discouraged and assume, mistakenly, that he will now feel this way—moody, irritable, unable to sleep, obsessed with cravings—all the time. But withdrawal symptoms are temporary. They usually occur within a few days of stopping the mood-changer and disappear within two weeks.

Not everybody experiences this syndrome, and those who do don't always experience it in the same way. Some even report a marked *improvement* in mood and mental state within the first week of abstinence.

Since many aftereffects are due to the mood-changer's disruptive effects on brain functioning (as detailed in chapter three), the person who seeks relief by using again only prolongs and intensifies these symptoms in the long run. Chemical addictions are the hardest to ride out, of course, because they have additional biological components.

Physical exercise and proper nutrition appear to reduce withdrawal symptoms. There is evidence that a daily regimen of certain vitamins (B complex and C in particular) and amino acids (tyrosine, phenylalanine, and tryptophan) facilitates the replacement of dopamine and other neurotransmitters that are depleted by certain chemical addictions such as cocaine.

The Pink Cloud

Some people experience a real exhilarating start in recovery—a pink cloud. As one recovering alcoholic describes it: "You're just so grateful not to be throwing up or waking up in strange beds that you feel like you're walking on air. All your senses come alive."

There's nothing wrong with enjoying this experience if it happens to you. But remember, "This too shall pass." This doesn't mean that you should think negatively and expect problems. Just strive for a balanced perspective. Without it you'll be setting yourself up for a fall, and it's a long way down from a cloud.

"The Healing Crisis"*

Whether or not you experience a pink cloud at some point after becoming abstinent, you may find yourself being overwhelmed by troubling or uncomfortable feelings. In all likelihood, these are the feelings you've been using the addiction to avoid. They might be feelings of fear, anxiety, self-hate, anger, depression, or inadequacy. Patti, the recovering alcoholic, anorectic, compulsive shopper and exerciser we met earlier in this chapter, relates how her feelings surfaced:

> I was brought up to focus on image: what I looked like, whether others approved of me, and all that. I learned to focus all my attention on controlling my appearance, because that way I didn't have to feel so inadequate, scared, and incompetent. I could always say to myself, "If only . . ." "If only I could exercise more . . ." "If only I was skinnier . . ." "If only I had a Rolex watch . . ."
>
> Now that I'm abstinent from this obsession, I don't have my image to focus on, and I'm acutely aware of these feelings. It's really painful . . . excruciating sometimes. It's like having no skin. They tell me in my recovery program that I'll grow new skin in time, so I have to trust that this will happen.

*A term used in *The Spiritual Dimensions of Healing Addictions*, Donna Cunningham and Andrew Rainer (San Rafael, CA: Cassandra Press, 1988).

If you're not prepared for this healing crisis or don't get help dealing with it, you might conclude erroneously that recovery isn't working for you. Or you may feel that it's not going to be worth it and ask "Why should I bother if I'm going to feel so bad all the time?"

In the middle of this healing crisis you may get some very strong cravings to use. The unconscious mind exerts a powerful pull back to the addiction, because going through this transition period is uncomfortable. Now you're really feeling the pain of believing you're not enough but you're not medicating that pain away. You have to go through these feelings in order to learn to cope with and, hopefully, resolve some of them without resorting to the mood-changers that damage your life. And this time you will have a support system so you don't have to go through it alone.

Try to stay focused on the fact that going through this unsettling period is part of the process of being *liberated.* Your whole being (mind, body, emotions, and spirit) is accustomed to being ruled by the addiction. Following any drastic change, there is a period of unrest before things settle down and become more stable.

Relapse Dreams

During the early phase of abstinence, some addicts have dreams about using their drug again. In some cases, the dreams are so real that upon waking, they feel guilty and depressed, as if they have actually relapsed. They think that the dreams are prophetic, proof that they are on the verge of relapse. "I must be secretly planning to do it or I wouldn't be dreaming about it," they say.

These interpretations, however, are unfounded. Dreaming about relapse usually means that you have *fears* about relapsing, not that you plan to do it. It may also indicate that you still long for the relief that your addictive substance or activity used to give you.

But if you misinterpret the meaning of a relapse dream, your feelings of discouragement *can* actually lead to relapse if not addressed. So talk about these dreams with someone in your support network. Such dreams tend to be stimulated by stress build-up in your life, so exploring the circumstances surrounding the dream is important.

Cravings and Urges

Cravings to use your drug again will occur and tend to be strongest during early abstinence. They are triggered by people, places, things, feelings, and situations previously associated with your addiction—anything that is a reminder of it.

People often mistakenly believe, especially early in abstinence, that having cravings means recovery isn't working for them, that they are "hopeless cases." Or, they believe that once a craving is felt, it will only keep intensifying until they give in and use. If you think you face only a constant, uphill battle such as this, you will likely become discouraged and even want to give up on recovery.

That's why it is important for you to expect cravings, learn about them, and prepare ahead of time to safely deal with them. Here are some key points to remember:

- Cravings can and do occur during recovery. They are the natural result of addiction and usually continue long after use is stopped.
- You are not responsible for the fact that you have cravings, since they are a symptom of addictive disease, but you *are* responsible for how you respond to them.
- Cravings are *always* temporary. They will pass on their own if you ride them out without relapsing.
- Cravings tend to reach their peak intensity within an hour of onset.
- Cravings do not *have* to lead to use. You can learn to change your old ways of responding to them.
- Willpower is a poor defense against cravings. It's best to remove yourself immediately from the circumstances eliciting the cravings and get in touch with your support network.

□   Relapse triggers can remain strong even after years of abstinence, so remain alert to cravings and don't become overconfident.

□   Every time cravings are followed by use, the likelihood and intensity of future cravings only increases. If you can respond safely to cravings without relapse, the cravings will diminish in frequency and intensity over time.

Conditioning

As a result of having engaged in your addictive activity hundreds if not thousands of times, your addictive behavior has now become paired or associated with many different people, places, and things in your environment, as well as to certain internal feeling states. These stimuli are called "cues" or "triggers" because they trigger the desire to use again.

Sometimes a trigger won't drive you to relapse immediately but will eat away at your resolve and increase the chances that you will give in soon afterward. Barry, a compulsive spender, decided to keep one of his charge cards in his wallet, "just in case." The first two times he felt like spending, he was able to resist, though he always thought about it. The third time, he gave in and charged several hundred dollars' worth of items he didn't need.

Conditioning is a three-part process, starting with a *cue,* that leads to a *behavior* and results in an *effect.* If the effect is a desired one, the conditioning is reinforced. For example, if a person feels bored, goes out and buys a new outfit, and feels a lift, the cue (boredom), the behavior (shopping), and the effect (the lift) become conditioned together. Each time a craving is followed by use it gets reinforced, and subsequent cravings become stronger and more persistent. The conditioning process thus perpetuates itself.

Additional factors can become associated with this chain, just because they occur "in the same picture." For instance, if shopping sprees take place at the mall you pass on the way home from work, just passing by that shopping mall can become a cue.

The passage of time by itself will not make cravings go away;

180

the only way to do that is to stop reinforcing them with use. You can be in recovery for the next ten years, and if you're still using—even now and then—you will continue to reinforce the conditioning and therefore continue to have intense cravings. Having cravings and *not* using weakens and eventually extinguishes the cues. This process is called "deconditioning," or "extinction."

In these first few weeks you need to begin deconditioning by doing two things: becoming aware of the cues in your life and avoiding them, and developing an action plan for dealing with cravings.

At the beginning of abstinence, it can be difficult to identify for yourself what situations pose a risk to you. Here's a list of some of the most common triggers for anyone in early abstinence:

Being in the presence of your *drug*

Seeing *people or things* associated with your drug (one compulsive gambler relapsed after seeing a limousine that reminded him of the one he often hired to go to Atlantic City)

Places where you got high (a recovering cocaine addict found he had to take a different route home in order to avoid walking past the after-hours club where he used to get high)

Negative moods, including feelings of rejection, loneliness, boredom, anger, guilt, fear, anxiety, and depression

Positive moods (when feeling good, you will be prone to experience a false sense of security about your recovery and may be less likely to reach out to your support system, thinking that you don't really need it anymore)

Vulnerable physical states (being run-down, physically ill, tired, hungry, or in pain can reduce your coping abilities and increase your vulnerability to giving in to cravings)

Memories (if there's a particular song, for instance, that you associate with getting high, it will be a cue)

Certain *times* (if you're used to using your drug after work, for example, that time of day will be a cue)

Sounds and smells (one recovering cocaine addict got cravings from smelling ammonia [a chemical he had used in preparing cocaine freebase] at the laundromat; for an alcoholic in early abstinence, the sound of a can of beer opening can set off cravings)

Seeing other people using (whether in person or in an advertisement, images of other people using your drug can be a cue)

Suddenly having a lot of *money* (applies to drug, alcohol, spending, gambling, and some sex and food addictions in particular)

Intentionally exposing yourself to addictive triggers in order to de-sensitize yourself is counterproductive. The willpower battle is a losing one. "Don't be strong, be smart" is good advice, because the more distance you can put between you and your drug the more likely you are to stay abstinent. Thinking that you can withstand high-risk situations without giving in to temptation is symptomatic of denial about your vulnerability to relapse.

There's no way to anticipate *all* the cues that could trigger cravings. You may be unaware that certain cues have the ability to trigger cravings. The conditioning can often be at a level below conscious awareness. Jason, a recovering cocaine addict, took all of the right steps: he got rid of his stash, threw out his paraphernalia, broke off with other users, and even moved out of the neighborhood where he had been getting high. But one day he experienced intense cravings for cocaine while driving past the highway exit to his dealer's home. That was one cue he just didn't anticipate.

The most difficult cravings to deal with are usually unexpected, set off by something or someone you run into accidentally. But if you have planned ahead how to deal with cravings and have an "action plan" in place, you will be less likely to give in to them.

The "Action Plan"

The goal when you get a craving is to ride it out, and prevent it from leading to relapse. The action plan you devise to short-circuit cravings should include the following:

1.   *Leave* the situation in which the craving is occurring. Get away from the person, place, or thing that is causing it.

2.   *Contact a member of your support network immediately.* Someone who understands addiction can talk you through the craving. (Always have phone numbers with you.)

3.   *Mentally detach* from the urge, and try to look at it as if you were an outside observer. Observe the craving from the perspective of "Isn't that interesting?" rather than from "It's going to get me."

Cecilia, a compulsive pot smoker and alcoholic in recovery, gives us this example:

> I still get cravings, but they're not as strong anymore. Now when I get them, I try to detach from them and notice what's going on with me that moment. I say to myself, "Oh, I'm having a craving. It's probably connected to a feeling; what's the feeling?" Once I note the feeling, I don't have to act on it. It doesn't drive me so much.

4.   *Plan* what you will do for the next several hours. How will you spend your time? Where will you go? With whom?

5.   *Get to a self-help group meeting* if possible, or read recovery literature. Alternately, get involved in something that will take your mind off the urge, for example, physical exercise or going to a movie, preferably with someone from your support team.

Additional tools for riding out cravings that have been used with success include

6.   *Think past the high* to what you'll get afterward if you give in and use. Focus on a negative memory or ugly reminder of your drug use, rather than dwelling on pleasant memories. Don't romanticize the high.

7.   *Write it down.* It may be helpful to carry a small notebook and write down the date and circumstance of any cravings you get and what you did to cope with them. You can then review each situation with a member of your support network soon afterward. This technique will help you become better at self-observation, a very important tool of recovery.

8.   *Use a relaxation exercise.* Cravings often have a physical component, including tensed muscles, increased heart rate, dry mouth, and sweating. Depending on the addiction, you may actually feel something in one particular part of your body: an overeater may feel his stomach in knots; a cocaine addict often gets a sensation of tenseness in her nose and throat. Relaxing your body can relieve these symptoms—and give you something to do while the craving passes.

9.   *Visualize yourself successfully handling cravings.* It is best to do this with a member of your support team, in case you need to talk it out afterward.

Social Pressure

The popular antidrug slogan "Just say no" is ineffective with addicts. It's not that easy. An addict is an addict in the first place because she *can't* say no, can't set boundaries, can't stick to limits. All her life she has sought acceptance and approval above *all* else (since she doesn't approve of herself). Why would it suddenly become so easy?

As you begin abstinence, you will frequently find yourself faced with an offer of your drug. It may be unexpected or come from people you feel self-conscious saying no to, and you may feel on the spot. If you're an alcoholic, you might be pressured by old drinking buddies to have "one for old times' sake." If you're an overeater, you might be urged to have some cake because the hostess "made your favorite dessert." If you're a workaholic, you may be asked to work through the weekend, postpone a vacation, or take on a new, all-consuming project. The temptations and decisions are endless.

It's crucial to develop *in advance* a comfortable, effective (face-saving if necessary) way to say no. Otherwise, when put on the spot, you'll be vulnerable to giving in. Learning to set limits, to say no appropriately, is a necessary part of the recovery process.

In early abstinence, you have an opportunity to "unlearn" this people-pleasing tendency rather than reinforce it, to take care of yourself. The truth is that most people don't care whether or not you partake or not, and if they do, they will quickly get over it. And even if someone is displeased, what is at stake for you is far more important.

Brainstorm the kinds of situations in which you are likely to feel social pressure, and prepare at least two or three face-saving but firm ways to say no in these situations. What do you think you will feel? A need to fit in? to please others? to avoid being different? to avoid making others uncomfortable? Allow any feelings of fear, anxiety, or ambivalence to arise.

Role-play each situation with one or more members of your support system. They can play the other people in your imaginary situations and give you feedback about how convincing your no is. You'll be surprised at how much role-playing will help. When you are on the spot, you won't have to invent this new skill right then and there. It will already be in your repertoire of skills, your "tool-box," ready to use.

The basic assertiveness technique is to face the person to whom you are responding, make eye contact, and say no—simply and firmly. Usually, a simple explanation is enough: "No thanks, I don't (smoke, drink, gamble, eat sugar)" or "No thanks, I get a bad reaction to that."

If the other person tries to argue, challenge, or debate you, don't allow yourself to be drawn into any further discussion. Use the "broken-record technique"; calmly but firmly repeat your original statement ("As I said, I don't want any"). Period. Say no more.

185

After each attempt to pull you back into discussion, just repeat the same phrase.

If someone still presses you after several of your broken-record responses, you can end the conversation. Just say, "I'm not willing to discuss it any further." Leave if you have to.

It's important to contact a member of your support system when faced with such internal or external pressure. Such situations are bound to create anxiety, ambivalence, and confusion that you'll need to talk about.

Tensions at Home

Just becoming abstinent does not always clear up all the family conflicts related to your addiction that have built up over the years. In fact, the first few weeks of abstinence can be *especially* tense at home, for several reasons.

If your addiction affected family members, they may have lots of leftover anger, shame, guilt, and other feelings, which don't go away just because you've stopped using.

They will be reluctant to trust your promise to quit if they've been let down many times before. Yet you're likely to feel insulted or hurt by their mistrust and cynicism.

If you neglected family responsibilities while active in your addiction, other family members may have filled in for you and resent your reform. For example, if you neglected certain parenting duties, your spouse or an oldest child may have taken over for you. They may resent your suddenly wanting to be responsible again, thinking, "Where were you when we needed you?"

If you go to a lot of self-help meetings, your family may resent the fact that you're never home and that your focus is so concentrated on your recovery (as it should be). This is true especially if they don't understand much about addiction and recovery.

If any family member served an enabling role in your addiction (see "What is 'Codependency'?" on page 190 and tables 3 and 4 on pages 192 and 193), she may unconsciously resent your recovery. That's because your getting better eliminates her role as "rescuer" or "manager," putting her in touch with feelings she'd been able to avoid by focusing on you.

The aftereffects (withdrawal) of your addiction may cause you to feel irritable, moody, and short-tempered right now, making it even more difficult for you to cope with normal family problems—and for others to cope with you.

All of these factors can exert a pull toward relapse. If a distrustful spouse or parent accuses you of having used your drug, you may feel so hurt and angry at being wrongfully accused that you'll feel justified in relapsing and blame him for it. You may think, "They don't believe me anyway, so I may as well do it."

But that's making your recovery contingent on the reactions of others, when it really has nothing to do with anyone but you. You're the one who will benefit from recovery and who will be hurt by relapse. Ultimately, it's not what others think but your *own* attitudes that will make or break your recovery, and this is what you should focus on.

Many addicts in early abstinence are sensitive to attempts by others to control their recovery. Bob, an alcoholic who had just begun AA, found that every day his wife, Susan, would ask him if he was going to a meeting that night. She even went so far as to call his sponsor one day when he was a half-hour late from work. Bob was furious about this and used it as an excuse to drink.

If you feel irritated by a person's attempt to monitor your recovery, talk it over with someone in your support network. Find a way to handle it other than using. The person may be "codependent," trying to control *you* the way you tried to control your drug (see "What is 'Codependency'?" on page 190).

Emotional detachment, to the extent that you can muster it, is probably the best way to handle such situations. Instead of *reacting* to them, try *acting* from what you know is right for you. Always doing the opposite of what someone else wants you to do in order not to be controlled by that person *is* being controlled by him. True independence is being able to do what *you* want to do—like staying abstinent—whether or not someone else wants you to.

It may help you to detach if you start looking upon the controlling behavior as humorous. Rather than "hooking in" and reacting with fury when your friend, parent, spouse, or boss starts trying to control you, take a step backward—in your mind's eye—and observe the situation. Say to yourself, "There he goes, doing his thing again." Seeing the humor in it takes the intensity out of the situation and helps you to see how self-defeating it would be to base your behavior on someone else's dis-ease.

In order to understand your family's reaction to your abstinence, it may help to understand how your addiction has affected them. Table 4 on pages 193–95 contains information *specifically* directed to those affected by someone else's addiction, and you may want to share this information with those people in your life.

Impact on the family. Most addictions affect families in the same destructive way alcoholism does. By the time you become abstinent, family members have accumulated many negative feelings, such as:

Guilt. Deep down, they may feel personally responsible for your addiction, thinking that if only they had done things differently, you might not have become addicted.

Shame. Having an addict in the family can be source of family shame ("We must be a crazy/bad/immoral family. I must be bad too.").

Grief. The person they once knew and loved hasn't been available. Even in recovery, you may be absent much of the time.

Anger. Family members are often angry about having been manipulated and neglected by you. If they don't accept that your addiction is a disease, they may feel angry that you've "chosen" to harm yourself and your family.

But the most profound and damaging effects on family members are more subtle. More and more, their attention will have shifted from their own lives and interests to your addiction, to trying to figure out if you're using, to reacting to your use, to reacting to your mood and behavior changes, to fighting about your use, to pleading with you to stop, to covering up to outsiders, to worrying about you, to handling legal, financial, and health crises when they occur, and so on.

Their own moods and behaviors will have progressively become contingent upon yours. If they resorted to nagging, pleading, and manipulating to try to control your addiction, they may have come to despise their own behavior, further lowering their self-esteem. All the while, they may be denying that your problem truly exists—just as you did—even though it has become a central theme in their lives.

Why do families deny? Because to admit that the problem exists means having to experience the feelings of shame, anger, grief, and guilt related to it. So instead, they block reality from their consciousness. Family members may also be overwhelmed by the problem ("There's no way out of this"). Feeling helpless to change it, it's easier to deny that it's happening.

Family members apply denial unconsciously in the form of a primitive belief/wish: "If I pretend there's nothing wrong, there won't be." This may actually work for a while, but the tangible evidence of the problem (lost jobs, missing money, arrests) will undoubtedly keep mounting, causing more and more anxiety in the person whose denial persists.

Because family members become invested in perpetuating the denial, they may unconsciously and without malicious intent begin trying to control and manage the addict's behavior and its ramifications. This has the inadvertent effect of enabling the addict's continued use. Enabling behavior takes various forms:

Shielding and protecting the addict from the negative consequences of his addiction: making excuses for him, taking over his responsibilities, bailing him out of trouble, paying his bills. This "damage control" is sometimes carried to extremes, even by ordinarily rational people.

Failing to set appropriate limits with the addict. Sometimes

WHAT IS "CODEPENDENCY"?

Codependency is a serious problem that results from being obsessively involved with an addict's problems. Codependents are typically so preoccupied with and so totally wrapped up in trying to rescue, protect, or cure the addict that they send their own lives into chaos in the process. The addict is addicted to mood-changers, while the codependent is addicted to the addict. A phenomenon usually seen in family members (parents, spouses, siblings) of addicts, codependency must be distinguished from a normal, temporary crisis response in people who genuinely care about the addict and try to help, although often unsuccessfully. Codependency occurs when the helping boomerangs into hurting for both the "helper" and the addict, but with the helper continuing this destructive behavior anyway. Codependents become trapped in a vicious cycle. It is an addictive loop where well-intentioned efforts to help only perpetuate the problem by enabling the addict, although all of the alternatives *appear* to be more frightening or hurtful.

Features of codependency follow.

1. In codependency the chief impetus for one's behavior comes from the addict rather than from oneself. The codependent lives by reacting to the addict rather than by acting from his own center.

family members give or loan an addict money, despite evidence that it's not being used for the stated purpose. The enabler blocks from consciousness the fact that the money will probably go toward the addiction.

Colluding with the user and actually helping him find, pay for,

2. Codependency is an addiction of its own. The codependent is addicted to the addict, just as the addict is
addicted to the mood-changing drug or activity. It has
the same symptoms as other addictions: obsession;
loss of control over behavior; continuing codependent behavior despite negative consequences; and
denial that one's behavior is a problem (see Table 3).
3. Codependency, like other addictions, is progressive.
Unless treated, it becomes worse.
4. At greatest risk for codependency are individuals who
already suffer from low self-esteem and who look to
the addict (or others in general) for confirmation of
their self-worth. Children of addicts (ACOAs) as well
as those who have been sexually or physically abused
are typically prime candidates for developing codependency problems.
5. Codependency is encouraged to some extent by our
culture. The wife who picks up the pieces behind her
alcoholic partner, for example, covering up the problem while holding the family together financially and
emotionally, often wins the admiration of other relatives and friends. People may say about her, "What a
saint!" Her addictive illusion of being all-powerful
and always in control helps bolster her own sagging
self-esteem.

or use his drug. Family members who collude in this way often do
so out of feeling like hostages to the addict's problem—they're
damned if they do and damned if they don't.

If these problems are not dealt with in professional counseling or in self-help settings, they can negatively affect both your and

your family's recovery. Bottled-up feelings can generate tension, impede communication, and keep any good feelings that *are* still present from being expressed—at a time when everyone involved needs them the most. Family members with unexpressed hostility may also (unconsciously) sabotage the addict's recovery. And if an addict knows that someone will rescue and shield him from the consequences of use, he is more likely to continue using.

It is apparent from our discussion of what to expect in early abstinence and how to handle it—from cravings and social pressure to tensions at home—that there's a lot more to breaking an addiction than just stopping use. Getting off, in fact, is only the first step. The real challenge is *staying off,* the focus of the next chapter.

TABLE 3.   The Addict and the Codependent: Parallel Addictions

Codependent	Addict
Avoids painful feelings by focusing on the addict	Avoids painful feelings by using a drug or activity
Moods depend on the addict's behavior	Moods depend on the drug's highs and lows
Denial increasingly employed to maintain the delusional belief that "everything's fine"	Denial increasingly employed to maintain the delusional belief that drug use is "under control"
Tolerance to addict's behavior develops; what once seemed shocking now seems normal and tolerable	Tolerance to drug develops; it takes more and more to achieve the same high
The addict's behavior and affairs become an all-consuming preoccupation	Getting and using the drug becomes an all-consuming preoccupation
Preoccupation with the addict leads to increased isolation and alienation from others	Preoccupation with the drug leads to increased isolation and alienation from others
Life becomes unmanageable; control over self and behavior is lost as the addict's behavior becomes an obsession.	Life becomes unmanageable; control over drug use is lost as the drug or activity becomes an obsession.

TABLE 4. For the Person Affected by Someone Else's Addiction*

Facts about addictive disease:

1. Addiction is a disease. It is describable, has specific symptoms, is chronic and progressive.

2. Its major symptoms are (a) cravings and compulsions for the mood-changer, (b) loss of control over use, (c) continued use despite adverse consequences, and (d) denial of the problem.

3. Addiction is not the result of moral weakness or a lack of willpower.

4. Because addiction is a disease, being reasonable or logical with the addicted person almost never persuades her to stop.

5. The addict is unable to control the disease. Therefore, it is not true that "She could stop if she really wanted to." Believing that is like believing a person could stop having heart disease or diabetes "if she really wanted to."

6. Addiction affects the user physically, psychologically, and behaviorally (loss of energy, mood swings, loss of self-esteem, value changes). These effects need to be seen as part of the disease process.

7. The addict is not responsible for having the addictive disease but is responsible for her behavior and recovery.

8. The disease of addiction is like an untreated allergy. It will always be there, and exposure to the "allergen" will set off a predictable reaction.

9. Addiction lasts a lifetime. It can be arrested, however, as long as the addict stays abstinent from all mood-changers.

10. Recovery is therefore possible, with abstinence and a change in attitude, life-style, and behavior.

Dealing with the addict who's still using:

1. Remember, you are not to blame for the addict's disease. Accepting blame for someone else takes away that person's right to be responsible for himself, and that enables his addiction.

2. The addict's disease is outside your control. Not only did you not cause it, but you cannot cure it.

3. The only person you can change or help is yourself. You are responsible for your own behavior.

*Adapted from Arnold Washton, *Cocaine Addiction: Treatment, Recovery, and Relapse Prevention* (New York: W. W. Norton, 1989).

TABLE 4. *(Continued)*

4. Addicts may not seek help until the pain of using becomes harder to bear than the pain of not using. Therefore, don't cover up, make excuses, bail him out of trouble, pay his legal fees, pay his bills.

5. This does not mean you should stop caring about and loving the addict. Detaching with love is not selfish. It gives the addict a chance to be responsible for himself—which holds the only hope of recovery.

6. Don't search for, hide, or throw out supplies or reminders of his drug. The addict will just get more anyway. Trying to keep him away from other users won't work either. He has to do it.

7. Don't use guilt on the addict; it doesn't work either. "If you really loved me, you would stop" only increases the addict's guilt, which can then be used to justify use.

8. Determine how you will live and what your boundaries will be. Set limits with the addict, and be consistent in enforcing them. "I will not lend or give money to you" is an example of an appropriate limit to set with a compulsive debtor, drug addict, alcoholic.

9. Remember that your relative's addiction is not a sign of family weakness or disgrace; it can happen in any family, just as any other disease can.

Dealing with the addict in recovery:

1. Remember that recovery is a lifelong process. Don't expect an instant cure.

2. You may have trouble trusting the recovering person for a while.

3. Expect ups and downs, maybe even relapses, as part of the recovery process.

4. Have a plan in mind for dealing with a slip (who you would call, what actions you would take). Once you have a plan, let go and live in the present. The point is not to expect a slip but to be prepared for one should it occur. Having a fire drill doesn't mean you live every day expecting a fire but that you're prepared if one occurs.

5. Don't try to protect the recovering person from normal family problems.

6. Don't try to control her recovery by checking up on appointments, calling sponsors, nagging about meetings. Don't pry into what is said in counseling sessions.

7. Do offer your support and love when you can. Encourage the efforts the addict makes now, even though you may sometimes feel it's "too little, too late."

TABLE 4. *(Continued)*

8. You may feel unneeded by the recovering person. After sticking it out through all the crises of addiction, you may feel left behind while she is active in recovery.

9. Don't expect the recovering person to be enthusiastic all the time now just because she's in recovery. Allow her to be irritable, anxious, unhappy.

10. Also allow her to *be* happy or enthusiastic. You may find yourself feeling she has no right to be happy after all the trouble her addiction caused the family. Let go, and just let her be.

11. Don't expect the addict's recovery to solve all the family's problems. In fact, other issues—some of which were ignored or avoided while the focus was on the addiction—may now become even more evident.

Your own recovery:

1. Learn to put the focus of your attention and the bulk of your energy back into your own life. Detach from the addict with love.

2. Examine your own behavior and attitudes. You are the only person you can change, so put your effort there.

3. Maintain your dignity.

4. Forgive yourself. Even if you have made mistakes in the past in dealing with the addict in your life, you didn't know any differently then. Have compassion for yourself.

5. Live in the present. Don't anticipate problems or dwell on the past, as doing so drains energy from dealing effectively with today's problems.

6. Get support in your life too. Don't remain isolated in your singular focus on the abuser.

7. Create a satisfying life of your own, one that includes recreation, hobbies, and plain old fun.

9

Staying Off

"I was on and off the wagon so many times I was worn out from climbing on and falling off. I wasn't able to stay sober for more than one month at a time. Then I added 'lacks willpower' to my low self-esteem baggage, since I thought anyone should be able to control his drinking."

—Frank, a recovering alcoholic

Mark Twain once wryly observed, "It's easy to stop smoking . . . I've done it hundreds of times!" He was referring to his own nicotine habit, but his point applies to all addictions. Typically, two thirds of those who try to break an addiction are back on their drug within three months.

Stopping, then, is not the biggest problem. Many people can get off their drug—whatever it is—for a few days, a week, even a month or two. But inevitably, cravings, denial, and addictive thinking return and—despite well-intentioned vows and promises—they somehow end up using again. Staying off, it seems, is even more challenging than getting off.

Still, despite the high stakes of relapse and the fact that it *is* preventable, the topic itself remains something of a taboo. Many newly recovering people seem to think that if they let themselves consider the possibility of relapse, it will become a self-fulfilling prophecy. Even addiction treatment professionals have avoided talking about relapse for fear of communicating an expectation of failure.

Ironically, it is this mistaken notion—that relapse is synonymous with failure—that contributes more than any other factor to high relapse rates. Because relapse is viewed as something to be ashamed of and treated as taboo subject matter, many people don't learn how to recognize their addictive attitudes and behaviors, avoid high-risk situations, identify the warning signs of a relapse, and cut one short if it occurs. These skills are the essence of relapse prevention.

The most important concept to understand to prevent relapse is that *abstinence is not synonymous with recovery.* In the absence of active, concrete prevention efforts, a tendency to relapse emerges automatically. Why shouldn't it? When an addict stops using, nothing inside has changed. The same pull back to the addictive substance—the compelling urge to anesthetize feelings when they become too uncomfortable—is still going to be there.

In other words, there's no standing still in recovery. If you're not moving away from the drug, you're automatically moving toward it. It's like standing on a down escalator. If you just stand there, you're going to go down, in this case back into addictive thinking and behavior. You've got to keep walking upward to counteract the escalator's—or addiction's—downward pull.

The good news is that with a conscientious relapse prevention effort, chances of recovery from addiction—arresting the compulsion and living a full, satisfying life—are very good. But as with any illness, just getting the diagnosis is not enough. A person will need to put his own effort into prescribed steps in order to see improvement, for recovery is active, not passive. In this chapter we will present many of the tools for avoiding relapse that have worked for others.

MYTHS ABOUT RELAPSE

Let's clear up some of the mistaken beliefs about relapse that abound and contribute to its high incidence:

MYTH #1:   *Relapse is a sign of recovery failure.*
FACT.   Having a relapse is not a sign that you are a failure or

197

that your recovery is flawed. It simply means you have made a mistake, one you can learn to avoid with greater awareness. Having a slip can be compared to falling on ice. If you slip and fall once, it doesn't mean that you are "hopelessly clumsy" or doomed to fall all the time; it means you need to take more precautions when walking on ice.

MYTH #2:   *Relapse is a sign of poor motivation.*
FACT: A tendency to relapse is a natural part of addictive disease, and even people who are highly motivated and sincere about their recovery can slip. No one is guaranteed a lifetime of total abstinence simply by embarking on recovery.

MYTH #3:   *Relapse starts the instant you "pick up."*
FACT: Relapse begins long before you actually return to drug use. A relapse starts when you "stuff" uncomfortable feelings or deny stressful circumstances in your life, return to addictive thinking, stop taking actions to cope effectively with problems, stop getting support, use another mood-changer, put yourself in a high-risk situation, and so on. Picking up your drug is actually the *end point* of the relapse, not the beginning.

MYTH #4:   *Relapse is unpredictable, and therefore unavoidable: It hits you out of the blue.*
FACT: Since relapse begins well before you actually return to use, there are many warning signs and chances to short-circuit the process before it culminates in use. Having an addictive disease means you have no control over your use once you reexpose yourself to the drug, because you escalate rapidly out of control. But you do have control over whether or not you put yourself in situations in which your vulnerability is raised—and that's where relapse prevention comes in.

MYTH #5:   *Relapse applies only to your drug of choice.*
FACT: Use of any substance, activity, or person that *you use to anesthetize your feelings* is a relapse, whether you've had a problem

with that particular mood-changer in the past or not. Other mood-changers such as money, gambling, sex, or other drugs can trigger cravings, lower your resistance to your drug of choice, or become new addictions.

MYTH #6: *A relapse cancels out all progress made up to that point.*
FACT: Having a relapse does not mean that all progress is lost. If you were abstinent for two months or two years before having a slip, you still have that experience in recovery. Those months or years don't cease to exist. A slip can be a temporary setback that ultimately serves as a reminder that you are still vulnerable. If you return as quickly as possible to abstinence, recovery can continue.

MYTH #7: *If a relapse isn't the end of recovery, then it's O.K. to have one.*
FACT: While a relapse is no reason to condemn yourself, it *is* always dangerous. Relapse is a return to the insanity and unmanageability of your addiction. Because of the progressive nature of addiction, the negative consequences of a relapse can be even more devastating than those that prompted you to quit in the first place. Some people never make it back.

THE RELAPSE CHAIN

The fact that you can be headed full-speed toward a relapse long before you actually pick up again might sound scary, but it's actually very encouraging, for it gives you time to recognize the warning signs and intervene. These warning signs are not only such dangerous emotional and physical states as depression, anger, boredom, loneliness, and fatigue but a return to old behaviors and ways of thinking.

There are many small, seemingly inconsequential "minidecisions" that the relapsing person makes long before actually picking up. The compulsive spender, for instance, might decide it's O.K. to

199

have a charge card again just for emergencies. The alcoholic might decide it's O.K. to drink nonalcoholic beer. The cocaine addict might decide to resume contact with a former drug buddy.

At the time such a minidecision is made, the addict plays it down. He doesn't mention it to anyone or talk about it in self-help meetings or therapy sessions. He just *does* it. At this point, denial is already at work. He denies to himself (and to others, if asked) that this little step has anything whatsoever to do with a relapse. He may well be out of touch with the feelings (and addictive beliefs) that are fueling these decisions.

Any such move in itself might not be so bad. But if the addict is not talking it over with anyone, eventually one minidecision leads to another and then another. Eventually, the minidecisions add up, and the temptations to use are simply too great to resist.

Think of the relapse process, then, as a chain of these decisions—made over a period of days, weeks, months, or even years—that together add up to backsliding in one's recovery. It's hard to say exactly where any one relapse begins, but the process might look something like this:

1. A Build-up of Stress

Negative or positive events and circumstances (work pressures, marital arguments, separation or divorce, career changes, financial problems, parenting problems, painful feelings or memories that surface because you're not anesthetized anymore) cause a build-up of stress.

2. Emotional Overreaction

Because the addict still has many of the addictive beliefs that made her vulnerable to negative moods in the first place, she tends to overreact emotionally to these events and circumstances. The feelings that are elicited—fear of abandonment, fear of inadequacy, anger and rage, loneliness—can overwhelm her.

200

3. Denial Sets In

Just as in active addiction, she craves relief from these feelings. If she doesn't yet know how to get support from other people, she may start to "shut down" emotionally. She's afraid to admit the problems she's having because she's afraid that if she reveals herself she will lose others' approval or love. So she denies that anything's wrong—even to herself—and puts up a front of being O.K.

4. Failure to Get Support

It's uncomfortable to feel negatively (confused, ambivalent, defiant, or whatever) while putting forth a positive image to others, so the addict starts cutting down on recovery meetings and stops talking about herself. Her silence or absence presents an incomplete or inaccurate picture to others. She is not getting the help she needs to face the stresses and cope with the overwhelming feelings. She may start having active cravings at this point.

5. "Little" Lies

At this point she begins telling "little" lies to herself and others. She makes up excuses for not going to meetings or counseling sessions or for going into high-risk situations. She is trying now to keep people "off her back." Since honesty is essential to recovery, she's on the way to relapse—unless she can interrupt it.

6. Increased Isolation

Because she is being dishonest, she wants to avoid other people more and more. As a result, she becomes increasingly isolated. As deep-down feelings of guilt, shame, isolation, and loneliness are reactivated, she might start thinking about contacting someone associated with her addiction, such as another user or a dealer.

7. Problems Grow Worse

The original problems grow worse because she is avoiding them, and new problems are created. For instance, if a source of stress is being behind on bills, and, instead of getting help dealing with her creditors, she blocks out the problem and avoids them, the situation may have escalated to the point where she is not only getting letters from collection agencies but summonses to court.

8. Hopelessness Returns

She feels totally incapable of doing anything about the situation, and once again experiences the hopelessness she thought she'd left behind. Self-pity sets in. Positive thoughts about the "good times" on the mood-changer start to cross her mind with increasing frequency. By now she has stopped going to meetings or counseling sessions, or she goes sporadically. The idea of using looks more appealing than it has in a long time and seems entirely justified.

9. Self-Sabotage

She increasingly "finds herself" in high-risk situations. She has frequent thoughts about getting and using the drug again but still resists. She may begin using other mood-changers, rationalizing that she has no problem with them. As her life skids out of control, she becomes increasingly isolated and alienated from her support system.

10. Use

Irresistible cravings and urges lead her to obtain or otherwise gain access to her drug. She uses, telling herself, "just this once." The relapse chain is almost complete, though she could still interrupt it—if she knew how.

11. Defeatist Reaction

Intense feelings of failure, shame, despair, and frustration set in immediately after use and further reinforce the relapse cycle. She tells herself, "I've already blown it, I might as well keep going."

12. Full-Blown Relapse

Feeling like a hopeless failure, the addict has cravings to use again and again that are almost irresistible. As one recovering overeater describes it, "It started with 'just one extra bite' off my food plan, and it ended with the despair of realizing I'd done it again. Then I couldn't stop."

KEEPING YOUR RISKS DOWN: LOWERING VULNERABILITY

A number of factors increase vulnerability to relapse: certain *physical states* (exhaustion, hunger, pain, or illness), *stressful events or circumstances* (work pressures, relationship or marital problems, financial crisis), *negative moods* (anger, shame, guilt, anxiety, depression), and *people, places, and things* (situations in which you might have easy access to the drug).

As you'll see later in the chapter, it takes time for the compelling urge to alter your mood to let up and even longer to modify the addictive attitudes and behaviors that are the common precursors to relapse. In the meantime, it's wise to avoid becoming vulnerable in any of these ways. Because once you're in a vulnerable situation, you've lit a match. All it takes is a little fuel (addictive thinking and denial) to light the fire.

Real Life: Constructive Coping in the Face of Problems

After a couple of months of abstinence, the particular crisis that prompted you to change your ways (a spouse threatening to leave unless you got help, for instance) may have subsided. At the same time, the newness and excitement of starting recovery may be wearing off. Suddenly, it seems, your problems start to weigh on you again: debt, a badly damaged relationship, an eviction notice, threatened divorce, whatever they are. And now that you're not anesthetized anymore, they seem more overwhelming than ever.

If you had the unrealistic expectation that just getting into recovery would solve all your problems, you can become discouraged at this point, thinking, "Look how hard I'm trying, and I still have all these problems," or "Is this what I got straight for?" This is a common motivational crisis, sometimes called "the wall." It is perfectly normal at this point in recovery. And if you remain open, it can be an opportunity to make a new, deeper commitment to your recovery and begin learning important coping skills—one step at a time. Here are coping tools others have used with success:

- □ *Don't hide out.* The most crucial aspect of coping with problems is simply to resist the impulse to run. Bring your problems out in the open, admit them to yourself and to people in your support network who can help you sort them out. Hiding from problems is a big part of addictive disease. You don't have to be perfect, just out in the open.
- □ *Keep problems in perspective.* People with addictions tend to overreact to problems because they interpret them as proof of their inadequacy and expect dire consequences. What's the worst that can happen from this problem? Will it really confirm that you're a worthless person—or simply that you're human? Can you be executed for it? Identifying the worst-case scenario can help you see that you can survive just about any problem, with support. But you might *not* survive a relapse, if you let it lead to that.
- □ *Talk about it.* Connect with your support system (people in your recovery group, nonusing family and friends). They may not have all the answers, but their nonjudgmental support can make the difference between letting it fester and being able to face it. And their feedback can help you

see when you are making decisions that are on the relapse track.

□ *Keep your recovery first.* The most responsible thing you can do to resolve any problem right now is keep your recovery first. That means minimizing vulnerability. Don't let problem-solving efforts interfere with your meals, rest, recovery meetings, and other baseline necessities. Losing your recovery because you're wrapped up in your problems makes no sense; it only makes more problems.

□ *Accept responsibility.* You may not have created a particular problem in the first place, but if it's affecting your life, it's now your problem and you must decide how to respond. Blaming others for your problems—and giving them the responsibility of solving them—is giving your power away. Accepting responsibility is not the same as accepting blame. It simply means, "I will not abandon myself, but will do what's in my power to resolve this."

□ *Commit yourself to resolution.* Even if there is nothing you can do to resolve a problem right now, make a commitment to do so as soon as you are able—keeping your recovery first. For instance, even if you can't repay a creditor immediately, make a commitment to *eventual* repayment. When you accept responsibility for a problem and commit yourself to resolving it, you no longer have to feel burdened by it—and it's not festering.

□ *Break problems down into small steps.* You don't need to figure everything out today, but identify what single, small step you can take that would be in the direction of resolution: make a phone call to the creditor, show up for a meeting with the attorney, fill out the application—whatever it is. Focusing on one little step rather than the big picture will help you avoid becoming overwhelmed.

□ *After you've taken the action, let go of the result.* One reason addicts have so much trouble facing problems is that they think they should be able to control the results. The secret is to take appropriate actions, and then let go of what happens. Just do what you can do. You can't control the results anyway.

- □ *Keep getting support.* Whenever you're feeling discouraged, isolated, or scared about a problem, it probably means you've fallen out of touch with your support team. It's amazing how sharing it can lighten the load. Share your successes with them too—not just your setbacks.

Thawing Out: Surviving Feelings
Now That You're Not Anesthetized

Bad moods (anxiety, shame, depression, loneliness, anger) are common precursors to relapse. After years of seeking the quick-fix for emotional pain, this process becomes a natural reflex. Uncomfortable feelings and urges to get high are *paired,* as Cathy, a recovering alcoholic, describes: "It's automatic. The urge to drink sneaks up on you to wipe out feelings. You don't think, 'I want to drink,' so much as you just *don't want to have these feelings."*

Studies bear out the connection between negative moods and slips. Overeaters, for example, have been found to be far more likely to relapse when bored, depressed, angry, or lonely. And a study of compulsive gamblers found that 47 percent relapsed on the heels of a bad mood. Obviously, learning to cope effectively with feelings is vital to avoiding relapse.

During the first six months of recovery, you may be even more susceptible to bad moods than usual. Mood swings, irritability, hypersensitivity to stress, and extreme anxiety are often the temporary aftereffects of addiction, caused by the disruption of brain neurotransmitters. In addition, since nearly every addict is a survivor of trauma—abuse, parental addiction, or emotional abandonment, for instance—intense feelings related to these experiences often surface abruptly, several weeks or months after getting off.

Many people experience emotional hypersensitivity in early recovery. Paula, a recovering alcoholic and compulsive eater, explains: "I wouldn't even call it 'feeling' in the beginning, it was more like total rawness, like having no skin. It was 'primal pain,' a lot of undefinable pain that had been squelched for so long."

Anger is a feeling that can easily cause cravings to get high in early recovery, either as a desperate attempt to find relief from it or to retaliate against someone you're mad at ("Look what you made me do"). As with other feelings, the addict's anger is often disproportionate to the current situation that provokes it. It's charged with the residual intensity of so many incidents in the past when the anger was stuffed. The anger and the impulse to get high are so subliminally paired that you may not even notice the transition. The feeling can remain below the level of conscious awareness and turn into a drug craving automatically.

Shame is another difficult feeling to tolerate early in recovery, for it strikes at the very core of one's being. Unlike guilt, which stems from believing one has *done* something wrong, shame stems from the belief that one *is* something wrong. Fueling it is that addictive belief "I am not enough."

Tools for dealing with feelings. Since negative moods raise one's vulnerability to relapse, it's important to develop some ways of coping with them—ways to relieve the intensity so that feelings can be tolerated.

1. *Just let it be.* When a feeling does come up, just let yourself sit with it, become *aware* of it, and go through it. Remember that you can't die from a feeling, and healing takes place just in feeling long-denied emotions. Remind yourself that you are safe.

2. *Keep breathing!* When you have a difficult feeling, take several slow, deep breaths. This helps you "center" yourself, to regain the sense of honor belonging to your true self.

3. *Remember that you don't have to act on it.* Having a feeling doesn't mean you have to do anything about it right now—or ever. A feeling can just be felt.

4. *Reach out.* For most people in early recovery, talking about what they're feeling with someone supportive is the key to coping. It helps to diffuse the urgency of the feelings and put them in

perspective. Instead of seeking to change the mood with your drug, let your support group be your mood-changer for a while.

5. *Don't judge feelings.* There are no "shoulds" when it comes to feelings. They are neither right nor wrong. Your feelings are automatically justified, just because you feel them—even if no one else validates them.

6. *Notice negative tapes* playing in your mind that reinforce the negative mood. Are you telling yourself that you're a "jerk," "stupid," "worthless," or otherwise verbally abusing yourself? If so, take a moment out to reprogram your internal computer. Tell yourself the kinds of things a loving parent would tell an unhappy, upset child. Try it, and see what a difference it makes to be respected.

7. *Stay in the moment.* Many of the addict's painful feelings are related to past hurts or fears about the future. That's why bringing yourself back to the present can help you cope better too. A baby does this automatically. She can be crying one minute from a wet diaper and smiling the next, as the diaper is changed. She's not hanging on to the past, or worrying about the future.

8. *Check out reality.* Because our most difficult feelings often stem from primitive, irrational beliefs and fears, they can have little to do with our current reality. For instance, when Gail was turned down for a job for which there were hundreds of applicants, she suffered profound feelings of rejection that far exceeded the reality of the situation. Fortunately, she was able to catch herself going out into unreality and cut the painful mood short.

9. *Remember, "This too shall pass."* Feelings, like cravings, are always temporary. No matter how uncomfortable, they do pass in time. Feeling something right now does not mean you will feel it forever from this moment forth.

10. *Let your feelings thaw out.* If you blocked off your feelings in childhood, you may be emotionally numb now, not even aware of what you feel anymore. In recovery, you may be in for some surprises, as Carl was:

> Fear has run my life, only I was out of touch with it until recently. Ironically, I was always into high-risk, dangerous behavior like auto-

racing, illegal activities, dangerous sports. I denied danger or that I was scared. On the outside it looked like I had no fear, but inside I'm wracked with it. In recovery it comes out with people—I'm scared to death of people. I'm scared to call anyone or reach out, or ask for a date. Fear, it turns out, is the driving force in my life. . . .

Getting in touch with your feelings again will be a process, not a one-shot event. As one recovering person puts it, "When you've been numb all your life, it takes a while to thaw out."

11. *Take it slow.* You don't have to feel everything you've stuffed for the past thirty years—right now. In fact, in early recovery, it's best to avoid situations guaranteed to elicit intense feelings, since enough will come up on their own. Lynn, a newly recovering alcoholic, tried to attend a group for adult children of alcoholics but found she had to back off. "Too much rage came up for me. It felt like it was racing through my blood—and the only thing that would quell it was a drink." She decided to put those issues on a back burner for the moment and concentrate on staying sober.

12. *Own your feelings.* Blaming someone else for "making" you feel something is addictive thinking; it's giving others power that's not rightly theirs. "But," you ask, "shouldn't other people be held responsible for their actions?" Yes, but how you choose to *react* to them is up to you. Far from letting others off the hook, you gain freedom with this new approach; you're no longer tossed about by everyone else's behavior.

13. *Use your feelings as signals.* Negative moods exist as a signal that something needs attention and possibly some action. They're like the fever that comes with a flu and tells you to take time out to heal yourself. Beverly, an overeater, says, "Now when I'm feeling unloved, which is when I want to eat the most, I say to myself 'O.K., this is not about food, it's about love. What do you feel bad about?' I think it's when I abandon myself that I feel the worst—and that's when I'm in the most danger of eating."

14. *Write.* Writing is a good tool for discharging overwhelming feelings. Write a letter to the person you're angry at or the person you feel abandoned by. Plan ahead of time not to mail it.

209

This gives you a focus for articulating your feelings, with the freedom of knowing you're not going to have to deal with the ramifications.

15. *Guard against relapse* when you're in a state of heightened emotional vulnerability. Barbara, a recovering cocaine addict, became aware that whenever she visited her parents she became anxious, self-doubting, and "off-center." It was after one such visit that she had a slip. Brainstorming ways to protect herself in the future, she saw that one option would be not to go home for visits right now. Another would be to take someone from her support system with her whenever she goes home. She decided on the second option—a plan that has worked beautifully so far.

16. *Watch out for self-pity.* Of course, it's possible to get stuck in a negative mood, to wallow in it unproductively. You may prolong a dark mood for secondary payoffs such as sympathy from others, to avoid taking the necessary actions to resolve it, or even to build up an excuse to use again. If you become aware of your mood, you can move on.

17. *Help someone else.* Sometimes the best antidote to painful feelings is to get out of yourself. If you're ruminating about a feeling and not getting anywhere with it, try helping someone else. If you're genuinely listening to someone else's problem, you can't be obsessing on your own. And you may find yourself telling them just what *you* need to hear!

18. *Change the way you view pain.* Addicts, and indeed our whole culture, look at pain as something that should always be avoided—at any cost. Yet it's the *resistance* to pain that's often the most painful. That's what addiction is, and look at the pain *it* has brought. In recovery, you can learn to meet pain head-on and, through meeting it, experience personal growth that is ultimately freeing. Cathy puts it this way: "There's no reason that pain has to be wired up in our heads as something to avoid. In recovery you learn that if you recognize it and feel it, pain can sculpt and shape you in a very beneficial way."

19. *Do something nice for yourself.* Nothing helps soothe sore feelings like T.L.C., and don't always wait for someone else to give

it to you. Give yourself a bubble bath, a nap, a manicure—whatever is nurturing for you. It reminds you that the "child within" is not being abandoned. And nurturing yourself is different from indulging: indulging is eating a whole box of cookies when you feel bad. Nurturing is making a delicious meal for yourself.

People, Places, and Things: Avoiding High-Risk Situations

"Don't go into the lion's den unless you're a lion tamer."
—Bonnie, recovering alcoholic and debtor

What Bonnie's remark means is, don't go into a high-risk situation when you are powerless against the danger. The most common high-risk situations for the recovering addict are those that involve people, places, or things that previously elicited cravings or provided access to your mood-changer.

For example, when Janis was ninety days abstinent from cocaine, an old boyfriend, Vincent, called and asked her to go away for a long weekend with him to Vermont—to the lodge where the couple used to go when they were getting high together. Vincent assured her he would not offer her any drugs nor use any himself. Janis wavered on the verge of accepting the invitation, telling herself that she needed the love and affection. In a moment of surrender to recovery, though, she called someone in her support group.

Ultimately, Janis had to admit to herself that it was a high-risk situation, and she chose not to take the chance. Why was she able to take this sensible step? She explains, "By this time, I could see that my own judgment and decisions hadn't worked so well for me in the past. This was an admission that maybe I didn't know it all."

Avoiding high-risk situations is the area of relapse prevention in which you have the most control. You will continue to be subject to denial and addictive thinking. That is not in your control, and the best you can hope for when you feel this way is to notice these feelings and take steps to interrupt them. But if denial and addictive thinking sneak in *while* you're in a situation which gives you

211

easy access to your drug, you're probably in trouble.

In other words, if you're an alcoholic and you sit around in bars drinking club soda, sooner or later you're bound to be there when denial and addictive thinking sneak back in, rendering you vulnerable. But if you're careful not to be in places where you have easy access to your drug, then a temporary lapse into addictive thinking or denial will not in itself be as dangerous.

Going into a high-risk situation when you are physically or emotionally stressed exacerbates the danger, because in that condition you are more vulnerable. One morning, Bruce, the sex addict mentioned earlier, had an upsetting argument with his wife. Right afterward, as he walked into his office, he got a call from a woman, Rose, with whom he'd once had a sexual affair. Rose is in the same business and was looking for free-lance work.

Thinking the situation over, Bruce realized it would be too dangerous for him to meet with Rose at this point in his recovery, especially given how he was feeling. "It would remind me of our past times together and stir up sexual cravings. And that would be real risky for me right now, since I'm already feeling abandoned by my wife."

High-risk factors, then, are cumulative. Let's look at a hypothetical situation in which Carol, a recovering cocaine addict, gets invited to a party. If she's feeling insecure, lonely, or otherwise "down" this evening, she is starting out at greater risk than if she were secure and "centered." Let's call her mood a risk factor of "2," with "10" equaling relapse. If she talked her feelings over with someone before going out, she could probably bring that risk back down to "0" or "1."

But suppose Carol goes to the party *without* first attending to her emotional state. Her vulnerability would now increase to "5" since she is not only (a) in a negative mood but also (b) out of touch with her support system and (c) running the risk of being exposed to cocaine. At the party, if Carol hears people talking about cocaine or if she has an alcoholic drink, her cravings for cocaine will probably be activated and she will totter at an "8" or "9." From there it's a short hop to using. Just knowing that people are getting high in the next room will be enough to take her over the edge.

One of the best ways to identify high-risk situations and prepare for them in advance is to imagine likely relapse scenarios. If you *were* to relapse, in what kind of situation might your relapse occur? Describe how the situation might arise, where you would be, what you'd be doing, and what kind of feelings you'd be having. If you have difficulty even imagining it, review episodes from the past, when you were on the wagon and fell off, noting what high-risk factors were operating at the time.

Once you've identified possible situations, go over the options that would be available to you today to minimize the danger. What is your action plan? Basic elements of it should be to leave the high-risk situation, talk with someone from your support team, and identify ways to lower your vulnerability immediately (eat, sleep, relax, exercise, go to a recovery meeting, meet with a friend). Role-playing these high-risk situations can be extremely helpful too.

Some high-risk situations cannot be avoided, however, and there are ways to weather them successfully. Bridget is a compulsive overeater who must attend work-related dinner parties even though they pose some risk to her. So she prepares herself in advance, using a number of tools (these can be adapted and applied to other addictions): she (1) plans her meals before the dinner so that she is not ravenously hungry when she arrives (*anticipates the risk*, makes certain she's not physically vulnerable to relapse), (2) contacts the host or hostess in advance to find out what's being served and makes arrangements for there to be safe food for her or to bring her own (*takes actions in advance* to insure her safety), (3) touches base with her sponsor before leaving for the party to go over her plan *(connects with her support system)*, and (4) reminds herself that she can always leave if she becomes uncomfortable—a very important key in dealing with high-risk situations *(leaves herself an out)*.

As you can see, the key to surviving high-risk situations that cannot be avoided is to anticipate and prepare for them.

213

ADDICTIVE ATTITUDES AND "MIND GAMES" TO BE ON THE LOOKOUT FOR

As we've seen, just getting off your mood-changer doesn't mean you're not operating in an addictive system anymore; it just means you're not using. The same addictive beliefs, thoughts, and behaviors are going to be there, exerting a pull toward using again. Often, they're quite insidious; you might not even notice them. This is how you're used to thinking and relating to the world, so it seems perfectly normal.

Marilyn, a recovering alcoholic and compulsive debtor, describes these addictive thoughts and behaviors as "a mental attack of negativity." Uninterrupted, these mental attacks will ultimately lead you to the addictive solution, which is to pick up: "You won't necessarily think, 'I want a drink, or a drug,' but you'll think, 'Nobody cares about me.' You'll feel lonely, isolated and desperate, and the desire to get high will just follow naturally."

In other words, leading up to a relapse, the addict has usually had certain familiar tapes running through his head. We call these "mind games." He may be telling himself, "I'm a hopeless case, I might as well get high," Or "I'm not really that bad, maybe I'm not addicted." Or "I can control it now." Or "I deserve it!" He literally talks himself into using.

In active addiction, these tapes may have driven you: the tapes ran, and you used. In recovery, unless you notice them and intervene, this can still happen. That's why it's so important to develop a "third ear": you need to hear these tapes running and intervene. Then, instead of there being one smooth reflex action—from addictive thought to negative mood to picking up—there will be an "advocate" who cares about your best interests and not just about the quick-fix. This outside observer can say, in effect, "Wait a minute. That's the disease talking. That's not in my interests."

To Beverly, a compulsive overeater who's lost 168 pounds in her recovery program, developing self-observation skills such as these has made the crucial difference between this and countless attempts to stop overeating in the past:

Now I'm not blanking out on what's going on. I might slip back into old ways of behaving and thinking, but I can *see* it now. I can see when I'm trying to get sneaky, or when I'm looking for an excuse to eat, or trying to drum up self-pity, or whatever little "trick" I'm trying to pull on myself. Then I can intervene, figure out what need I have that's not being met, or what feeling I'm trying to escape, and take care of it.

As Beverly implies, the particular mind game you're playing can often tell you something about what you really need. For instance, if you're playing the tape "I deserve to get high," it should tell you that you've let stress build up and are feeling deprived and needy. Reading this signal, you can then find positive, recovery-based ways of fulfilling your needs. Instead of indulging your child, you can give him real gratification.

Obviously, for such self-observation to work, you have to be *honest* with yourself. This isn't always easy in the beginning, since self-delusion is probably the most insidious aspect of addictive disease, but it's a skill that can be cultivated. But, as one recovering gambler puts it, as long as you stay honest with yourself, you're "somewhere in the ballpark." The Self-Observation Checklist in table 5 can help identify your high-risk factors on an ongoing basis.

The good news, then, is that with awareness, self-observation, and self-honesty, these addictive behaviors and mind games can be interrupted. So long as you remain aware of the many disguises addiction wears, and of the fact that you too are vulnerable, then you can *observe* yourself falling into these traps, honestly call them what they are, and *interrupt* them. You can stay on a recovery track but only by recognizing your continued vulnerability and actively countering it with these tools.

Because these addictive attitudes and mind games are so predictable, we are able to identify the most common ones here. As you read, you may recognize yourself and be tempted to judge yourself harshly for still thinking or behaving addictively. This would be counterproductive, however, for it would keep you in the addictive cycle. Addictive behavior and mind games have nothing

TABLE 5.   Self-Observation Checklist

A.   Am I experiencing any of these negative moods right now?

__ Angry	__ Scared
__ Depressed	__ Inadequate
__ Anxious, nervous	__ Humiliated/embarrassed
__ Lonely	__ Rejected or abandoned
__ Guilty	__ Bored, empty
__ Ashamed	__ Other: _____

B.   Am I experiencing any of these other high-risk factors?

__ Urges and cravings

__ Impatience

__ Overconfidence

__ Expecting too much of myself

__ Expecting too much of others

__ Blaming others

__ Defiance

__ Defensiveness

__ Desire to indulge myself

__ Exhaustion

__ Feelings of giving up

__ Inability to have fun without my drug

__ Feelings of neediness, deprivation, overstress

__ Feelings of elation but off balance

__ Feelings of invulnerability to relapse

__ Doubts that I'm really an addict

__ Fantasies about controlled use

__ Feeling sorry for myself

__ Waiting to be cured

__ Feeling like a hopeless case

__ Romanticizing the good times on my drug

__ Feeling overconfident

__ Feeling like celebrating

__ Feeling cured

__ Feeling justified in getting high

__ Feeling plagued by painful memories

__ Relapse dreams

TABLE 5. *(Continued)*

___ Wanting magical solutions to my problems
___ Being harshly critical of myself
___ Thinking maybe I'm not addicted any more
___ Planning to drop out of treatment or recovery program
___ Dwelling on past mistakes
___ Putting myself in high-risk situations
___ Acting impulsively
___ Focusing on someone else's problems or recovery
___ Coming late to meetings or counseling sessions
___ Throwing myself into a new relationship in an obsessive way
___ Not putting my recovery first
___ Not exercising
___ Not eating properly
___ Not getting enough sleep
___ Not having fun
___ Not taking care of my medical or dental needs
___ Lacking structure in my day
___ Allowing stress to build up
___ Lying
___ Isolating, withdrawing from people in my support network
___ Not talking about my problems with anyone
___ Using other drugs, activities, or people as mood-changers
___ Rationalizing
___ Rejecting suggestions of others in recovery
___ Saying what people want to hear but secretly feeling otherwise
___ Cutting corners in my recovery program

to do with how smart you are or how motivated to recover; they are simply another symptom of addictive disease.

The harder you are on yourself, in fact, the less you'll be able to observe and to interrupt your particular addictive traps. If you believe they're just more proof of your failure and unworthiness, you won't want to let them into your conscious awareness—and that will keep you stuck in unhealthy patterns. *Recovery is observ-*

ing yourself with compassion—then taking appropriate action, as Cindy, a recovering codependent and bulimic describes:

> I've come to look upon my addictive disease—and all its forms of expression—as a sane reaction to the insane environment I grew up in. I don't think that it was so bad anymore that I used food and other things to avoid pain. That's a pretty natural instinct, and I didn't know any other way to deal with the painful feelings then.
>
> Now when I find myself slipping back into my old ways, I try to see it in the same light. Instead of thinking, "Oh, look at what you're doing again; when will you ever learn?" I think, "Oh, there must be something I don't want to feel because it's painful . . ." and I go on to figure it out. Ultimately, I find that the more compassionate I am with myself, the easier it is to interrupt these slips of attitude. It becomes easier to be honest.

"Back-Door" Setups

People headed for relapse often put themselves in high-risk situations "accidentally." Through a series of subtle, seemingly inconsequential minidecisions, the person puts himself in a high-risk situation where the return to use seems justified because the temptations become too great. He suddenly finds himself in a situation that virtually guarantees an encounter with the drug—but in a way that appears to absolve him of any responsibility for it.

For example, a recovering cocaine addict may accept a party invitation knowing full well that at least one person there will probably bring cocaine. The person setting himself up like this will usually downplay the risks inherent in what he's doing, saying it's "no big deal." The cocaine addict, for example, may later claim it was just bad luck to run into a former cocaine-using friend who was sitting there getting high and how the temptation was simply too much to resist. The relapse, he may say, "came out of the blue."

These "back-door" setups usually indicate a person is in heavy denial again, wants to use, but doesn't want to take responsibility for it. He wants to continue to look good and to play out the role of the "innocent victim of circumstances."

Many recovering women say they are prone to using sex and love relationships as foils for their own desire to use again. Pam explains:

> I used men to set myself up. The first thing I did when I was first off cocaine was to start going out with a guy who was using it. He would go and cop, and I would go with him. He would smoke pot in front of me, he would snort coke in front of me! And I would say to myself, "As long as I'm not doing it, it's O.K." But it was crazy! I'd be sitting there, grinding my teeth. It was the biggest setup.
>
> When I finally gave in and used, I thought it wasn't my fault. It felt beyond my control, like I had nothing to do with it. The guy was to blame—not me! That's what I thought. My denial was ten feet thick.

Three to four months into recovery is a particularly vulnerable time for most recovering addicts and a time when self-sabotage often starts. Up until then, he's been concentrating on just staying abstinent. Now, his problems start to become apparent again, and this is often the first time he's faced them without his drug in a long while. Unconsciously, he may be yearning for a way out. Rather than assume responsibility and address the problems (a day at a time), he begins unconsciously sabotaging recovery.

But it's not just feeling troubled that can precipitate self-sabotage. In many ways, feeling good is even harder for the newly recovering addict to tolerate. When things start to come together and he's feeling good about his abstinence—healthy, behind himself, acknowledged by others—the urge to return to the familiar territory of addiction will be strong too, precisely because he's made a decision to change.

Says Bruce, a sex addict who has experienced this fear of feeling good: "It's like climbing a mountain. If I feel good, it feels like I'm too high up. It feels like I can't make it, because I've never made it before. I just want to get back down to the bottom so I can get rid of this anxiety. Feeling all the guilt and shame again feels right, it feels like me."

Hidden dependency feelings can play a part in back-door setups too. All his life, the addict has tried to appear independent, even though, as we have seen, he has strong, hidden dependency feelings underneath. The setup can be an attempt to put himself back in a dependent position, to insure again that someone else will have to take care of him.

There are some warning signs of a back-door setup. The person may start *letting stress build up*. He may become *increasingly isolated* as he withdraws from or pushes away people in his support system. *Abrupt, impulsive decisions* are another sign. In a fit of anger or frustration, the person may quit a job, end a long relationship, start an affair, drop out of a recovery program. *Reinitiating contact with people who make the drug available* is yet another sign that a person is trying to position himself to "accidentally" get high again.

Because he's in denial, the person on a self-sabotage track gets defensive when confronted about these accumulating danger signs. He may dismiss someone's stated concern as unjustified, meddling, or alarmist. A recovery group can be particularly helpful in confronting self-sabotage; the unconditional support combined with gentle confrontation by others who've been there can help pierce the denial.

Substitute Addictions: Same Disease, Different Symptoms

As we've seen, getting off an addiction means having to feel the feelings you've been anesthetizing all these years. The pull to obliterate them in some other way is very strong. The most common "second-round" addictions are food (overeating, anorexia, bulimia), spending, gambling, exercise, and work. Let's look at some examples:

Jackie was a heroin addict who got straight in an eighteen-month in-patient therapeutic community. She did so well, in fact, that she was asked to take a staff job. Jackie threw herself into the work, putting in twelve hours a day, plus carrying a second job. Her fellow staff members marveled at her seemingly infinite energy, taking her industriousness to be a sign of her strong recovery. What no one realized—including her counselor—was that Jackie was still a very active addict; she had merely switched from heroin to work-aholism. Inside of two years Jackie was shooting dope again, lost her job, and plummeted anew into the nightmare of heroin addiction. It was inevitable; nothing had changed except that she was staying busy.

In another example, Patti stopped drinking in AA but began obsessing about her weight, starving herself, and exercising compulsively. Abstinent from alcohol, she'd merely substituted obsessions. Looking back now, she sees that the only reason she was even willing to give up the booze was because she had these other mood-changers to rely on. Unfortunately, it took Patti several more years of suffering before hitting bottom as an anorectic and being hospitalized.

Cliff's story is similar. He didn't start running up debts with his spending until he got straight in Cocaine Anonymous. Before that, he jokes, whatever money he had went directly to his dealer's pocket, and he didn't even qualify for credit cards. Once straight, though, Cliff's compulsion with money escalated rapidly in three years to the point where he wound up many thousands of dollars in debt and was arrested for passing bad checks.

These second-round addictions are often sneakier than substance addictions: they're more socially acceptable, harder to define, easier to rationalize, and harder to detect. As Patti says about her obsessions with food and exercise, "There was no telltale smell on my breath anymore, and I wasn't staggering around. My behavior was off the wall and erratic, but no one knew what to attribute it to."

So if you're abstinent and find yourself working excessively, becoming compulsive with food, money, or exercise, consider whether this escalating new behavior is serving a purpose for you. Is it distracting you from feelings such as fear, loneliness, inadequacy, anxiety, anger? Is it taking up your time so you have an excuse for not risking new activities or socializing? Is it giving you some way to act out your need to control? Is it an attempt to give your day structure, something to do? Is it really just the same addictive "dis-ease"—expressing itself now in a new way?

If you answered yes to any of these, you're being honest—which is a great first step. The next step is to acknowledge this substitute addiction to someone in your support network. Saying it out loud to another person will help keep denial from getting in the way of dealing with it.

Perfectionism

People with low self-esteem (most addicts) are often harshly judgmental of themselves and feel they have to do everything perfectly—superlatively—or they are failing. It's that black-and-white addictive thinking again: I'm either perfect or worthless. There's no middle ground, which means there's no room for reality.

This perfectionism is, as we've seen, one of the traits that makes one vulnerable to addiction in the first place, and it doesn't disappear with abstinence. During recovery, perfectionism can keep a person from admitting problems and mistakes, causing them to fester and become overwhelming.

Carl, for example, had been in recovery for two years and working in a government office for one year when he made a mistake on some legal records. Rather than admit the mistake, he changed other records to cover it up. He was scared to admit he'd made a mistake. To make a long story short, Carl was eventually indicted for tampering with public records and perjury, lost his job, nearly went to jail, and was left tottering on the brink of relapse—all because he thought making a mistake was the end of the world. *That* turned out to be the real mistake.

Perfectionism can also make it difficult to develop the kind of self-observation and inventory-taking that is crucial to preventing relapse. The perfectionist won't admit having thoughts about getting high again, as he thinks he should have a perfect recovery.

Experiencing cravings or having a slip can cause him intense self-loathing. He compares himself to other people in recovery, who he sees as being more recovered and concludes that he is a hopeless case—"What's the point of trying?"—and gives in to an urge to use. So perfectionism in recovery ends up being a setup to fail.

Before you can change an unwanted behavior or trait, you have to first accept yourself right where you are. Where you are now is exactly where you need to be, in fact, to learn what you're learning about life. No one achieves perfect recovery; slips do occur even when one is using the tools of a program. The maxim "Progress, not perfection" conveys much wisdom. The person who applies this measurement is far more likely to recover—however imperfectly—than the person who insists on recovering flawlessly.

In time, as your recovery continues, perfectionism will simply lose its appeal. Since perfection is impossible to achieve, its rewards are equally elusive. Surrendering to who you really are (imperfections and all) turns out to be much more rewarding.

Isolating

Isolating is a very common precursor to relapse. Addicts have a tendency to isolate, as we've seen. They isolate when feeling good ("I don't need anybody now") and when feeling bad ("Nobody wants to hear my problems"). It's often simply more comfortable for an addict to isolate than to deal with the challenges of relating to others. The resulting inevitable loneliness feels right and familiar and provides a good excuse for a relapse.

It's hard to interrupt this addictive behavior, but it can be done. Just remember that if you're in a negative mood and you're *not* doing something about it, you're isolating. And if you're doing things that you don't want to tell anyone in your support network, you're isolating too. If you keep in the back of your mind that isolating is a precursor to relapse, then when you see yourself doing it, you'll be more likely to take action: go to a recovery meeting, call someone on your support team, make social plans with a safe

223

person, schedule a counseling session.

Of course, if you're isolating, you're not going to *want* to reach out. But experience shows that if you want to avoid a relapse, it is the necessary medicine. The good news is that once you have taken this step and interrupted your tendency to isolate, you will usually feel better and be glad you swallowed the remedy. Isolating is another example that you have to *proceed on what you have learned* about addiction and recovery—not on your natural inclination.

Corner-cutting

Corner-cutting usually starts out small: coming late to meetings or counseling sessions, leaving early, not sharing as actively as you once did, not bothering to call people in your support network when a problem arises. At first, any one of these alone seems like no big deal. If anyone confronts you about it, you're likely to feel unjustly accused.

But corner-cutting, like addiction itself, is progressive. It starts small but, unchecked, leads to a complete collapse in your recovery program. Eventually it can escalate to skipping meetings you once considered essential, rejecting the need for total abstinence as something that doesn't apply to you, resenting the commitment of time and energy you've been making to recovery, and suddenly coming up with schedule conflicts that prevent you from attending meetings, counseling sessions, and other recovery activities—conflicts that *could* be resolved if you really wanted to.

Joe, an alcohol and amphetamine addict, had several years of abstinence when he started cutting corners on his recovery. A long-distance truck driver, he stopped going to his group meetings regularly because, he said, he couldn't coordinate them with his work schedule. He checked in with his support group even less. Gradually, Joe slipped into what he calls a "dry drunk." He wasn't drinking, but his attitudes became less than sober; he was becoming dishonest, selfish, grandiose—all the things he'd been when he was drinking. This became clear to him the day he started an engine fire in his truck in order to get paid time off on the road.

"Because I was used to looking at my behavior by this time, I saw myself on the 'reruns' of the day and said to myself, 'There's a drink here somewhere. I don't know when or where, but I know there's a drink here.' I was living like a drunk, and when you live like a drunk, eventually you gotta drink." Joe attributes his dry drunk entirely to cutting corners in his recovery. "I stopped going to meetings, and the mental part of my disease reared its head. It's as simple as that."

Superficial Compliance

The person with this addictive behavior may appear perfectly pleasant, cooperative, and compliant on the surface, accepting guidance from his counselor and others. But he is all talk and no action when it comes to making the long-term life-style and attitude changes necessary for lasting recovery. Secretly, he discounts or disregards what others say and fails to follow through with their suggestions, quietly planning to go on doing things his own way.

Often, it is the addict in early recovery who adamantly claims to have *no* desire to use anymore, who will have *no* problem giving up people, places, and things associated with his drug, who will *never* have a slip—who is complying only superficially. He may not want to admit his true feelings of ambivalence because he wants to please others (spouse, therapist, self-help group members) or keep them off his back. So he gives the impression of being very gung-ho and then does what he wants.

The problem with this behavior is that if a person doesn't own up to his reservations and ambivalence, there is the strong possibility of a "boomerang reaction"—of going from extremely positive to extremely negative (relapse). It is important to allow the real you— resistance, ambivalence, and all—to be expressed. Only then can these normal, addictive attitudes be worked through and the risk they pose to recovery avoided.

"White-Knuckling"

Occasionally it happens that an addict is able to stay abstinent for an extended period of time without making substantial changes in life-style or attitudes. This is often called "white-knuckling," as we've discussed, and, as the term implies, there is much strain involved. Abstinence is maintained through sheer determination, requiring constant vigilance against and resistance to urges and cravings.

In alcoholism treatment this person might be said to be dry but not sober, because while he isn't using, he might as well be. His attitudes and approach to things are still those of an active user. And he's still trying to outwit the addiction with his own willpower.

Hanging on so tightly to abstinence, trying to do it all himself, makes for a very uptight, joyless person who has to avoid many situations (to avoid anxiety and other uncomfortable feelings). His life ends up being quite boring. It's only a matter of time before he feels deserving of getting high again. He hasn't gained enough pluses in recovery to balance out the strain that abstinence is for him.

The "Cure-Me" Attitude

"When I first went to a treatment program, my attitude was O.K., I'm here, fix me! Tie me to a chair, do whatever you gotta do, but make me not get high."
                                        —Jeff, recovering cocaine addict

Because it is part of the addictive belief system to view people and things outside yourself as having the power you lack, this magical thinking can get applied to recovery too. This mind game holds that some doctor, counselor, or recovery program is going to fix you if you just present yourself. Those who go to professionals for help are especially prone to this cure-me mentality. They feel they're paying for a service and expect the counselor to provide it.

Of course, this attitude is usually unconscious, not something the newly recovering person says when he walks in the door. More likely, the attitude gets expressed through his behavior, usually in his passive approach to recovery. He is literally waiting for it to be performed on him, like an operation. But recovery requires internal shifts in attitude, values, and priorities—something you can only do for yourself. So recovery is the end of the quick-fix road; there *is* no such thing as a fast solution to addiction.

People with the cure-me attitude may have (conveniently) misinterpreted what is meant by the disease concept of addiction. When they learned that they were powerless over addiction they took it to mean that they were powerless over *everything*.

Because deep down he believes that recovery shouldn't require any effort, the person waiting to be cured often will not take the concrete actions such as breaking off with dealers and users, getting rid of supplies, and so on. Then, when inevitably faced with an opportunity to use, the person playing this mind game feels like an innocent victim: "What could I do? I asked him over for dinner, and afterward, he put cocaine right under my nose." A counselor or other support person usually gets the blame for any slips too: "If she was doing her job, this wouldn't have happened."

In reality, recovery is like taking a hike up a mountain: counselors, sponsors, and other helpers can serve as guides, but you still have to do the walking yourself. Because no matter how skilled a guide you have, if you're not putting one foot in front of the other yourself, you can't possibly get anywhere.

"WHY ME?": The Self-Pity Trap

"Sometimes I feel, 'Why me? I've been dealt a bad hand. My mother really screwed me up. Other people have it so easy.'" These are the thoughts that sometimes plague Joel, three months into his recovery, making him want to throw in the towel and get high again. Joel is caught in the self-pity trap, a mind game in which he spews out a steady list of reasons why he *should* be miserable. Sooner or later, these can become excuses to pick up.

The person prone to self-pity tends to look negatively at his life, focusing on the problems he still has and overlooking the progress he's made so far in recovery. He may chronically complain yet reject all advice that would help lift him out of his misery. Other features include blaming other people for his problems, focusing on others' shortcomings while remaining blind to his own, and holding on to the conviction that life is meaningless and/or recovery futile.

People who operate in this self-defeating, help-rejecting complainer mode usually wind up alienating most of the people in their support system. Then when they are left feeling that there's no one who cares, this too provides a justification for relapse.

The best approach to self-pity is simply to become aware of it in yourself. Hear the self-pity tapes as part of the self-defeating addictive disease, but accept it in yourself. Having self-pity is nothing to be ashamed of, it's just another symptom to bring out into the open. After all, you should *expect* to have addictive attitudes: if you didn't, you wouldn't be addicted! And secrecy about one's addictive attitudes is more dangerous than the attitudes themselves. All you need to do now is bring them out in the open. That's when they will start to change, and not before.

"I'm Unique": Grandiosity in Recovery

As we've seen, the flip side of the addict's low self-esteem is her tendency to think she's unique, special, different from others. The person with this addictive attitude often compares herself to other addicts and finds them so much "worse off."

She may conclude from this that because she's a different kind of addict, she doesn't have to go to the extreme measures these others might. "They" might have to attend self-help groups or therapy, but not her. "They" might have to remain totally abstinent, but not her. "They" might have to call each other up and ask for help, but not her. She may think she's more intelligent or sophisticated than these others.

The degree of self-delusion in this can be mind-boggling. Joel, despite his twenty years as a heroin addict and alcoholic, looked around at his first Narcotics Anonymous meeting and thought,

"Wow, I'm here with a bunch of addicts!" He didn't think that he was like them at all.

A good thing to remember to counter this mind game is that it's not how much of your drug you used, or how often you used it, *it's what you used it for.* Being an addictive person has much more to do with one's overall approach to life, to how one deals with feelings, problems, and other realities, than it does to the substance or activity itself.

"It Can't Happen to Me": Overconfidence

One evening, Patrick, five months off his nicotine habit and newly divorced, was on a date with a beautiful woman—who smoked. After a nice evening of dinner and dancing, they stopped at an open field to star-gaze, and she lit up a cigarette. Patrick had a craving. "We'd had such a good time and I was feeling *so* good that I said to myself, 'How could one cigarette bother me?' " Patrick asked her for a cigarette—and by the time he started for home later that night, he'd smoked about half a pack.

To become overconfident like this is to forget or deny one's continued vulnerability. This overconfidence is often accompanied by a relaxing of self-observation and monitoring. Suddenly, it seems, you're smoking that cigarette, or snorting cocaine in the bathroom at a party, or doing whatever your "thing" is again. Because of overconfidence, some people start putting themselves in dangerous, high-risk situations, which can lead up to a slip.

Most people have to avoid *all* cues—people, places, and things—associated with their addiction for at least a year and often much longer, until their inner attitudes have shifted so substantially that they are less vulnerable. The problem is that people in the early phase of recovery often *think* they have achieved invulnerability before they really have. The newly abstinent person can mistakenly believe that because he's been able to stop using for a little while—perhaps for the first time—he's now cured. He may make uncategorical statements, such as "I'll never relapse," or

"There's no way I'll ever do that again." He might even do things to prove that he's not in any danger anymore.

Overconfidence is a common trap for the person abstinent for a long time too. In his life, things seem to be working well now: major crises are resolved, he's able to be productive again at work, and he probably enjoys more harmonious relationships than ever before. As one long-recovering alcoholic says, "You feel so normal, it seems like you should be able to drink normally now too."

Learn to anticipate this kind of thinking. It's part of the addictive process and never goes away totally. When it does creep in, tell someone. Once again, the simple act of being honest and admitting you are overconfident takes away the power of this type of thinking.

The "Maybe I'm Not Addicted After All" Mind Game

Cathy, a recovering alcoholic with five years' abstinence, was standing on a subway platform several months ago waiting for a train, when all of a sudden the thought came to her that maybe she'd been brainwashed in her recovery program and wasn't really an alcoholic after all.

> I said to myself, "Wait a minute, I *love* drinking! I've been duped. I'm not an alcoholic!" It was so bizarre, and so powerful, this sudden thought. I'm lucky there wasn't a bar right there.
>
> But by this time in my recovery, I had learned the different ways the disease approaches. I knew that it can be very cunning. I was able to see what was happening, and was in awe of the power of it. All I have to do is look at my record and I believe I'm an alcoholic. But if I hadn't been able to catch myself, to see it was the disease talking, I could've been in big trouble.

It's common to have thoughts like Cathy's during recovery. Often, these haunting doubts are exacerbated by friends or family members who don't understand addiction (or who are addicts themselves, in denial). Joel, after twenty years as a heroin addict and alcoholic, was chided by friends when he went into Narcotics

Anonymous who told him he didn't need it. Now, when Joel gets discouraged in recovery, he wonders if they were right. "I say to myself, 'Maybe I *don't* have to do all this. I didn't feel like doing drugs today, so why should I go to a meeting?'"

This questioning of one's ongoing vulnerability also tends to be accompanied by other self-delusions, such as believing your problem was limited to the use of one particular chemical or activity that's now under control, believing your problem was merely the result of certain external problems (a nagging spouse, a high-pressure job) that have now been resolved, and questioning whether your life was really ever unmanageable in the first place.

"These Are Special Circumstances": Intellectual Rationalizations

Sometimes a recovering person is lured by her own addictive disease into believing that she *has* to use the drug again in order to "do well at work," "have good sex," "talk with people," "meet women/men," "succeed in my career," or whatever else. Intellectualization is the defense that combines with denial here to create a "rational" case for returning to use.

Often this belief occurs when a person is having a crisis in motivation, when she's overwhelmed by stress and other problems she's not talking about. She *wants* to use, but doesn't care to admit that, so convinces herself that there's a good reason in this "special circumstance."

When Joel, the recovering heroin addict and alcoholic, was just two months abstinent, he was offered marijuana by someone he describes as a "celebrity." Joel is a musician and had been invited to Mr. X's house to work on a musical arrangement, and he was flattered. When his celebrity friend handed him the joint, he panicked. He hadn't thought ahead about how to handle such a situation. The tape that ran in his head was saying, "It's in my best interests to keep on his good side." Joel took the joint.

In reality, of course, it was not in his best interests to use a mood-changer that could—and did—precipitate a relapse. But ad-

231

dictive thinking in a situation such as this can be so powerful as to cancel out one's own best intentions. Joel probably didn't have enough time in recovery at that point to be able to recognize his addictive thinking as a justification, as his disease "talking."

Relapse rationalizations often masquerade behind a sense of obligation to others ("It will hurt her feelings if I don't eat the cake she made for me"), a desire to avoid making others feel uncomfortable ("I can't go to a business luncheon and not have a martini, it will make them ill at ease"), or some sense of having to face up to the realities of the work world ("I have to sleep with him—that's how you get ahead in this modeling business)," or Joel's "It's in my best interests to . . ."

It helps to brainstorm ahead of time some justifications *you* might be tempted to use. Think of those you've used in the past or can imagine yourself using in the future. Explore each one, uncovering the denial and addictive thinking inherent in it. Then, if one of those rationalizations does enter your mind, you'll be better able to recognize it as that and take appropriate action to protect yourself.

"I Deserve to Get High": The Deprivation Mind Game

Elaine, a recovering alcoholic, has a fair amount of stress in her life on a good day—between her work as a police officer and the occasional trials of being a gay woman in a small, country town. When Elaine's companion, with whom she'd been living for ten years, was taken seriously ill last year, it nearly pushed Elaine over the top of the stress scale. Driving home from the hospital one night, she passed a local pub and hangout. The urge to pull over and go in was incredible.

"I was thinking, 'Goddamn it, I've had it . . . I deserve a break! A beer would taste so good right now.'" Fortunately, Elaine had another "voice" going through her head, one she'd acquired in recovery. This one was saying, "If you go in there, it's not gonna be one beer." She kept driving, but she had had a close call.

Broken abstinence often comes on the heels of such stress

build-up and feelings of deprivation. One of the most common rationalizations for relapse, in fact, is the belief that one's desire to indulge is justified. This usually results from feeling stressed, overworked, deprived, or otherwise in need of relief from the demands of everyday life. Because your drug has often been the only form of gratification you allowed yourself regularly, it's natural to crave it more strongly under high stress.

To avoid stress build-up, *take the pressure off where you can.* Identify the specific sources of stress in your life, then take actions to reduce them. For instance, if you're trying to stay abstinent while holding down a very high pressure job, it may behoove you to request a temporary change of assignment. If a particular relationship you're in creates high levels of stress that trigger cravings, this may be the time to put it on hold too.

Let go of trying to control everything. It's very draining and stressful to be pouring all your time, attention, and effort into trying to control other people, your addictive dis-ease, and other circumstances beyond your control. If you can come to accept the things you cannot change or control, you will no longer be driven by the addictive beliefs "I should be perfect," "I should be all-powerful," and "The world should be without limits."

Try using a stress-reduction technique. Possibilities include getting regular exercise and fresh air every day; pursuing sports, hobbies, and other leisure activities; getting plenty of rest; giving up caffeine and other artificial stimulants; taking up meditation or prayer; doing muscle relaxation exercises; delegating responsibility; getting organized at home and work; getting proper nutrition; talking about your feelings and problems with supportive people; and taking periodic vacations.

Avoid the deprivation-splurge cycle. Barbara, a compulsive overeater, would always lose weight on diets but only after much straining, girding, and obsessing. Eventually, she would feel so deprived, she'd give in to the feeling that she deserved something—like a whole box of cookies. Finally she learned a different approach, one with more balance:

"Now, when I'm in the supermarket and I feel like I want to

eat everything there, I say, 'O.K., I'm having a hard time. What's going on?' And I try to make it easier on myself. I might decide I can have an extra bowl of popcorn that night—but not a whole bag of candy. That way I feel satisfied, and not just 'controlled.' "

The Secret Plan to Return to Controlled Use

Another relapse pitfall is the hidden hope and plan to someday become a controlled or social user of the drug again (gamble "a little," do cocaine "now and then," be a "social drinker").

This desire to return to controlled use occurs to most recovering people at some time and is itself a symptom of addictive disease. Since this contradicts both what has been learned about addictive disease and probably your own history, it is clear that you can arrive at such a self-deceiving theory only through denial. The fantasy of controlled use only goes so far as the high; left out of the fantasy in the mind is the likely aftermath of using.

It's important when one is entertaining the desire to test control to *tell someone.* Again, this is the medicine you will not want to take at the time, for this plan to return to controlled use is almost always harbored in secrecy. Other recovering people will undoubtedly understand and not reject or ridicule you for having this fantasy, and they can help expose the denial that is at work behind it.

Addiction is a one-way street. If you try to return to controlled use, even after an extended period of nonuse, you may be in control for a short while, but you will very soon be obsessed again. Remember this, and, if you can, accept it on blind faith. You'll save yourself a lot of headaches.

"Those Were the Good Old Days": Romanticizing the High

After a brief period of abstinence, a tendency to idealize the high—to remember only the pleasurable effects of your drug and selectively forget all the adverse effects—often emerges. This is most likely to happen once the negative consequences caused by the addiction are not so immediately obvious and the bad memories—

the arguments, car accidents, health problems, eviction notices, public humiliation, missed promotions, lost jobs, wrecked marriages, nightmare arrests, and lost fortunes—have begun to fade into the past.

When people romanticize the high, they often stop right there—with the high. They remember the good feelings they got early on in their use—feelings of confidence, "freedom," sexual stimulation, release from pressures—however temporary, artificial, and illusory these may have been. They fail to think about the whole picture, of what—realistically—comes after the high. Instead, they might start thinking, "Maybe it wasn't so bad after all. I might have exaggerated it. It really was a good time." That's addictive thinking: denying reality.

This selective forgetting is more likely to occur when a person is under stress or otherwise unhappy, because the desire to escape bad feelings is strongest then and the addict is conditioned to look for relief. Since the net effect is to maintain or heighten the allure of the drug, this mind game can contribute to eventual relapse. Here are some techniques you can use to avoid getting seduced by idealized memories:

Learn to *think through the high*. When you get a nostalgic memory, take your thoughts beyond the high you might (or might not) get if you used again to the consequences that would surely follow it—the "crash," the guilt, the shame, the losses, the isolation, and the rest of it.

Beverly, the compulsive eater, used this technique when she suddenly found herself in emotional crisis, having received notice of a lawsuit filed against her: "My first thought was, 'I want to eat.' My second thought was, 'Yeah, but it'll make you feel worse.' I thought about the bloating, the lethargy, the shame, the guilt, the excruciating humiliation, and said to myself, 'It's only going to feel good while you're doing it, and you can't keep doing it indefinitely.' "

Review your original reasons for quitting. This will help you put together a more realistic picture of how this drug has affected your life. Out of this list of consequences, choose a few of the worst

235

and create a *memory file* for them so that you can call them up whenever you find yourself romanticizing your drug, as Pam, a recovering cocaine addict, does:

> When I'm actively caught up in glorified fantasies about cocaine, I go back in my mind to the worst moments I can remember—like the time I watched a subway train coming into the station and seriously thought about throwing myself in front of it, the rent eviction notices, the harassing calls from bill collectors. I remember the terror, the times I got beaten up because I couldn't get coke for somebody . . . the times I was sick and had no one to help me.

Keep concrete reminders of your addiction's consequences as visible as possible: a cast from an injury, that eviction notice, whatever it is. One recovering cocaine addict, for example, decided to hold off repairing the fender on his new car—damaged in a cocaine-related accident—until he had six months of abstinence. Just seeing that fender every day, he says, helped set him straight whenever he started romanticizing past times on cocaine.

THE DEFEATIST REACTION TO SLIPS

No one wants to have a slip, and just thinking about it makes some people very nervous. But denying the possibility altogether and refusing to think about it and prepare an action plan just in case is addictive behavior itself.

Part of people's fear of talking about slips is their mistaken belief that a slip and a relapse are the same thing. *A slip is the isolated event of returning to the addictive behavior.* If a slip is interrupted immediately, it can be a temporary loss of abstinence—one piece of cake, one cigarette, one bet. *A relapse is a full-blown return to the addictive behavior,* usually resulting in the person dropping out of recovery. A relapse occurs if a slip is not interrupted. Whether or not a slip is interrupted depends on your reaction to it—whether you steer yourself immediately back into abstinence or have a defeatist reaction.

The defeatist reaction is a complex of negative feelings and thoughts that flood a person as soon as he picks up again. These include profound feelings of failure, guilt, self-loathing, and shame for having given in. Most important, the person experiencing the defeatist reaction usually tells himself, "Well, I've blown it now. I might as well keep going."

Also part of this reaction are intense guilt feelings for having "let other people down," the belief that this proves you can't do *anything* right and that you've been only a fraud in recovery. You feel frustrated and hopeless because it appears that all your progress up to this point has been lost and will never be regained. If you don't short-circuit these negative feelings, the likelihood is great that a single slip will escalate into a full-blown relapse and cause you to drop out of recovery.

A familiar, everyday example of the defeatist reaction is the person on a diet who gives in and eats a piece of cake, then immediately afterward feels very guilty and discouraged and declares, "Well, I blew it, now I might as well pig-out and get back on my diet tomorrow." Sometimes he gets back on tomorrow, but, more often, he's off for a while. The "defeat" itself becomes a reason for continuing to overeat.

This distorted view—that we are either successfully recovering or are a total failure at it—is addictive, black-and-white thinking. In reality, having a piece of cake doesn't mean that the addict has blown recovery, it only means that he has had a piece of cake. By making it into a failure, he elicits the shame, guilt, and hopelessness which then propel him further into a full-blown relapse. Ironically, the overreaction itself is what causes the relapse.

Other traits of the addictive personality contribute to the defeatist reaction. Perfectionism, for instance, causes the addict to have unrealistic expectations for a flawless recovery. His tendency toward isolation and secrecy increases the likelihood that he will not want to tell anyone. And if he's under the illusion that he's cured and has boasted, "I'll never have a relapse," he will feel that he has lost face if he slips, and the humiliation will be intense.

Slips occur among even the most motivated recovering people. Sometimes it even takes a slip for someone to accept that what he's dealing with is a lot more powerful than he is. If you use a slip to your advantage, it can bring you closer to acceptance (and thus to lasting recovery) than you were before.

As with all other pitfalls in recovery, the best prevention is to be informed ahead of time about this common pitfall and be prepared with a specific *action plan* to counter it should you have to.

1. Your main goal, should a slip occur, is to *cut it short*. Simply don't do it anymore. Get back on your recovery track *right now*. This is a new moment, and right now you can abstain, even if you didn't five minutes ago.

2. *Leave the situation* in which the slip is occurring.

3. Immediately *call a member of your support team.* Identify ahead of time who it is you would call. And remember, if you're having a defeatist reaction, you won't want to call anyone. So make it part of your plan to take these actions anyway, even if you don't want to.

4. Remember, *a slip is not a total nullification of progress.* If you are two months abstinent, you still have two months of experience with abstinence. Those two months don't cease to have existed. The slip is a rough spot on the road to recovery, but you're still on the road. Jeff, a recovering cocaine addict, learned this after a slip: "The main thing my counselor told me was, 'It's not over. You were straight for a month, you took a couple of hits—O.K., that's what happened. Starting now, don't do it anymore.'"

5. *Don't beat yourself up about it.* The feelings of self-loathing that follow a slip are actually in the service of the addiction; it's the disease talking. Berating yourself and wallowing in self-hate, guilt, and shame will only perpetuate the slip. Recovery is furthered by giving yourself *compassion*—and taking *action* to interrupt the slip.

6. *Learn from your mistakes.* While a slip is not evidence that you are a failure, hopeless case, or bad person, it does indicate that you have made a mistake, failed to observe yourself slipping back into addictive thinking or to recognize relapse warning signs. Look upon the slip as an opportunity to problem-solve. By learning from

it, the slip will become *part* of the recovery process and not antithetical to it.

7. *Work in additional support.* Having a slip should tell you that you need more support than you are currently getting: perhaps more meetings, a commitment to reach out more to others, or additional counseling. Repeated or frequent slips may signal a need for an in-patient addiction recovery program.

Being prepared for a slip is like having a fire drill. It doesn't mean you expect a fire but that you are prepared to take responsible action should one occur.

NOW THAT YOU'VE GOTTEN OFF your drug and learned techniques for staying off, you might think your recovery is complete. It isn't, and for one simple reason: recovery is a lifelong venture. After all, you can't just go back to being the person you were before recovery: that person became addicted! Once you've established stable abstinence, it's time to turn your attention to creating a healthier life-style, one in which addictive solutions simply lose their appeal. It's time to start getting better.

10

Getting Better

WHEN YOU STARTED RECOVERY, you may have had one simple goal: to stop using your drug. But since the drug by itself is not the whole problem, getting off and staying off is not the whole solution. Unless you deal with the *source* of the problem—the dis-ease within that made mood-changers so appealing to begin with—you'll remain vulnerable to relapse or to switching addictions, or both. Like the bump in the rug, your inner dis-ease will keep expressing itself in one way or another. It will pop up wherever it can.

Think of yourself as having had the inner conditions in which the dis-ease of addiction thrives, the way bacteria thrives when certain conditions are present. Now you must change those inner conditions so they are no longer favorable to addiction. You can create a healthier culture in your own life, one in which addictive solutions lose their appeal. That's what getting better is all about.

But what does this entail? Basically, it means changing how you think about yourself and how you live your daily life. It means building into your life sources of positive gratification so that the short-lived excitement or relief offered by the quick-fix doesn't hold such allure. It means learning to live according to certain life-affirming principles, such as honesty rather than denial and delusion, humility rather than grandiosity, accountability rather than irresponsibility, community and service rather than self-preoccupation, and—most important—self-acceptance rather than self-hate.

But this shift to a healthier, nonaddictive life-style is not something you have to try hard to accomplish. It will take root naturally if you're working on a recovery program like the one outlined in this book, one that includes group support and a spiritual foundation. Because if you stay in recovery, you will inevitably find that it affects your whole life. It transforms you from within—naturally, gently.

For some people, the idea that recovery changes your life is very frightening. They are afraid that they will lose their individuality, be changed into zombies or carbon copies of other recovering people. If this is your fear, you can relax, because that's not what happens. In recovery you actually have the chance to become *more* of who you really are than ever before. As you get better, you will become more autonomous, less dependent on others for approval, and more self-expressive.

Larry, when he first joined Alcoholics Anonymous, didn't want to change anything about himself. He says that he wanted to go on "living like a drunk," minus the active drinking. And he did for a while. But after a couple years in recovery, Larry's life-style started to change on its own, without his forcing it. His former way of life—full of chaos, crisis, stress, and negative attitudes—simply lost its appeal, he says, because it was replaced by "better ways." "It wasn't really an effort to change how I lived, gradually my values just shifted. Things that were once important just weren't that important anymore."

This reordering of priorities is one of the most fundamental and far-reaching changes that occurs in recovery. The person brought to his knees by an addiction has a rare opportunity to reassess his life and as a result gains a new appreciation for what matters most. Another recovering person described the shift this way: "Important things have become important to me now: people, my family and friends, living in the moment, helping someone else, seeing the beauty around me—things like that."

Strange as it may sound, people with a few years of recovery often consider themselves fortunate to have become addicted, because it has given them this opportunity to discover what matters in life. The life-style they adopt in order to stay abstinent, it turns

241

out, yields far more satisfaction than the way they were living. What started out as hitting bottom now seems more like a stroke of luck. Rose, who stopped using heroin and cocaine ten years ago, describes the rich rewards of recovery this way:

> It's hard to say what are the greatest things I've gotten from recovery, but freedom is one of them: freedom from fears, freedom from self-consciousness, freedom from the need to control, freedom from self-absorption, and the freedom that comes from accepting that I'm just one of the human race, that things are going to go wrong for me as well as anyone else, and that I can cope with it when they do.

Over the long haul of recovery many addictive personality traits begin to change. (Table 6 on pages 243–44 recaps the addictive personality traits and how they change over time in recovery.) The changes are sometimes astounding:

> I lived my entire life as a shame-based person, and now I'm not. I'm now living my life based on joy and freedom and hope. This is unbelievable!

> I spent a good bit of my life expecting somebody to "find out." I don't know what it was they were going to find out, but by God, they were going to find out if I didn't hide it. And now, I can't think of anything anyone *could* find out. It's a feeling of being free.

> I didn't know who I was when I was using. I had a persona. I was this perfect, wonderful person: very intelligent, very accomplished, who could achieve, achieve, achieve. But I had to use cocaine to sustain that. Now I'm finding out who I really am. I'm peeling away the mask, and it's a great sense of freedom—and discovery.

> The big difference today is being able to express my feelings and not having to chase after relationships. I don't feel I have to apologize for being myself anymore—and as a result, my relationships are of much better quality.

> One of the greatest changes in me is that I now welcome responsibility, where before I was always avoiding it. One reason why I used to like to get drunk, in fact, was so that everyone else would

TABLE 6. How Recovery Heals Addictive Personality Traits

Getting Better	Addictive Dis-ease
Traits that develop naturally in recovery	**Traits that made you vulnerable to addiction**
Aware of intrinsic worth	Feelings of shame
Self-forgiving	Perfectionism
Aware of inner potency; able to let go of control; flexible	Hunger for power and control to compensate for feelings of powerlessness and shame; rigid manipulation
Honest with self and others	Dishonest; self-deluding; denying
Able to think in gray areas	Thinking in black-and-white extremes
Able to be there for others	Self-obsessed
Self-possessed; self-honoring	Self-less
Feeling whole	Inner emptiness
Guided by a sense of meaning and purpose; able to be useful to others	Without meaning and purpose
Genuine; truly self-expressive	Excessive approval-seeking; obsessed with image
Appropriately open with others	Self-censoring
Not driven to use guilt as smokescreen for other feelings	Guilt-ridden
Able to deal constructively with anger and conflict	Trouble managing anger
Self-accepting and expressive, therefore less likely to be depressed	Underlying depression
Able to identify feelings and use them as signals	Emotional numbness
At ease with self; serene; able to enjoy own company; able to relax	Inner tension
Takes appropriate risks; able to tolerate "failure" in self	Afraid of taking appropriate risks; inordinate fear of failure and rejection
Acknowledges needs and takes responsibility for meeting them; autonomous; interdependent *with* others	Hidden dependency needs

TABLE 6. *(Continued)*

Getting Better	Addictive Dis-ease
Less in need of being right and in control, thereby reducing trouble with authority	Trouble with authority figures
Able to self-observe and accept responsibility for self	Blaming; taking on passive/victim role
Faces and resolves problems, willing to get help	Poor coping skills
Willing to live in the real world, to put in effort	Wishful thinking
Takes on adult roles and feels adequate	Never wanting to grow up
Sets boundaries and limits	Without boundaries
Able to delay gratification	Need for immediate gratification
Self-caring	No internalized "good parent"
Able to form intimate relationships	Intimacy problems
Sense of connectedness with others	Lack of community
Living a full, gratifying life	Trouble having real pleasure

take care of me. But now I've discovered that it's *fun* being responsible. It's exciting! Not only do you gain the respect of other people, but you feel so much more in command of your life. And it's one of the things that recovery gives you—automatically.

Of course, personal transformation isn't something you can ever achieve perfectly. Recovery, after all, is a lifelong adventure, not a performance. If you approach it as something else to "achieve," you're still operating within an addictive system. Obsessing on your recovery relentlessly, trying to make it happen "better" or "faster," is just more self-preoccupation. The whole point is to get on with the business of living!

What you can do is foster certain conditions in your life that are the natural *antidotes to addiction,* that make you less vulnerable to the appeal of mood-changers. These include self-acceptance, honesty, humility, and letting go of control. If you cultivate these conditions in your life, you will grow more resistant to addictive disease.

PRACTICE HONESTY

Addictive dis-ease thrives in dishonesty. After all, two key features of addiction are denial, which is dishonesty to self, and secrecy, which is withholding the truth from others. Getting better, then, requires cultivating honesty and integrity in your everyday affairs. Those with long-standing sobriety and serenity verify the central role that honesty plays in their recovery. Arthur, a recovering alcoholic and amphetamine addict, can't emphasize it enough: "I know if I'm not honest, I'll eventually drink again. So I don't try to justify my behavior anymore, or rationalize. Whatever mistakes I make, I just admit them now, call a spade a spade. But I don't rake myself over the coals about my mistakes either—I just admit them honestly."

Arthur's last point is important. The reason addicts have such trouble with honesty is that if they acknowledge a mistake or a shortcoming, they feel it makes them worthless people. It can be enormously freeing to discover that telling the truth about yourself is just admitting, "I am human, I have flaws." Nothing more. And it's not a crime to be human! Arthur talks too about the freedom this has given him:

> It turns out that being honest isn't a drudge, like I used to think. Because every time I get another piece of the truth, I get freer. It becomes easier to laugh. Yeah, that's a by-product! I'm not carrying around so many secrets anymore; I can afford to let my guard down. And out of that, I'm free to laugh with you, I don't have to be vigilant, on my toes, waiting to cover up something.

NURTURE THE SPIRIT

"By understanding accurately his proper place in Creation, a man may be made whole."
—Wendell Berry, *The Unsettling of America*

Spirituality is another antidote to addictive dis-ease. Among societies with low stress levels (and low rates of addiction), most are firmly grounded in religious or spiritual beliefs. Nurturing a belief in a higher power gives addicts greater meaning, security, and joy in their lives and helps them to avoid relapse.

By coming to know his proper place in creation, the addict is healed from the (addictive) belief that he should be omnipotent. He gains perspective. He need no longer feel ashamed of not measuring up because his standards are no longer impossible to live up to. He need only be human. Without shame as a motivator he is in less need of relief and his drug loses its compelling appeal.

Spirituality is a hard concept to pin down. But the word *spirit* derives from the Latin "spiritus," which means, variously, "breath," "courage," "the soul," and "life." So in long-term recovery this means adopting a way of life that is creative, alive, courageous, and life-affirming rather than life-destructive. Spirituality has to do with honesty too, for seeking the truth in oneself and in the world is by definition a spiritual quest. Author Paul Martin suggests that when people tell the truth, try to find the truth, or acknowledge the truth, they are engaged in a spiritual practice.

Nurturing the spirit also implies fostering respect for and connectedness with the earth and the rest of nature, for our interdependence with other living things *is* a truth of life. Many recovering people find spiritual inspiration in nature, as this comment by a recovering alcoholic illustrates: "Nothing improves my conscious contact with God like looking up at those mountains every morning." There *is* a lot of mystery in life. Getting humble and acknowledging our modest place in the larger scheme of things is honest and carries with it tremendous power.

Prayer and meditation are two ways of cultivating the spirit. Glenn, a recovering cocaine addict, described how vital prayer and meditation are to his recovery:

> The key in recovery, I find, is to gather all parts of myself back in: my intellect, spirit, and body; to be right here, living in this moment. It's when the externals, the anxieties, the worries and the desires, and

246

the focus on money and all the rest of it, take over that I become scattered. Then the inner strength that I do have is dissipated and I'm no longer myself; I'm what everybody else wants me to be. So pulling myself back in is what I have to do every day. And that's why I start every morning in meditation and prayer, because it helps me to stay in that frame of mind.

CULTIVATE HUMILITY

". . . humility consists less in thinking little of yourself than in thinking of yourself little."
—Reverend Joseph J. Gallagher, *Pleasure Is God's Invention*

Humility grows automatically out of a spiritual foundation. To be humble is to acknowledge your humanity, your place in creation. Humility is a state of mind that says "I don't have to be perfect or powerful. I have limitations, just like everyone else—and that's O.K." To be humble, then, is to *accept* yourself—as you are.

Many people confuse humility with humiliation, but these are very different experiences. Humiliation comes from having overblown expectations for yourself, such as "I should be all-powerful and perfect, and if I'm not I'm a failure." Humility frees you from such black-and-white thinking. With humility, you accept yourself as an imperfect human being rather than insist on being better than everyone else. Notice that humility *unites* you with all of humanity, whereas humiliation alienates you from it through the illusion that your limitations are something unique to you, something that sets you apart from others.

Cultivating an awareness of a "power greater than ourselves" helps to develop humility. If we believe there is a higher power, we don't have to "play God" anymore while being secretly afraid of being found out. What a relief it is for us to stop trying to project this superhuman image and regain the freedom that comes with being *ordinary*.

PRACTICE "SELF-FORGETTING"

If addictive dis-ease is preoccupation with the self, recovery is a process of "self-forgetting," of becoming less and less preoccupied with yourself. As you heal, this occurs naturally, because you no longer need to keep licking your wounds, which is what the self-preoccupation of addiction is. If you hurt less, your attention and energy are naturally freed up and you can start to look beyond the end of your nose to the rest of the world around you. The rewards of this process are described by Eileen, a recovering marijuana smoker we met in the last chapter:

> To the extent that I'm successful at self-forgetting, I just bop along in life. Nothing really bothers me anymore, because none of it is that important. It's when we're all tied up in our own importance, that every little slight snub or cross-eyed look someone gives you takes on enormous importance. Self-forgetting is freedom.

The idea of self-forgetting can be confusing to some, especially the codependent, whose very addiction involved putting others' needs first all along. But the selflessness of codependence and the self-forgetting of recovery are two very different things. In codependency, the selflessness has a secondary motive of being in control, of avoiding rejection by making oneself needed. It is, in reality, another form of preoccupation with self, even though it appears focused on the other person.

On the other hand, self-forgetting in recovery springs from genuine interest in others, without seeking secondary gains. A person who's getting better can achieve this because if she's been in recovery long enough, she's feeling pretty whole as she is; she doesn't need to shore herself up with illusionary self-importance or grandiose feelings of power and control. Her own wounds are simply less acute now and therefore less consuming.

This is where the service component of self-help groups comes in. Doing service—helping others along in their recovery by listening to them, sharing your experience, or serving in some other way (even by making coffee at a meeting)—promotes self-forgetting by helping remove you from the imprisonment of self-obsession, which in Alcoholics Anonymous literature has been called "the bondage of self."

Giving service is an antidote to addictive dis-ease, because the moment you serve another human being, you are no longer an isolated, inwardly focused unit but part of an interdependent community. The sense of belonging and usefulness that comes from contributing to and participating in a community with others is an example of one of the "better ways" referred to by recovering alcoholic Larry that simply replaces reliance on a mood-changer. You no longer need to numb yourself from feelings of isolation or to depend on the pseudocommunity offered by addiction.

"STICK WITH THE WINNERS"

As this popular AA slogan implies, you should seek out healthy role models. By "winners" we mean people who are *already* living the kind of life you want to live. Why follow a path—even a well-worn one—if you don't know anyone who's gotten out of the woods that way? If you're really serious about recovery, find people who have found it already—and seek out their company.

At the same time, avoid those people who are "addicted to their addiction," people who seem to wallow in their dis-ease and never get on with the business of living. One recovering addict calls this "terminal self-help": "If someone's been sober for a year or two and ain't laughin' yet, he's missed the boat. I better not try to follow him!"

Seeking out healthy role models is crucial for two reasons. One, it can give you hope that vibrant recovery is possible. Two, you can save yourself a lot of time and aggravation by learning recovery tools that work from people who have successfully used them. One recovering person compared it to seeking help in any area of life: "The notion of sticking with the winners is the same as getting a competent lawyer or accountant. It just makes sense to have someone help you who knows what she's doing. The whole idea is to make your life *easier*—not harder."

REPROGRAM YOUR BELIEF SYSTEM

Another antidote to addictive dis-ease is to become aware of the beliefs that fuel your behavior and "reprogram" yourself with healthier, recovery-promoting beliefs. At one time, we acquired addictive beliefs because they helped us survive in a dysfunctional family or because they were promoted by our society. Now, however, these beliefs are making us dysfunctional, and we must transform them.

Changing internal values, beliefs, and attitudes is the most important factor in breaking addictions, according to new research, because how we conceptualize things has a lot to do with what we feel. If we *think* we should be perfect and then we make a mistake, we will *feel* like a failure. With the belief that we should be perfect we *are* a failure. But if we alter the belief, come to believe that we are O.K. as we are, then making a mistake does not produce such painful feelings.

What are healthy, recovery-promoting beliefs? Generally, they are life-enhancing, conveying honor and respect for ourselves and others, whereas an addictive belief is life-destructive. A Nonaddictive Belief System includes the following:

1. "I am not perfect, and that's O.K."
2. "I am not all-powerful, and that's O.K."
3. "Limits are necessary; they give us structure."
4. "Pain and loss are a part of life."
5. "I am enough just as I am."
6. "I can cope with the problems life brings me (with support, a step at a time)."
7. "People, drugs, money, and other mood-changers cannot give me self-esteem, power, or anything else that's not within their power to give."
8. "Feelings are not dangerous; denying them is."
9. "Honesty is more important than image."
10. "*I* am responsible for seeing that my needs are met."

Most people experience the shift in perspective from life-destructive to life-enhancing as a tremendous relief. The addictive way of thinking held some allure in terms of thinking of yourself as potentially very powerful and perfect, but it also gave you much pain when you (inevitably) fell short. With a healthier belief system, you give up thinking of yourself in such superlative terms, but now you automatically measure up.

Anthony, a recovering cocaine addict and alcoholic, describes the relief he felt when he started to see the difference between the illusion of power he had been holding on to in his addiction and the personal potency that grew out of his new perspective:

> When I was using and dealing cocaine, I had what I thought was a lot of power. I had people around me who I had a certain kind of control over. I could snap my fingers and get things to happen. But I've come to realize that that is not correct power, that correct power is not something you deal or wield by being stronger or richer or more intimidating than the next guy. Correct power is something you command from inside of you. It flows automatically from self-esteem. It's a much better feeling to have inside of you; much better.

ACCEPT RECOVERY

Just as you had to accept the fact that you had an addictive dis-ease in order to get off and stay off your drug, you now have to accept recovery if you're going to keep getting better. This is not as easy as it sounds. It's been said that for an addictive person, the only thing worse than not getting what you want is getting it!

As you proceed in recovery and start to enjoy the riches of it—greater self-esteem, improved relations, prosperity—you may find that your self-critical tapes play louder than ever in your mind. You may have such thoughts as "Who do you think you are? You don't deserve this!" Continued recovery demands consciously expanding your view of yourself to include the possibility of having these riches.

Why would anyone have trouble accepting such "good stuff" in her life? A number of issues can contribute. For some, getting better means having to let go of "survivor guilt." If you're from a dysfunctional family, you may find that as you start getting better, other family members resent or envy your new-found happiness (or you may assume they do even if they don't). "Holding on" to your dis-ease can be a way of avoiding the guilt you'd feel if you continued moving forward. It can also be a way for you to stay connected to your family and not risk rejection.

For others, it's a matter of identity. If your role in the family, for instance, was that of the "eternal, irresponsible adolescent," you may find yourself sticking to that script, even when you've long outgrown it. And if it's the script of others in your family to either scapegoat you as the "one who's never amounted to anything" or come to your rescue whenever you "bottom out," you may resist getting too much better so as not to throw a wrench into the family "production," to remain loyal to your supporting cast.

Then too, it can feel safer to stay in the dis-ease than to reap the riches of recovery, for the moment you start letting yourself have more good stuff—self-esteem, improved relationships, financial prosperity, meaningful work—you run the risk of losing them and you're not in control of that. It's this lack of control, as we've seen, that the addictive person fears most.

Just becoming aware of what it is that blocks you from accepting the riches of recovery is a first step toward dismantling these barriers. Eventually, as you proceed, you'll find yourself automatically letting more and more of the good stuff in. As you come to accept yourself—flaws and all—there's no more reason to be deprived. You can't make a case for it anymore.

PRACTICE "LETTING GO"

"Do you know how much energy *it takes to control the whole world, to cause everybody to have the correct opinion of you?"*
—Mitchell, recovering workaholic and compulsive eater

One of the most profound changes for those in long-term recovery is learning to let go of control. Earlier, we wrote about surrender to one's powerlessness over addiction, but there are many areas of life in which the addictive person clings to the illusion of control. Often, she thinks she should be able to control how other people behave, what happens at work, whether someone likes her—even how fast the traffic moves! But once the addict realizes she's not in control of any of these things, she gets her life back. After all, if it's not in her control anyway, then she might as well let go and enjoy the trip.

A lot of suffering comes from trying to control matters beyond our control. For one thing, as Mitchell's comment illustrates, it saps us of energy that could be put to better use. Holding on to control also makes it difficult to receive support and love from others, for we can't be open to receiving and be in control at the same time. Similarly, it prevents us from taking risks and being spontaneous, as doing so also requires letting go. This is not to mention the damaging effects that trying to control has on others (children, spouses, friends), for when we try to control them, we are rejecting who they really are.

Some people associate surrendering control with defeat and humiliation. But giving up control does not mean you are being defeated at all—it means you are *winning*. When you stop wasting all your energy on things outside your control, you win the chance to live your life. When you realize you're not in charge of every outcome, you win the chance to take risks. And when you give up trying to control the future, you win the opportunity to live in the present.

Some people mistake letting go of control with being irresponsible. They think if they're not trying to manipulate the outcome of every situation, worrying and obsessing about it, they will somehow be abdicating their responsibility. But surrendering control and being irresponsible are two different things. When you're trying to control everyone and everything, you're not *being* responsible, though you may look as if you are. How responsible is it, after all, when your ultimate motive is to get people to do what you want? Genuine responsibility comes from honoring yourself and others, doing the best you can in your endeavors, and letting go of the results. Being responsible is staying "right-sized" and avoiding grandiose fantasies about your power.

It's a tremendous relief when a person finally realizes she doesn't have to try to control everything. Eileen says she used to smoke pot to help herself let go, and now, in recovery, she is learning to let go by herself.

> Now I'm learning to let go of trying to control and predict everything, of obsessing, of worrying, of grasping, of holding on . . . as opposed to flowing. To the degree that I can go with the flow, it's such a relief. Now I'm trusting myself more, and trusting that there's a flow in the universe that is working in a positive way through me, if I just let go into it. And it's becoming easier all the time.

GRIEVE—AND LET GO OF THE PAST

"I don't walk around like a wounded child anymore, like I'm branded. At last I've been able to gain freedom from the past. I can be a grown-up now."
> —Lowell, recovering alcoholic

All addicts have ungrieved losses. When you are no longer anesthetizing yourself through addictive behavior, you may find that intense feelings of grief start to surface. If you let yourself go through this grief, feel it rather than block it, inner healing will occur, for only by fully experiencing the depth of our pain can we be healed from it—and be done with it.

In early recovery, it may have been important for you *not* to feel too many painful feelings from the past, to monitor them so as not to get overwhelmed. At that point, negative feelings and moods were dangerous because they could trigger cravings to use your drug again. Now, after some sustained abstinence, the next step in recovery is to *let* yourself feel grief, and "work it through" so it doesn't keep influencing your present behavior.

What exactly are the losses that have to be grieved? Charles Whitfield, in *Healing the Child Within*, writes that we experience loss whenever we are deprived of or have to go without something that we have had, valued, needed, wanted, or expected. Allowing ourselves to feel the pain of such a loss is called "grieving."

When we grieve, the pain of the loss eventually dissipates on its own and we get back to living our lives. But when the pain is blocked (with a mood-changer or in some other way), it does not dissipate but festers like an abscess below the surface of our consciousness. Then there is always the threat of its erupting again if we don't "keep a lid on it."

Suppressing grief requires a good deal of energy. If enough of it builds up, the person remains in a chronic state of stress. He is not present, not fully available emotionally, because all his energy must go into keeping that "lid" on. This state of internal, unconscious preoccupation results in free-floating anxiety (the person has to be on guard against anything that could loosen the lid), emotional numbness, feelings of emptiness, and symptoms of physical stress. Resisting grief thus adds to the disease that makes us vulnerable to addiction.

The biggest threat to a person with a lot of unresolved grief is a new loss, because each time a rejection, abandonment, or other type of loss occurs it taps into the reservoir of unresolved grief from the past and threatens to bring it to the surface. Hence the person avoids situations that could potentially result in loss (especially intimate relations) in order to avoid the risks. (That's why the active addict is emotionally unavailable. He can't afford to risk surrendering his heart to someone, for if he loses in love, it would be unbearable, given the additional weight of the past.)

When we fail to acknowledge a loss and work it through, we establish a smoldering resentment against the person we blame for it. We then have to carry this resentment around with us like a piece of baggage, draining our energy and consuming our attention. The word "resentment," in fact, derives from the Latin *resentire*—"to feel again." So when we fail to acknowledge grievance or loss, we are fated to feel it again and again.

It is necessary—albeit painful—to go back and reexperience these ungrieved losses in recovery in order to cleanse them from our systems and move on. Fully grieving the past allows us to live fully in the present. Usually this inner work begins after a year or two of abstinence has been established. It cannot begin earlier because there is so much else to do first to establish a stable, sustained abstinence, the foremost goal.

What the recovering person needs to do at this point is accept the fact that whatever he wanted, desired, expected, or hoped for as a child and didn't get cannot be obtained *now*—as that child, from those people. That time is gone forever. There is no benefit to holding on anymore; it is hopeless. There is lots of hope for the future, though, if he lets go. Once the addict gives up hope of getting what he could not get in the past, he can begin to get what *is* available to him in the present. There is no making up for losses in childhood; there is only building adulthood.

But why would anyone insist on holding on to the past when it obviously cannot be redeemed? For addicts, there can be a number of reasons, and becoming aware of them can make it easier to let go. Some follow:

You may be so used to carrying the baggage around that you have come to identify it as part of you. To set it down now and leave it behind would feel strange, even wrong.

You may be afraid to let go of the baggage of your past, however uncomfortable it is to lug around, because it maintains at least *some* connection to your family. (You *must* belong, you're carrying the family baggage!)

You may be holding on to the childlike fantasy that the people you blame for your problems will eventually "see what they've done to you" and give you what you want. But ironically, if your family members do change their long-established patterns of behavior, it will probably be because *you* have changed.

You may be holding on to resentment as a way to avoid *feeling* previous losses. As long as you focus "out there" and tie up your energy with blaming externals, you never have to sit with the feelings.

As long as you carry the resentment around, you avoid taking responsibility for yourself, because once you've let go of the baggage, there is nothing else holding you back. You have to change.

Once you identify your barriers and let go, your sense of being becomes "lighter." Now when you experience a rejection, abandonment, or other loss (as we all must in the natural course of life), you will be dealing with the present incident and not with the additional hundreds that preceded it. Of course, this "clearing process" is never one hundred percent complete, but more and more, you become able to process each emotion as it occurs.

A word of caution: as with any feeling, you must first *know* what you feel—"own" it and experience it fully—before you can proceed to the next step of letting go of it. So much is said about forgiveness these days that it's possible to jump ahead to this stage prematurely. True forgiving and letting go of past hurts and losses cannot occur until you have allowed yourself to feel them. Otherwise, you're repressing, as you did before, and the feelings will go back underground and continue to drive your behavior.

And there are no shortcuts to this process. Letting go of the past is a gradual process, not something that happens all at once or quickly. If it's real letting go, it's not a quick-fix solution but a genuine acceptance and working through of the feeling. Premature forgiveness can even be a new way you try to avoid grieving.

RECLAIM YOURSELF

"The company of prison wardens does not encourage lively development. It is only after it is liberated . . . that the self begins to be articulate, to grow, and to develop its creativity."
—Alice Miller, *The Drama of the Gifted Child*

257

The recovering person has a dilemma: in order to recover, he needs to love and accept his true self unconditionally, yet he has this tyrannical false self—this "prison warden" as Alice Miller calls it—that blocks him every step of the way. The warden is akin to the self-critical tapes we've talked about. When you get close to knowing and loving your true self in recovery, you're likely to hear these tapes running in your mind again, saying things like, "Who are you kidding? You'll never amount to anything," or "When people get to know you, they'll see through you." These are the voices of the false self that you erected in order to keep from revealing your true self at a time when it wasn't safe to.

Your task in recovery is to come back into "possession" of your self, for self-possession is another antidote to addictive disease. *When you are self-possessed, you will no longer need to be self-obsessed.* That's what addiction is, in a sense: a self-defeating and all-consuming attempt to relieve the pain that comes from self-alienation.

The first step in reclaiming your self is to avoid reinforcing the inner voice of the prison warden. Therefore, maintain distance from any people in your life who reinforce your self-hating tapes.

The second step is to start developing an inner "advocate" who makes contact with and provides nurturing and encouragement to your imprisoned self. And to do this you must cultivate self-forgiveness. For just as you need to let go of what other people have done to you in the past, you have to forgive yourself too. Think of this as declaring "amnesty" for your imprisoned self. You were, after all, a political prisoner in a sense—jailed not for real crimes but for who you were.

One of the great rewards of long-term recovery is improved relationships with others, and coming back into possession of yourself is key in this. That's because the traits of the addictive person—the need to be in control, perfectionism, grandiosity, self-preoccupation—are all *antithetical* to the traits needed to develop and maintain intimacy, and almost all stem from the person's self-rejection.

When you come back into possession of yourself, you become

more capable of intimacy because you can then share yourself with another (you have a self to share); tolerate ambiguity and frustration (there's not so much riding on every outcome, because you have your self); be honest (you have nothing to hide); set boundaries and limits (it's not so risky); let go of control (you've got what you need, you don't have to manipulate others into giving it to you); enjoy your own company (so you're not so desperate for someone else's); take responsibility for yourself (and not put that pressure on someone else); and be there for someone else (you're not so preoccupied with licking your own wounds).

BECOME YOUR OWN "GOOD PARENT"

It helps many people to think of their true self as an "inner child" and to treat themselves with the nurturing, understanding, and compassion with which they would treat such a child. For Amy, recovering from bulimia, contacting and reassuring her "child within" has been key in her recovery:

> For me, recovery has been all about finding my inner child and accepting her. I had to start out accepting the cute little kid I remember myself as before I got fat. From there I moved on to accepting the fat, "unacceptable" kid I became around the third grade. Now, when I get any kind of overwhelming feelings, I just sit down and connect with this kid. I listen to her, hear her out, put my arm around her, love her, and tell her, "Don't worry, I'm not going to abandon you—ever again."

You can't go back and change anything that happened to you growing up, but you do have the power to give yourself all the support, forgiveness, reasonable limits, good nutrition, and whatever else you might need now. How you are treated today is within *your* control. You can't change the past, but you don't have to keep repeating it either.

In addition to giving yourself nurturing and compassion, another part of becoming a "good parent" to yourself is becoming appropriately self-protective. That means setting limits and boundaries with other people. Addicts usually have difficulty doing this. They tend either not to set limits at all or do so rigidly and arbitrarily. Marie relates how this is changing for her in recovery:

> I learned as a child that *I* was not important, that what was important was pleasing other people. So I grew up not communicating what I wanted or what I needed, didn't set any boundaries with people. I was whatever they wanted me to be, did whatever they wanted me to do—and that played a big part in my sexual compulsion too. I thought if I established a boundary with someone, I wouldn't be liked anymore. And God forbid, because if one person doesn't like me, then I'm a failure.
>
> Now, after a couple years of recovery, I can set limits with people and not worry whether they like me or not. I've applied this in dozens of situations. Just two weeks ago, I asked my boyfriend to get an AIDS test. I never would have asked for something like that, something that would make me feel safe but might annoy or inconvenience someone else. But it was so simple! I just said, "Would you do this?" And he said, "Yes." I felt this flood of self-love afterward, like I was really not going to abandon myself anymore . . . and it felt so good.

Like Marie, we can trust ourselves and others more once we know that we can and will take care of ourselves. That's what setting boundaries does: it creates a safe environment for your true self to thrive in.

Creating a safe environment for yourself means learning to trust your inner voice when it tells you something feels wrong. For instance, if you find yourself feeling exploited, abused, dishonored, or otherwise unsafe around a particular person, trust those feelings and set the necessary boundaries. Learning to be open and honest doesn't mean you do so without discrimination. In fact, being open and vulnerable (and therefore available for intimacy) *requires* that you discriminate between situations in which it is safe to open up and those in which it is not. As Robin Norwood, author of *Women Who Love Too Much*, writes:

No matter how willing to be genuine you become with recovery, there will still be people whose anger, hostility and aggression will inhibit you from being honest. To be vulnerable with them is to be masochistic. Therefore, lowering our boundaries and eventually eliminating them should happen only with those people—friends, relatives or lovers—with whom we have a relationship bathed in trust, love, respect, and reverence for our shared, tender humanity.

There may be people in your life who resent your becoming more self-caring and autonomous in recovery. They may fear being abandoned by you as you get healthier, or they may feel that you're not as easy to control or exploit now that you are setting your own limits and boundaries. One recovering debtor and alcoholic, after she'd been in recovery a while and was setting appropriate limits, was told by her mother, "You're not nice anymore." But if being "nice" in someone else's terms means being without limits and boundaries, then practice being "not nice."

This is where taking responsibility for yourself comes in again. Leaving the addictive system means surrendering the fantasy that other people will or should take care of you or treat you as you would like—all the time. The fact is that if someone is exploitive or abusive in her own life, she won't be different with you just because you want her to be. You have to become a reliable, protective good parent to yourself, one who is wise enough to spot an unsafe or menacing situation and come swiftly to your protection.

LEARN TO TAKE RISKS—AND LIVE!

To live creatively, we must be willing to encounter the world, to feel passionate about something, and to take risks. It's not easy to do this, living as we do in a time when the prevailing attitude seems to be to *avoid* this encounter, to "play it safe," and to resign oneself to a rather deadening existence—and then "relax" with a mood-changer.

Not taking risks is a way we protect ourselves. If we don't try something, we can't lose—or so we think. But by playing it safe, we run the highest risk of all: not having much satisfaction in life and feeling incomplete, empty, bored—and all the more attracted to a mood-changer. So learning to take risks is another antidote to addictive dis-ease.

But taking risks requires letting go of control, and, as we know, this is hard for addictive people. If you stick with the familiar, no matter how unfulfilling it is, you can at least feel in control. When you take risks, you are, by definition, not in control of the results.

To get to the point where you can start taking appropriate risks in recovery, there are a number of steps you can take:

1. *Stretch your identity.* Most people from dysfunctional families were exposed to repeated negative messages about themselves which eventually became part of their identity, such as "I'm good for nothing," or "I'm stupid." They may have also gotten the message that certain satisfactions in life (meaningful work, creative hobbies, fun, pleasure) are for "other people" and not for them. Or they may be pessimistic about their ability to change: "I'll never change . . . I'll always be a ____." Now, to really live fully, this identity has to be stretched.

2. *Resurrect your dreams.* A man wore a button at an addictions conference recently that read, "Discipline is remembering what you want." We all have dreams, things we want to do, if we let ourselves remember and not censor them. The main difference between people who achieve their goals and those who don't is the willingness to try.

3. *Take action.* Allowing yourself to have your dreams is not enough if you do nothing to bring them into reality. So the next step is to put in the footwork: ask for the date, go for the audition, sign up for the course, whatever is necessary. If you don't take action, your dream will be like a flower that never bears fruit. The potential was there, but it was not brought to life. Taking action is the equivalent of "fertilizing" your dreams.

Action begets attitude. In taking action, psychic change occurs. You begin to see yourself as a person who "shows up" for life, not because you have no fear about it but *in spite* of the fear.

4. *Let go of the results.* Once you've taken whatever action you can, you might as well let go of the results. You're not in control of them anyway. And even if the results are not outwardly successful (you get turned down for the date, don't get the part, find the course isn't for you), you *are* a success—in the only way that really matters—just for having given it your best. No one can do more than that.

5. *Reframe failure.* Believing we should never fail is a part of the addictive belief that we "should be all-powerful." To give up this grandiose belief and accept that we—like everybody else—are going to fail at times *because we are human* is to leave the addictive system and accept ourselves.

The real prize is that once we accept our fallibility, we no longer have to avoid failure so staunchly. We become free to take risks, because the outcome does not carry so much weight. For even if the outcome *is* "failure" in some societally defined sense, it no longer means we are exposed as the "worthless person we are" but instead as a vulnerable human being who at least had the courage to try. To fail no longer means we stand apart from our fellows but are united with them in the very fact that we have failings and limitations too. The only true failure is not accepting the possibility of failure in ourselves. That will guarantee us a failed life.

Not only is failure inevitable, but it can be a great teacher. It can, if we use it right, help us discover where our mistakes lie so that we can correct our course and thus be brought ever closer to reaching our destiny. Risk-taking then becomes an automatic "win," as recovering alcoholic Arthur believes:

> There's only lessons and blessings. So when life presents you with an opportunity, you give it your best shot. There are no guarantees. But even if it turns out to be a mistake, it wasn't wasted. There's a lesson there, I guarantee you. And if it does turn out the way you hoped, it's a great blessing. Either way, you win!

6. *Persist!* The recovering addict will often venture out to take a risk, but if he gets turned down, rejected, or "fails" once—that's

263

the end of it. He uses his failure to reinforce the self-critical tapes: "See, I knew it wouldn't work!" But to recover we must be willing to encounter the real world, and in the real world (not the addictive fantasy world) things don't always fall magically into place the way we want them to. To think that they should is to fall back into addictive thinking ("Life should never be painful, uncomfortable, or require effort").

The real magic that's available in life is embodied in persisting, because if you desire something, accept the idea of having it, take the actions to get it, let go of the results, *and keep applying yourself,* the results will be quite amazing.

SEEK PLEASURE

"Sobriety is not a Greek tragedy."
—Warren, a recovering alcoholic

There is nothing wrong with seeking pleasure. Pleasure-seeking becomes addiction only when it has negative consequences for us or others. In fact, as we have seen, a drug high has all the more appeal if it is the only source of pleasure we have. Addiction is, in a sense, compartmentalized pleasure-seeking: "Well, the rest of my life is drudgery, so I deserve to 'have fun' with my drug."

As an antidote to addictive dis-ease, then, *seek pleasure everywhere!* The more pleasure you have in your life, the better you will be able to deal with frustration, for it is an inner sense of deprivation that feeds the addict's inability to delay gratification "one minute more" (his quick-fix mentality). The more real pleasure you build into your life, the less appealing the quick-fix pleasures will be.

Addictive people typically have a couple of barriers to letting more pleasure into their lives. One is the need (once again) to be in control. Jed, a recovering sex addict, describes how always trying to be in control of how he looked to others kept him from really having fun—until he got into recovery and began learning to let go:

Most of my life, people thought I was on top of the world, having a great time—but I really wasn't. I was trying to *look* like I was. First of all, fear and joy can't be in the same place, and I was so fearful, so controlled. Even my "spontaneity" was planned, if you know what I mean. I always felt like I had to be performing. That's where I was at, whether I was having sex, water skiing, or having a conversation with a friend. I didn't think joy was something I deserved . . . not real joy. I thought the best I could do was to perform well and get approval.

Another barrier to experiencing pleasure is a tendency to live either in the past (bemoaning what happened yesterday) or in the future (worrying about what will happen tomorrow). But since pleasure is an experience, it is *only available in the present.* Sharon, a recovering compulsive spender and workaholic, shares with us her excitement upon discovering this age-old truth and how it has increased her "pleasure ratio" greatly:

I was always one of those people who was too focused on getting to the "station" to enjoy the ride. I bought into the popular myth that when I got the new car or the next house or the third TV set, I'd finally be happy. But I never was. After a couple of weeks, the car was just a car and the TV was just another TV. And my husband and I fought as much in the new house as we did in the old. I kept looking to the future to bring me pleasure, and it never could.

Thanks to what I've learned in recovery, I now know that today, *this moment*, is what counts. The reality is, there's never going to be a "station" to arrive at. And if I miss the journey, I've missed the whole thing. It's a simple concept, but it's made a major difference in my life.

Now I rejoice in the simple pleasures that are available all the time: the wildflowers I see on the side of the road, a star-lit sky, a moving piece of music, the smile on a friend's face. And I don't take myself so seriously. Now I can laugh at myself.

Like so many changes that occur in recovery, becoming open to greater joy and pleasure in your life happens automatically, as your priorities change. To a large degree, how satisfied we are with our lives depends not on the circumstances we encounter but on our attitude toward them. Rather than focusing on what you *don't* have, learning to see the cup as half full (and being grateful that it is) will keep you in awe of how much abundance you actually *do* have in your life.

And as a recovering person, you are rich indeed, for you have the opportunity to create a more satisfying life-style—something many people would benefit from but rarely do. And the best part is that you don't even have to try to make it happen; you only have to surrender to the process of recovery and let the addictive ways be replaced by "better ways." Arthur, the recovering alcoholic and amphetamine addict, sums it up for us:

> It's not a conscious decision to develop your sense of humor or anything; it's just that less and less is important to you. You undergo some kind of value change. Maybe the laughter is really the outward manifestation of gratitude, I don't know. I just have to tell you that very little bothers me today. *Life is good!*

Looking Forward with Hope

ADDICTION IS FULL OF PARADOXES. Perhaps the most fundamental paradox is that within the addict lies both the seeds of personal destruction *and* self-transformation. The choices you make will determine which seed grows. The addictive person can either continue to search for quick-fix solutions (first-order change) or can surrender to powerlessness over addiction and thus embark on a new set of challenges offered by recovery (second-order change). The choice is yours.

The unexpected surprise of recovery is that what starts out looking like a humiliating defeat—hitting bottom—turns out to be the gateway to a victorious and more fulfilling life. No one sets out to become addicted—wishes for this challenge—but once the problem appears in your life, what you make of it is up to you.

In recovery lies hope. There is the promise not so much of giving something up as of gaining a great deal, and most important, the potential to move forward. That hope is what we have tried to provide in this book. Through the experiences of other recovering persons, we have tried to help you discover not only where vulnerability to addiction comes from, but how this crisis can be used to make your life better. Finally, recovery gives you the hope, not of returning to the person you were before your addictions appeared, but of thriving, of becoming all that you are capable of becoming.

The epidemic of addiction in this country presents us with the same opportunity of choice. As a nation we can go on groping for more magical solutions to our explosion of addictions or we can use this crisis to transform ourselves and our culture. If there is a silver lining in our addictions epidemic, it is this: as more and more of us begin rejecting addictive solutions to our problems, we begin to create a healthier culture in our society. In this sense, recovery is revolutionary. Unlike other revolutions, however, recovery transforms from within naturally, organically, gently. It is time.

Bibliography

The authors gratefully acknowledge the following books and articles that served as references for this book.

"A Travelogue With M. Scott Peck, M.D.," *Changes,* March–April 1988, p. 20.

BECKER, ERNEST. *The Denial of Death.* New York: Macmillan, 1973.

BERRY, WENDELL. *The Unsettling of America.* New York: Avon, 1977.

BLASZCYNSKI, ALEXANDER P. "A Winning Bet," *Psychology Today,* December 1985, pp. 38–46.

BRADSHAW, JOHN. *Bradshaw On: The Family.* Deerfield Beach, FL: Health Communications, 1988.

CARNES, PATRICK. *Out of the Shadows: Understanding Sexual Addiction.* Minneapolis, MN: CompCare, 1985.

CASALE, ANTHONY M., with LERMAN, PHILIP. *USA TODAY: Tracking Tomorrow's Trends.* Kansas City, MO: Andrews, McMeel & Parker, 1986.

CLARK, NANCY. "The Compulsive Athlete," *Cycling,* December 1986, p. 5.

CONANT, JENNET. "Scalpel Slaves Just Can't Quit," *Newsweek,* Jan. 11, 1988, pp. 58–59.

CUNNINGHAM, DONNA, and RAMER, ANDREW. *The Spiritual Dimensions of Healing Addictions.* San Rafael, CA: Cassandra Press, 1988.

CUSTER, ROBERT, and MILT, HARRY. *When Luck Runs Out.* New York: Warner, 1985.

DERBER, CHARLES. *The Pursuit of Attention.* New York: Oxford University Press, 1983.

ETZIONI, AMITAI. "Say 'I'm Sorry' Like a Man," *The New York Times,* March 23, 1988.

FLOWERS, CHARLES. "Sex Addiction," *Changes,* September–October 1987, p. 23.

FREY, JAMES. "Gambling: A Sociological Review," *The Annals of the American Academy:* 474: July 1984, pp. 107–121.

FRIEL, JOHN, et al. *Co-dependency and the Search for Identity.* Deerfield Beach, FL: Health Communications, 1984.

GALLAGHER, REV. JOSEPH J. *Pleasure Is God's Invention.* Center City, MN: Hazelden (booklet).

GODBEY, GEOFFREY. *Leisure in Your Life.* Coopersburg, PA: Venture, 1985.

GORSKI, TERENCE. *Denial Patterns,* Hazel Crest, IL: CENAPS, 1976.

———. *The Denial Process and Human Disease,* Hazel Crest, IL: CENAPS, 1976.

———, and MILLER, MERLENE. *Staying Sober.* Independence, MO: Independence Press, 1986.

GOTTLIEB, ANNIE. *Do You Believe in Magic?* New York: Times Books, 1987.

HALPERN, HOWARD. *How to Break Your Addiction to a Person.* New York: McGraw-Hill, 1982.

HATHAWAY, BRUCE. "Running to Ruin," *Psychology Today,* July 1984, pp. 14–15.

HATTERER, LAWRENCE. *The Pleasure Addicts.* San Diego, CA: A. S. Barnes, 1981.

HIRSCHMANN, JANE, and MUNTER, CAROL. *Overcoming Overeating.* Reading, MA: Addison-Wesley, 1988.

HODGSON, RAY, and MILLER, PETER. *Self-Watching.* New York: Facts on File, 1982.

HOLDEN, CONSTANCE. "Against All Odds," *Psychology Today,* December 1985, pp. 31–36.

HYDE, MARGARET O. *Addictions.* New York: McGraw-Hill, 1978.

KUSYSZYN, IGOR. "The Psychology of Gambling," *The Annals of The American Academy:* 474, July 1984, pp. 133–145.

LARSEN, EARNIE. *Stage II Recovery.* New York: Harper & Row, 1985.

LASCH, CHRISTOPHER. *Haven in a Heartless World: The Family Besieged.* New York: Basic Books, 1979.

LESIEUR, HENRY, and CUSTER, ROBERT. "Pathological Gambling," *The Annals of the American Academy,* 474, July 1984, pp. 146–156.

LOWEN, ALEXANDER. *Fear of Life.* New York: Macmillan, 1980.

———. *Pleasure: A Creative Approach to Life.* New York: Penguin, 1980.

MACHLOWITZ, MARILYN. *Workaholics.* New York: New American Library, 1980.

———. *Whiz Kids.* New York: Arbor House, 1985.

MARLATT, G. ALAN, et al. *Relapse Prevention.* New York: Guilford, 1985.

MAY, ROLLO. *The Courage to Create.* New York: Bantam, 1975.

———. *Freedom and Destiny.* New York: Dell, 1981.

MILLER, ALICE. *The Drama of the Gifted Child.* New York: Basic Books, 1981.

MILLER, PETER. *Personal Habit Control.* New York: Simon & Schuster, 1978.

MORGAN, WILLIAM. "The Mind of the Marathoner," *Psychology Today,* April 1978, pp. 38–49.

MULE, S. JOSEPH, ed. *Behavior in Excess.* New York: Free Press, 1981.

NAKKEN, CRAIG. *The Addictive Personality.* Center City, MN: Hazelden, 1988.

NORWOOD, ROBIN. *Women Who Love Too Much.* New York: Simon & Schuster, 1985.

O'GORMAN, PATRICIA, and OLIVER-DIAZ, PHILIP. *Breaking the Cycle of Addiction.* Deerfield Beach, FL: Health Communications, 1987.

ORBACH, SUSAN. *Hunger Strike: The Anorectic's Struggle as a Metaphor for Our Age.* New York: Avon, 1986.

"Patterns of Addiction," *Ms.,* February 1987, p. 35.

PECK, M. SCOTT. *The Different Drum.* New York: Simon & Schuster, 1988.

———. *The Road Less Traveled.* New York: Simon & Schuster, 1978.

PEELE, STANTON. *The Addiction Experience.* Center City, MN: Hazelden, 1980.

———. *How Much Is Too Much?* New York: Prentice-Hall, 1981.

———. *The Meaning of Addiction.* Center City, MN: Hazelden, 1985.

———, with BRODSKY, ARCHIE. *Love and Addiction.* New York: New American Library, 1975.

ROSELLINI, GAYLE. *Stinking Thinking.* Center City, MN: Hazelden, 1985.

ROTH, GENEEN. *Breaking Free From Compulsive Eating.* New York: Bobbs-Merrill, 1984.

ROUNSAVILLE, BRUCE, et al. "Interpersonal Psychotherapy Adapted for Ambulatory Cocaine Abusers," *American Journal of Drug and Alcohol Abuse,* 11: 1985, pp. 171–191.

SCHAEF, ANNE WILSON. *Co-Dependence.* New York: Harper/Winston, 1986.

———. *When Society Becomes an Addict.* San Francisco: Harper & Row, 1987.

SCHAEFFER, BRENDA. *Is It Love or Is It Addiction?* New York: Harper/Hazelden, 1987.

SCHATZMAN, MORTON. *Soul Murder: Persecution in the Family.* New York: New American Library, 1974.

SEYMOUR, RICHARD, and SMITH, DAVID. *Drugfree.* New York: Facts on File, 1987.

SLATER, PHILIP. *The Pursuit of Loneliness.* Boston, MA: Beacon, 1970.

SMITH, ANN. *Grandchildren of Alcoholics.* Deerfield Beach, FL: Health Communications, 1988.

SMITH, DAVID E. "Decreasing Drug Hunger," *Professional Counselor,* November–December 1986, p. 6.

STEINER, CLAUDE. *Healing Alcoholism.* New York: Grove Press, 1981.

STONE, NANNETTE, et al. *Cocaine: Seduction and Solution.* New York: Crown, 1984.

SUBBY, ROBERT, and FRIEL, JOHN. *Codependency and Family Rules.* Deerfield Beach, FL: Health Communications, 1984.

THARP, VAN. "The Compulsive Trader," *Stocks & Commodities,* January 1988, pp. 8–14.

———. "The Compulsive Trader, Part 2," *Stocks & Commodities,* April 1988, pp. 31–34.

Twelve Steps and Twelve Traditions. New York: Alcoholics Anonymous World Services, Inc., 1983.

WASHTON, ARNOLD. *Cocaine Addiction: Treatment, Recovery, and Relapse Prevention.* New York: W. W. Norton, 1989.

———, and BOUNDY, DONNA. *Cocaine and Crack: What You Need to Know.* Hillside, NJ: Enslow, 1989.

WATZLAWICK, PAUL, et al. *Change.* New York: W. W. Norton, 1974.

WEGSCHEIDER-CRUSE, SHARON. "Co-dependency: The Therapeutic Void," in *Co-Dependency: An Emerging Issue.* Pompano Beach, FL: Health Communications, 1984.

WHITFIELD, CHARLES. *Healing the Child Within.* Deerfield, FL: Health Communications, 1987.

WINSTON, STUART, and HARRIS, HARRIET. *A Nation of Gamblers.* New York: Prentice-Hall, 1984.

WURMSER, LEON. *The Hidden Dimension: Psychodynamics in Compulsive Drug Use.* Northvale, NJ: J. Aronson, 1978.